THE ORIGINS OF THE EQUAL RIGHTS AMENDMENT

THE ORIGINS OF THE EQUAL RIGHTS AMENDMENT
American Feminism Between the Wars

Susan D. Becker

Contributions in Women's Studies, Number 23

Greenwood Press
Westport, Connecticut • London, England

Library of Congress Cataloging in Publication Data

Becker, Susan D
    The origins of the Equal Rights Amendment.

    (Contributions in women's studies ; no. 23
ISSN 0147-104X)
    Bibliography: p.
    Includes index.
    1. Women's rights—United States—History.
2. National Woman's Party—History. 3. Feminism—
United States—History. I. Title. II. Title:
Equal Rights Amendment: American Feminism between the
wars. III. Series.
HQ1426.B423   305.4'2   80-23633
ISBN 0-313-22818-3 (lib. bdg.)

Library of Congress Catalog Card Number: 80-23633
ISBN: 0-313-22818-3
ISSN: 0147-104X

First published in 1981

Greenwood Press
A division of Congressional Information Service, Inc.
88 Post Road West, Westport, Connecticut 06881

Printed in the United States of America

10 9 8 7 6 5 4 3 2 1

CONTENTS

PREFACE

The National Woman's Party was not actually a political party but rather a feminist pressure group organized to lobby Congress, to educate other women about discriminations against them, and to attempt to convince the Democratic and Republican parties to include the Equal Rights Amendment in their platforms. This book uses the terminology that the NWP and its members preferred, both in reference to the Party and Party offices such as chairman, and to titles and forms of address such as Mrs. Harvey Wiley, Jane Norman Smith, or Miss Doris Stevens.

I have benefited greatly from the cooperation and assistance of the staffs of the Arthur and Elizabeth Schlesinger Library at Radcliffe College, the National Archives, and the Stack and Reader Services division of the Library of Congress. William O'Neill of Rutgers University, Burl Noggle of Louisiana State University, and Edwin Trainer of the University of Tennessee have read earlier versions of this book, and although I have not always followed all their suggestions, I very much appreciate their advice. I also owe a debt of gratitude to a number of friends: David B. Van Tassel, of the History Department at Case Western Reserve University, who guided my initial research on the

National Woman's Party; Lois Scharf, Director of National History Day, and Marian Morton of John Carroll University with whom I have had many constructive discussions about the nature and assumptions of twentieth century feminism; Mary Giunta of the National Historical Publications and Records Commission who facilitated my use of the uncatalogued Women's Bureau papers at the National Archives; and finally, Charles Johnson, Michael J. McDonald, and W. Bruce Wheeler, my colleagues in the History Department at the University of Tennessee, who encouraged me steadily throughout the process of several revisions and listened to me complain every step of the way.

ABBREVIATIONS

AAUW	American Association of University Women
BPW	Business and Professional Women
ER	*Equal Rights*
ERIFW	*Equal Rights Independent Feminist Weekly*
LC	Library of Congress, Washington, D.C.
LWV	League of Women Voters
NA	National Archives, Washington, D.C.
NCL	National Consumers' League
NWP	National Woman's Party
SL	Arthur and Elizabeth Schlesinger Library, Radcliffe College, Cambridge, Massachusetts
WTUL	Women's Trade Union League

THE ORIGINS OF
THE EQUAL RIGHTS
AMENDMENT

PROLOGUE

In January 1917 the first "silent sentinels" appeared in front of the White House, holding banners inscribed with woman suffrage slogans. Crowds passing by were curious but sympathetic, and the authorities did not interfere. Even a moving picket line around the White House on March 4, inauguration day, encountered no difficulties from either the police or the public. But as the American war effort accelerated and the accompanying war proganda intensified, the slogans on the banners became sharper. "Kaiser" Wilson was informed that "Democracy Should Begin At Home," and by June, mob violence had erupted against the pickets. Arrested and charged with obstructing sidewalk traffic, the suffragists were sentenced at first to a few days in jail, then to six weeks, and finally to six months in prison. Two hundred eighteen women from twenty-six different states were arrested; nearly one hundred went to prison. They protested with hunger strikes and their jailers responded with forced feeding; only the sensational and unfavorable publicity that nearly crowded the war news off the front pages caused the authorities to relent. Late in November all the pickets were unconditionally released and the following March the District of Columbia Court of Appeals invalidated both the original arrests and the subsequent sentences.[1]

These suffragists were members of the National Woman's Party, a militant offshoot of the more respectable National American Woman Suffrage Association (NAWSA), which hastily denied any approval of such tactics. The aim of the National Woman's Party suffragists was to force Woodrow Wilson to use his power as head of the Democratic party to push the Susan B. Anthony suffrage amendment through Congress. Led by Alice Paul and influenced by the Pankhursts' tactics in England, they nevertheless stopped short of the British suffragettes' wide scale destruction of private and public property. Members of the NWP were content with symbolic destruction, dropping posters with Wilson's phrases printed on them into "watchfires." But like the British militants, their American counterparts were quite ready to "die for the cause" if that should prove necessary.

The American suffrage movement had split twice in its history, but only the second schism was a traumatic, irreparable break. The first split, which occurred in 1869 between the Stanton-Anthony faction and the Stone-Blackwell faction over the Fourteenth Amendment and the abolitionist pleas that it was "the Negro's hour," was healed in 1890 with the organization of NAWSA. But the suffrage movement then entered a period of "doldrums," and between 1896 and 1910 no new states enfranchised women. After 1910 the pace began to quicken again, and finally Carrie Chapman Catt, with her superb administrative and organizational talents, took over the leadership of NAWSA. But it was too late to prevent the younger, more immediatist suffragists who wished to work only for the federal amendment from taking their "organization within an organization," the Congressional Union, out of NAWSA. The break came after the Congressional Union had violated the nonpartisan credo of NAWSA by working against the Democratic candidates in the western states during the midterm elections of 1914, had organized the Woman's Party in states where women had the vote, and had decided to campaign against Wilson and the national Democratic slate in the elections of 1916. Although in 1916 Mrs. Catt revealed her "winning plan" and NAWSA was finally committed to the federal amendment, the difference between the two suffrage groups over tactics was still great. Compromise efforts failed, and the pickets of January 1917 belonged to the new organization that represented the combined Congressional Union and Woman's Party.

NAWSA leaders objected to the Woman's Party tactics for a number of reasons. Such tactics were futile, they argued, because Democrats sympathetic to suffrage would be alienated by such apparent partisanship, because President Wilson did not have the power to force the amendment through Congress, and because there was no party in power that controlled the necessary two-thirds of both Houses. But as Aileen Kraditor has perceptively noted, their opposition to these tactics went much deeper; it was based on principle. They believed that the suffrage cause would be debased by such tactics, saw the cause of suffrage as above party politics, preferred reason and persuasion to force or coercion, and always approached legislators as individuals. Furthermore, they had a traditional distaste for partisan politics, seeing women as humanitarian reformers whose arguments for the vote could not fail to convince men of good will. The Woman's Party, by trying to make woman suffrage politically expedient, implied that all such arguments were obsolete.[2]

Although historians of woman suffrage have disagreed about the relative importance of the contributions of the Woman's Party and NAWSA to the final victory, it can be argued that the work of the two organizations at least partially complemented one another. Yet the fight for the Nineteenth Amendment was long and hard, even toward the end. Although the amendment passed the House in January 1918, it did not get through the Senate until June 1919. Then the campaign for ratification began, and women were not finally enfranchised until August 1920. The legacy of animosity engendered among the membership and leadership of the two rival suffrage organizations would last far longer than the next two decades.

The 1920s marked, if not the end, certainly the beginning of the end of two remarkably intertwined movements. Similar in outlook, mood, tactics, and even sharing some of the same personnel, feminists and Progressive reformers would find the twenties increasingly hostile to further social change. Although much weakened, the Progressive and feminist impulses did survive and, in fact, partially merge in the decade of the twenties. Indeed, J. Stanley Lemons had shown that some women, the social feminists, became the era's major proponents of such Progressive reform measures as the Sheppard-Towner Maternity Act, the amendment prohibiting child labor, and the various measures intended to bring more efficiency to government. Many of these social feminists continued their activities as part of the New Deal reform programs, while the equalitarian feminists of the National Woman's Party who had sponsored the Equal Rights Amendment in 1923 began to secure their first real support from professional women's organizations in the 1930s.[3] However, overtaken by the worldwide depression in the thirties, most women and men alike would turn their attention first to the economic crisis within the United States, and then to the growing threat of fascism throughout the world. In both the twenties and the thirties, feminism seemed increasingly old-fashioned, perhaps even irrelevant, to most Americans.

Taking changes in style for changes in substance, the majority of both contemporary observers and later historians have emphasized the importance of the "new" woman in the 1920s. This emancipated middle-class female leaps out at the reader in various forms: the "Flapper Americana Novissima" from the pages of *Atlantic Monthly*, the unhappy and confused Carol Kenicott from the best selling novel *Main Street*, or the carefree young women portrayed in the lively, if often inaccurate, journalistic account *Only Yesterday*. Some historians have questioned the timing of the "new" woman's emergence, suggesting that her prototype, at least, was present in the pre-World War I era. Other accounts of the "new" woman, while tending to place her more firmly in the 1920s, differ primarily by insisting that her "newness" was merely that of the "sexy saleslady" or of the wife who had moved "from the nursery to the bedroom."[4] But aside from questions about who she was, what she was like, and when she emerged, almost no contemporary or historical accounts have doubted her existence, and most have made her the central female figure of the decade. Then, just as suddenly as she emerged, the "new" woman seems to have disappeared—a casualty, it would seem, of the Great Crash of 1929, quickly replaced by the "forgotten man" of the thirties.

This emphasis on the so-called "new" woman has tended to distort the realities of most women's lives during the twenties,[5] as well as to obscure the very real continuation of the woman's movement during the twenties and thirties. Regardless of whether they were feminists, nonfeminists, or antifeminists, most women during this period still expected to marry and have children. The consumerism of the twenties and the economic insecurity of the thirties only heightened the material aspirations of the American middle class and of those who wished to be middle-class. Yet women encountered increasing obstacles in gaining access to equal economic opportunity throughout these two decades, and experienced considerable confusion concerning the multiplicity of roles that seemed to be offered to them.

Equally puzzling to both contemporary observers and later historians has been the problem of what happened to the American woman's movement after the Nineteenth Amendment was ratified. Only the broad outlines of an answer are visible: the strength and vitality of the earlier women's organizations declined and the suffrage coalition broke down; many Americans believed that equality, or as much equality as was good for women, had been achieved; the post–World War I political climate was not conducive to further reform; popularized Freudianism encouraged the concept that the usable past was that of the individual rather than that of the community; and the new generation of women "inherited a legacy of female independence but without the political context in which it had been born."[6]

The demand for woman suffrage, oversold as it may have been, expedient as the arguments in its favor may have become, was never totally severed from its origins in that important feminist manifesto of 1848, the Seneca Falls Declaration. The only one of the original resolutions to be hotly debated, women's "sacred right" to vote was inherently a radical demand.[7] Ironically, in 1920 the right to vote was the only one of the Seneca Falls resolutions that had been completely attained, for in most ways women were still considered inferior to men and, on that basis, denied equal opportunities with them. It was the National Woman's Party (NWP) that recognized this persistent and pervasive denial of women's equality and that, admittedly with limited success, devoted itself to the task of eliminating the remaining legal discriminations against women during the next two decades. At the heart of the equalitarian feminists' program lay another federal amendment, the Equal Rights Amendment.

During the 1920s, postsuffrage feminist issues were gradually defined. Throughout most of the decade the NWP stood nearly alone in its advocacy of the ERA as the best method for eliminating the remaining legal discriminations against women, primarily because of the threat to special protective legislation. But there were many other specific legal issues on which feminists could agree, and to some extent, cooperate. The drive for jury service for women continued unabated throughout the twenties and into the thirties, yet in the thirties about half the states still barred women from serving on juries. In fact, the state-by-state campaigning became so disheartening that in 1937, many women welcomed the alternative offered by the introduction into Congress of a federal jury service bill. During the 1920s, questions arose concerning a married woman's right to retain her birth name for professional purposes, to establish her own domicile, to have equal rights of inheritance and guardianship, and to possess citizenship independent of her husband. On these questions there was little disagreement among women's groups, and there was also generally widespread support among organized women for such measures as mothers' pensions or endowments, the federal maternity act, and the child labor amendment.

Yet the disagreement over how to achieve economic opportunity for women made any genuine wholehearted cooperation among such groups as the NWP, the League of Women Voters, the Consumers' League, the Business and Professional Women, and the U.S. Women's Bureau impossible. Since the first Woman's Rights Convention in 1848, feminists had stressed the important connection between the economic opportunity for financial independence and the attainment of women's emancipation. Such theorists as the American women's movement possessed, particularly Charlotte Perkins Gilman, had consistently emphasized how essential it was for women to be able to earn their own livelihood. Thus economic independence had become a key assumption in the mainstream of both British and American feminist thought. Since the economic interests of women were so fundamental, it was not an area in which conflicting viewpoints about how to secure these interests could be reconciled easily.

One of the major underlying issues of the 1920s was women's right to paid employment, particularly married women's right to work.[8] The economic dislocations caused by rapid demobilization after World War I were eased to some extent by the lingering patriotism that encouraged married women to relinquish their jobs for the returning soldiers. But the general trend continued to be the movement of women into the work force and this was perceived by both organized labor and the general public as an encroachment, especially during the depression decade of the 1930s. Organized women divided bitterly in the 1920s over the question of how best to secure optimum conditions for women's employment. While the NWP maintained that any special legislation restricted women's employment opportunities, other groups such as the Consumer's League, League of Women Voters, and the Women's Bureau argued that special legislation protected women and made them better able to compete for jobs.

This same issue was also present within international feminist organizations. In the struggle for ideological leadership of both the American and international movements, the NWP had the advantage of being a "single issue" group devoted to equal rights, while the League of Women Voters was more diffuse in its aims and clung to its early primary goal of citizenship education for voters. But the NWP experienced organizational difficulties and its internal disagreements prevented the Party from taking full advantage of its "hard core"[9] feminist position. The Party stood alone throughout these two decades in its single-minded dedication to obtaining legal equality between men and women. All its activities on the state, national, and international levels were directed toward the achievement of this goal, which its members believed would have a tremendous impact on women's economic opportunities and social status.

In spite of serious divisions within its own ranks, the NWP remained a committed feminist organization, active throughout the twenties and thirties on behalf of women's rights. Conservatives, moderates, and reformers within the Party shared a belief in the urgent need for such an organization and voiced a consistent concern over the meaning of feminism. Increasingly forced on the defensive by hostile public opinion during the late twenties and thirties, the Party held firm to its belief that the world needed the contributions of woman, which could only be realized fully when she was freed from artificial legal restrictions that prevented her from developing her potential as a human being. Members were never aware of any inconsistency in their acceptance of the Victorian emphasis on the differences between men and women, and their demand for absolute equality between men and women. There were other women outside the Party who became increasingly concerned with the meaning of and the need for feminism in response to the growing economic insecurity, the rise of fascism, and what appeared to be a widespread conviction, supported by general public opinion, that women should return to their proper "place" in the home. But the NWP's feminism was an exclusive fortress, standing on a narrow legalistic base, and insisting on allegiance to the ERA as the sine qua non of "true" feminists. This made it impossible for most of these feminist sympathizers outside the Party to cooperate with the NWP.

The Party did have more success during the thirties than during the twenties in convincing some women's organizations to support the Equal Rights Amendment. At first, in the early twenties, they clung to their old tactics that they believed had been responsible for the Congressional passage of the Nineteenth Amendment. Yet the circumstances were different in the twenties and the issues were rarely clear enough for militant confrontations, except occasionally in the international arena. Publicity had always been their forte, according to both admirers and enemies alike, yet by the thirties the press coverage was often openly hostile to the Party. The equalitarian feminists also abandoned their tactic of holding the party in power responsible for the fate of the ERA after the NWP's nearly disastrous participation in the election of 1928. However, they continued to endorse women for both elective and appointive positions in government, to promote the writing and teaching of women's history, and to commemorate women's past achievements. Yet none of these tactics was very effective. The times had changed, feminism had fallen into disrepute, and the NWP feminists were divided from the social feminists in the American and international movements both by temperament and personal antagonisms, but more importantly, by a fundamental disagreement over the meaning of equality.

The NWP's strong bid for a dominant leadership position in both the American and international feminist movements failed, but this failure cannot be attributed completely to its own internal Party difficulties and the opposition of the social feminists. The NWP's feminism was too narrowly defined to appeal to many women, whose concerns often centered on the apparent conflicts between their positions as wives and mothers and the economic and personal attractions of a job or career. A close examination of the ideas expressed by NWP members and leaders during the 1920s and 1930s reveals an underlying assumption that all women should have jobs or careers outside the home, and a definite ambivalence toward marriage and motherhood, based on a distrust of men. But the equalitarian feminists never developed a systematic ideology with regard to women's roles as wives, mothers, and workers, nor did they move beyond Charlotte Perkins Gilman's turn-of-the-century analysis of marriage and the home. Instead, equalitarian feminists repeated again and again that there was no need to choose between a job and a marriage with children, when evidence to the contrary was becoming more difficult for both the general public, and married women in particular, to ignore. Unable to retain the younger women it attracted during the interwar period, by 1941 the NWP had become more ingrown in its membership, less democratic in its structure, and increasingly rigid in its ideology. The tragedy was that, just as its members had so often insisted, the NWP was the only "true" feminist organization in America during the twenties and thirties.

But the woman's movement, most notably the part of the movement that demanded legal equality between men and women, did survive. In this context, it becomes significant that during the "revival" of feminism in the 1960s, the Equal Rights Amendment was also revived; however, it was only one of many feminist goals, most of which called for a reexamination of women's relationships with men and with other women, as well as for a new analysis of women's roles in marriage, motherhood, and work. This study will focus on the equalitarian feminists, particularly on the members of the National Woman's Party and their allies, as well as on their opponents during the 1920s and 1930s, in an attempt to suggest answers to several related questions. What was the nature of American feminism between the wars? What were the origins of the Equal Rights Amendment and on what bases did people support or oppose it? What, if anything, had been achieved as a result of the women's movement by the time World War II broke out?

NOTES

1. The best general account of the suffrage movement is Eleanor Flexner, *Century of Struggle* (Cambridge: Harvard University Press,

1959). Accounts by active members of the Congressional Union and NWP include Inez Haynes Irwin, *The Story of the Woman's Party* (New York: Harcourt Brace, 1921) and Doris Stevens *Jailed For Freedom* (New York: Boni and Liveright, 1920). For a balanced yet sympathetic analysis of the NWP's role in the suffrage struggle, see Loretta Ellen Zimmerman, "Alice Paul and the National Woman's Party, 1912–1920 (Ph.D. diss., Tulane University, 1964).

2. Aileen Kraditor, *The Ideas of the Woman Suffrage Movement, 1890–1920* (Garden City, New York: Doubleday, 1971), pp. 198–201.

3. J. Stanley Lemons, *The Woman Citizen* (Urbana, Ill.: University of Illinois Press, 1973). Although his thesis is the lack of carry over, see also Otis Graham, *Encore For Reform* (New York: Oxford, 1967).

4. G. Stanley Hall, "Flapper Americana Novissima," *Atlantic Monthly* 129 (June 1922), 771–80; Sinclair Lewis, *Main Street* (New York: Harcourt Brace, 1920); Frederick Lewis Allen, *Only Yesterday*, (New York: Harper, 1931); June Sochen, *The New Woman: Feminism in Greenwich Village, 1910–1920* (New York: Quadrangle, 1969); James McGovern, "The American Woman's Pre-World War I Freedom in Manners and Morals," *Journal of American History* 55 (Spring 1978), 315–33; Henry F. May, *The End of American Innocence* (New York: Knopf, 1959); Mary P. Ryan, *Womanhood in America* (New York: Franklin Watts, 1974); and Sheila Rothman, *Woman's Proper Place* (New York: Basic Books, 1978).

5. Paul Carter, *Another Part of the Twenties*, New York: Columbia University Press, 1977).

6. William Chafe, *The American Woman* (New York: Oxford, 1972); William O'Neil, *Everyone Was Brave* (Chicago: Quadrangle, 1969); Lemons, *The Woman Citizen;* Loren Baritz, *The Culture of the Twenties* (New York: Bobbs-Merrill, 1969), xli; Jo Freeman, *The Politics of Women's Liberation* (New York: David McKay, 1975), pp. 18–19.

7. William O'Neill, "The Failure of Feminism as a Radical Ideology," in *Dissent: Explorations in American Radical History* (DeKalb, Ill.: University of Northern Illinois Press, 1968); Kraditor, *The Ideas of the Woman Suffrage Movement;* Ellen C. DuBois, *Feminism and Suffrage: The Emergence of an Independent Women's Movement in America, 1848–1869* (Ithaca, N.Y.: Cornell University Press, 1978).

8. Lois Scharf, *To Work and To Wed: Female Employment, Feminism, and the Great Depression* (Westport, Conn.: Greenwood Press, 1980).

9. William O'Neill's term for Party members because they put women's equality first, as opposed to "social" feminists who were willing to work for other reforms of a humanitarian nature before women had achieved equality. See O'Neill, *Everyone Was Brave.*

1

THE NEW NATIONAL WOMAN'S PARTY

The equalitarian feminists of the NWP did not return directly from the polls in 1920 to begin working for the Equal Rights Amendment—they understandably wished to commemorate the end of the long and arduous suffrage campaign. They also needed to regroup their supporters, reorganize their Party, and perhaps recruit some social feminist allies. Most of all, they needed to bury the old antagonisms that the intensity of the final stages of the suffrage struggle had exacerbated.

The National Woman's Party underwent a period of extensive reorganization between 1920 and 1923, and emerged with the new objective of complete legal equality between men and women. The three instruments to which the equalitarian feminists eventually committed themselves were the Equal Rights Amendment, its international parallel, the Equal Rights Treaty, and the more limited Equal Nationality Treaty which dealt only with citizenship. All their major activities during the remaining years of the twenties, as well as during the depression decade of the thirties, were efforts to secure support for and passage of these equality measures.

Although publicly identified as leaders of the Party, neither Alice Paul nor Mrs. O. H. P. Belmont actively directed the NWP after its initial reorganization. The real position of power within the Party was that of national chairman, a position held by only seven women during the twenties and thirties; all but one of these women, along with Doris Stevens and a small number of other activists, continued to provide the stable core of NWP leadership during this period. Although both Party membership and Party finances fluctuated during these two decades, the overall pattern was one of decline. Yet ironically, at the same time, support for the Party's kind of equalitarian feminism was increasing in both the United States and Europe.

Since the thirty-sixth state did not ratify the Nineteenth Amendment until August 1920, the suffragists had little time to organize and register women for the presidential election of November. Carrie Chapman Catt had worked to keep the suffrage structure intact by creating the League of Women Voters in states where women had previously obtained partial or total suffrage. In states where suffrage was obtained through the federal amendment, the National American Woman Suffrage Association (NAWSA) continued to function until well after the presidential election. The NWP made no attempt to reorganize until its annual meeting in 1921, although late in the previous year Alice Paul had indicated that she was open to suggestions for postsuffrage programs. Among the various proposals were strong pressures on the Party to work with the growing peace movement, a specific feminist program advanced by Crystal Eastman, and the suggestion that the NWP disband permanently now that the vote had been won.

Disbanding the NWP was never a real possibility. In contrast to NAWSA, the NWP members and leaders had never put all their faith in the vote, but rather had considered suffrage as a means to further feminist advances. The question then became the direction or focus these further feminist gains would take. The peace movement was more a humanitarian than a feminist effort, although women were in the forefront of most peace groups. Alice Paul and other NWP leaders showed little interest in the comprehensive Eastman program, which was an attempt to provide social, political and economic equality for the "new" woman.[1] Instead, the NWP leadership was inclined to focus on the remaining legal disabilities of women.

Mrs. O. H. P. Belmont, the Party's major financier, had never doubted that there was a need for further work leading towards equality for women. She had made her views known at a conference of the national officers and state chairmen in early September 1920, at the Belmont home on Long Island. Distrusting the existing political parties, Mrs. Belmont strongly advocated a woman's party that would use the strategy and tactics of the NWP's suffrage campaign to obtain real equality for women. Yet even at this early conference, echoes of dissent were present. Mrs. Belmont, fearing that women might be taken advantage of by the existing parties, argued that an independent feminist party could support or oppose candidates according to their stand on women's issues. Harriot Stanton Blatch, who would leave the NWP briefly but become active again in the late 1920s, opposed a separate woman's party because she thought the vote could be used more effectively as a tool for reform through the existing political structure. Florence Kelley, who later became one of the most outspoken critics of the NWP, favored broad nonfeminist reforms such as peace work, the antilynching campaign, and the improvement and modernization of Congress. Others urged the improvement of education, the abolition of poverty and disease, and the need for a campaign against prostitution and venereal disease. Some thought that any action that might perpetuate sex antagonism should be avoided until it was clear that there would be a distinct difference between men's and women's political interests, while others promised continued support for the NWP if it would work for the removal of the remaining civil disabilities of women.[2]

These disagreements among the members were only mild indications of what was to come, and the 1921 convention was to be the turning point. The NWP had invited all other women's organizations to present their programs at the Party's annual convention in 1921, hoping to avoid duplication of effort but primarily to sound out support for its own tentative decision to concentrate on removing legal discriminations against women. Nearly fifty national women's organizations were represented at the memorial service which opened the convention on February 15, 1921, in Washington. Crystal Eastman covered the meeting for *The Liberator*, and her reaction was representative of the era's radical feminist left. Eastman was not moved by the stirring rhetoric, asking instead why so little time had been devoted to the future of the feminist movement. She also criticized the extreme respectability of the convention, noting that "all doubtful subjects, like birth control and the rights of Negro women, were hushed up, ruled out, or postponed until the affair at the Capitol was over." At the conclusion, the NWP executive committee resolved that the reorganized Party would work "to remove all the remaining forms of the subjection of women," and an attempt to introduce a minority resolution as a substitute failed because "the time limit and a very efficient steam roller disposed of it before the discussion had fairly started." Always a perceptive observer, Eastman believed that Alice Paul's real, but unspoken, message to the delegates was that they should go home and not worry, since they would be told later what to do.[3]

Florence Kelley, who had been a vice-president of NAWSA and then worked with the Woman's Party during the militant phase of the suffrage campaign, also reported on the NWP convention. Kelley was quick to realize the potential threat to protective legislation for working women in the NWP's new emphasis on total legal equality. She was unwilling to see jeopardized that hard-won state protective legislation which limited women's work week, prohibited night work for women, established minimum wages for women and children, and provided certain special work facilities for women.[4] Kelley's fears would soon be shared by other social feminists.

After the 1921 reorganization conference, events moved rapidly. In February Alice Paul announced her intention to retire as Party leader, in April NWP delegates called on President Harding urging him to support an end to discrimination against women, and in May the Party completed negotiations to buy a historic Capitol Hill house in Washington as the headquarters for its national activities. Mrs. Belmont, whose contribution had made possible the purchase, was elected president of the new National Woman's Party and a national council and executive committee were established. In September the NWP's women lawyers began meeting to discuss the drafting of an equality amendment to the federal Constitution, and by December their preliminary report was made public.

The NWP would never wholly abandon state work because of the continuing interest of its members in such measures as jury service for women, equal inheritance and guardianship rights, married women's control over their earnings and property, and equal opportunities for women in education, business, and the professions. Since the League of Women Voters' method for ending the remaining discriminations against women was "specific bills for specific ills," this often meant a certain overlapping of the efforts of the two organizations on the state level, and sometimes jealous competition over which group should receive the credit for any accomplishment. Furthermore, in addition to the federal amendment method and the specific bill method, there had seemed at first to be a third legislative alternative.

In July 1921, Wisconsin had passed a blanket state equal rights bill for women, but unlike the proposed Equal Rights Amendment to the federal Constitution, the Wisconsin law contained a clause exempting protective legislation for women. Therefore it was not vigorously opposed by other women's organizations, although Florence Kelley later criticized the law. As the NWP's position against protective legislation became more uncompromising and outspoken, the open opposition of other women's organizations to a possible Equal Rights Amendment and to blanket state equality bills intensified. By the spring of 1922, public debates were being held between members of the NWP and their opponents, and the League of Women Voters had countered with a committee to work on removing women's legal disabilities. The National Consumers' League, along with the National Council of Catholic Women, had announced it would fight the NWP's legislative plans for any blanket bills and began soliciting money for that purpose, while the NWP launched a fund-raising drive of its own. The first major clashes took place in New York, where both the NWP and the Consumers' League had relatively strong state organizations and where Alfred Smith had just been elected governor.[5]

The Equal Rights Amendment, sometimes called the Lucretia Mott Amendment, was adopted unanimously by the NWP convention which met in Seneca Falls, New York, in July 1923. Later that year, the ERA was introduced into both houses of Congress. Drafted by Alice Paul, the Amendment read: "Men and woman shall have equal rights throughout the United States and every place subject to its jurisdiction." At the convention, Paul pointed out that the state-by-state method of attaining equal rights was intolerably slow and insecure. "We shall not be safe," she said, "until the principle of equal rights is written into the framework of our Government." At this same meeting, two representatives of New York working women asked whether equality before the law would also apply to women in industry, and Paul replied affirmatively. Other early reasons advanced for the federal amendment method were that it would have permanent results, was a dignified way of attaining feminist goals, cost less to campaign for in terms of time and money, and would force national politicians and parties to take clear stands and prevent them from dodging the issue of equality. Later these arguments were expanded greatly during the course of debates with opposing women's organizations. But in 1923, the NWP could simply maintain that the federal amendment method was the most effective and expedient, while "to await State action is to take the most difficult and most roundabout way of approaching our goal." "It shoots straight at the mark," editorialized the Party journal, "it proves that women have at last thrown off the shackles of serfdom and lifted their faces from the dust."[6]

There were several other important aspects of the NWP's reorganization during the three years following the ratification of the Nineteenth Amendment. Having determined that the immediate goal was to be the abolition of the remaining legal disabilities of women, it established a legal research department in 1921 which began the laborious task of compiling state-by-state digests of laws discriminating against women. The two most important members of this department were Burnita Shelton Matthews, who later became a federal judge, and Emma Wold, who was appointed technical advisor to the American delegation at the 1930 Hague Conference on the Codification of International Law.

The NWP also established twenty-five permanent councils "to sweep away the prejudice and tradition which still restrict the activities of business and professional women." The Party used the broadest possible definition of business and professional women, who ranged from actresses, architects, and farmers to homemakers, osteopaths, and teachers, and invited prominent women to head these councils.[7] Since its official organ, *The Suffragist*, had ceased publication in 1921, the NWP had been relying on a newsletter format, *Equal Rights: Weekly Bulletin of the National Woman's Party*. Because this newsletter obviously would be inadequate for its needs in sponsoring the Equal Rights Amendment, the NWP made arrangements for a new full-sized journal, *Equal Rights*, which began publication in 1923.

NWP members, like other women, also became very concerned during the twenties about the gap between themselves and the newer generation. They were committed to spreading feminist ideas among the younger women, but were no more successful in their attempts to recruit them than other women's groups. The Party had originally appealed to many younger members of NAWSA, although quite a few of their activist members had been older women even in 1913. Yet NWP members thought of themselves as "young" because they believed themselves open to change, optimistic, and courageous, all qualities which they associated with youth. Looking about for some way to integrate younger women and girls into the NWP, they decided to form students' councils. The Inez Milholland Memorial committee was created for this purpose in 1923, and it began its organizational activities with college women. Milholland was chosen as the symbol of inspiration for the organization of younger women because of her early dramatic death while campaigning for suffrage.[8]

The committee's goal was to interest college women in working for the equality of the sexes among both students and faculties. The initial organization was based heavily upon members' own daughters, however, which meant that the women's colleges of New England and New York were overrepresented. By 1924, there were only about 100 student members, and student officers were generally the daughters of NWP veterans, like Elizabeth Selden Rogers II and Cornelia Bruere Rose, Jr. The Party provided materials showing the discrimination that existed in colleges, and in 1925 the students' goals were to form more councils, do research on discrimination, work for academic equality for women students and faculty, and help forward the passage of the ERA. The student organizations were never large or widespread, but continued into the 1930s. In order to interest more college women in the struggle for equal rights, the Party sponsored intercollegiate undergraduate essay contests judged by prominent women, and awarded prizes ranging from 100 to 500 dollars. "The cause is never lost so long as each succeeding generation is ready to help carry it on," maintained the president of the Goucher student council in 1933, and the NWP continued its active attempts to recruit younger women throughout both decades.[9]

By 1923, then, the NWP had taken on its new form and objectives and had acquired both a headquarters and a solid financial base. It had an equalitarian feminist program that had already pushed its natural allies such as the League of Women Voters into opposition, and a new journal to circulate the Party's views. It also had a nucleus of seasoned, dedicated leaders, and a small but active and articulate membership. In comparison to the experience of other women's groups during the twenties and thirties, the NWP weathered the period well. The upper middle class, well-educated women who provided leadership for the NWP formed a small rather exclusive elite group, but the same might be said of most of the social feminist leadership of the period.

During the twenties, the NWP engaged in several equal rights strategies, all intended to achieve some tangible results, such as the election or appointment of women to office, as well as to educate women about the discriminations against them. In 1924, the Party mounted an extensive Women for Congress campaign designed to elect women to the House of Representatives as the first step toward the creation of a "women's bloc." Organizers, speakers, and money poured into Pennsylvania, where five of the ten women nominated for Congressional seats that year were campaigning. Not one of the Pennsylvania women was elected, however, in spite of the NWP's efforts. Moreover, although the Women for Congress campaign had received a great deal of publicity, much of it criticized the NWP for engaging in partisan politics.

In 1926, the NWP was one of the many women's groups participating in the Conference of Women in Industry called by Mary Anderson, head of the U.S. Women's Bureau. The equalitarian feminists' demand that the Bureau consider the disadvantages, as well as the advantages, of special legislation for women disrupted the conference and later destroyed the committee appointed to study the question. The Women's Bureau report, finally published in 1928, insisted that special legislation helped rather than harmed women, but the controversial issue refused to die. In fact, the disagreement between the social feminists who advocated protective legislation for women and the equalitarian feminists who opposed such laws spilled over into the international feminist movement in the late twenties.

Post–World War I economic dislocations were far more severe in Europe than in America, and when the NWP representatives arrived in Paris a few months later for the congress of the International Alliance of Women, they found that many European feminists were very concerned about the restrictive effects of so-called protective legislation on women's economic opportunities. The League of Women Voters was the only organization representing American women within the Alliance, and it successfully spearheaded a social feminist drive to deny Alliance membership to the NWP. The cost of this denial was great, however. Several active European feminist organizations opposed to special legislation and protective conventions for women withdrew from the International Alliance of Women, and the Alliance, previously able to speak for international feminism, was much weakened by their defection. Those who withdrew from the Alliance quickly organized new groups such as the Open Door International and the Equal Rights International to lobby for complete civil equality between men and women at the League of Nations, World Court, and International Labour Office. With feminist leadership divided, women found themselves increasingly unable to resist the impact of the deepening worldwide depression and the rise of fascism.

By 1928, the NWP was aggressively challenging American social feminists and their European allies for leadership of the international woman's movement. Doris Stevens, the NWP's major activist in the twenties and thirties, led most of the international efforts during the period. Stevens was a graduate of Oberlin College, had been both a social worker and a high school teacher, and had done state suffrage work before joining the Congressional Union in 1913. As an organizer for the NWP she managed its California campaign in 1916, and was arrested twice as a result of her participation in suffrage demonstrations in Washington, D.C., and New York City. After suffrage was granted, she wrote *Jailed for Freedom*, married, and continued her NWP activities full time. In 1935, she married for a second time. Stevens served on the national council almost continuously for the entire two decades, managed the Party's Women For Congress campaign, and presented the NWP's equality treaties at international meetings. In the late twenties an admiring article in *Time and Tide*, a militant English feminist journal, accurately characterized Doris Stevens as "An Apostle of Action."[10]

Stevens attended the Sixth Pan American conference which met in Havana in 1928, and presented the NWP's new Equal Rights Treaty, modeled on the ERA, to the delegates. They responded favorably, much to the chagrin of the American social feminists, and named her to head their advisory committee on the status of women, the Inter-American Commission of Women. Since the problem of married women's citizenship was on the agenda of both the Hague Codification Conference and the League of Nations, the InterAmerican Commission decided to study that aspect of women's status first. In the meantime, without consulting their membership, NWP leaders announced that the Party would present its new Equal Rights Treaty to every government and international conference. Arriving in Paris late that summer, Doris Stevens led a group of equalitarian feminists who interrupted the Kellogg-Briand talks with their demand that the French goverment endorse the Equal Rights Treaty. One of the few militant confrontations in which the NWP engaged during the postsuffrage era, this action proved to be divisive in the long run. Although many of the old guard NWP members praised such international activism, other members questioned it, believing that the Party should concentrate its efforts on achieving equality for American women first.

Most Americans probably were more interested in domestic matters than in international affairs that year. The presidential contest between Herbert Hoover and Al Smith also attracted the attention of the NWP leaders, who decided to support Hoover for presidency. Although Hoover had not endorsed the ERA, his campaign rhetoric emphasized equal opportunity for all Americans; Smith, on the other hand, openly advocated protective legislation for women and children only. Engaging in partisan politics turned out to be a serious error for the NWP, however, for the Party contained prominent and active Democratic women who were alienated by this strategy. Furthermore, although Hoover won the election, his failure to support economic equality for women and the NWP's inability to hold the Republicans to account on this issue thoroughly disillusioned those equalitarian feminists who had believed in the British tactic of holding the party in power responsible for its actions.

In the 1930s, feminist issues were very nearly submerged by the worldwide economic depression and the rise of fascism. Yet both depression and fascism involved a special threat to women's status, because basic to both was a back-to-the-home movement. The equalitarian feminists of the NWP had survived the unsympathetic climate of opinion of the twenties, when feminism had seemed increasingly irrelevant and old-fashioned. But they were to face outright hostility and strong resistance during the thirties when they championed women's right to work outside the home. In this struggle, they would be hampered not only by the continuing division between the equalitarian and social feminist viewpoints, but also by a serious schism in their own Party.

During the 1930s, the NWP continued its international efforts to obtain approval for the Equal Rights Treaty. Lobbying focused on the League of Nations; although the U.S. was never a member nation, NWP feminists utilized their own memberships in international women's groups and their friendships with Latin American representatives to bring equalitarian feminist views before the League. The International Labour Office, especially its Women's Work division, remained a stronghold of the social feminist viewpoint. Social feminists, of course, opposed the Equal Rights Treaty because it would destroy international protective labor conventions for women.

In 1935, the Juridical Commission of the League of Nations debated the Equal Rights Treaty for several days, but the outcome was disappointing. The treaty was referred back to individual governments, women's organizations, and the ILO for further study. After it joined the ILO in 1934, the U.S. was represented by a prominent social feminist, and in the late thirties NWP members were excluded both from the women's coalition group formed in America to study the treaty and from the new committee appointed by the League of Nations to investigate the status of women. Although Alice Paul united European equalitarian feminists into the World Woman's Party in 1938, the outbreak of World War II in Europe soon overwhelmed the new organization.

Nor was the NWP able to retain its leadership position in Latin American feminism during the thirties. After joining the other women's groups at the 1930 Hague Codification Conference in an unsuccessful attempt to obtain independent citizenship rights for married women, the InterAmerican Commission of Woman had formulated an Equal Nationality Treaty. This treaty was accepted by the Pan American Conference which met in Montevideo in 1933, debated in the League of Nations in 1935, and recommended for adherence to the League's member nations later that year. But the success of such a blanket means, even when the end—independent citizenship—was a desirable goal, spurred American social feminists to cooperate in a successful effort to eliminate the NWP influence in Latin America. Social feminists representing the U.S. effectively blocked any further consideration of equality measures at the 1938 Pan American Conference in Lima. The following year, Franklin Delano Roosevelt appointed an American social feminist to replace Doris Stevens, and by 1940, the InterAmerican Commission had been completely reorganized and reflected a social feminist outlook.

The thirties were also characterized by a growing disagreement within the NWP over priorities. Increasingly, newer members who had joined the Party primarily in response to economic discriminations against women, such as the Government Economy Act of 1932, the National Recovery Act codes, and the interstate labor compacts, wished to expand and democratize the NWP. These women believed that a large, broadly based Party would be better able to educate the public and counteract such discriminations. But the old guard faction of the NWP wanted the Party to remain much the same structurally and to concentrate on centralized lobbying for the ERA and the Equal Rights Treaty. These differences, along with others, eventually led to a schism within the Party which lasted from 1935 to 1937. Unfortunately, the differing factions were not really reconciled by a series of revisions in the NWP's constitution that technically reunited the Party in 1938.

Nevertheless, throughout the 1930s, NWP feminists continued to try to convince uncommitted women of the need for the Equal Rights Amendment. The equalitarian feminists debated the social feminists not only in the pages of middle class women's magazines, but also within American women's organizations, such as the General Federation of Women's Clubs, the Business and Professional Women's Federation, and the American Association of University Women. The only major women's organization to endorse the ERA by the end of the decade was the Business and Professional Women, although numerous smaller organizations also came to support the Amendment. On the other hand, the movement for protective legislation for women had slowed nearly to a standstill in the twenties, and support for such laws eroded even more rapidly in the thirties. In fact, the two groups fought each other to an impasse—most uncommitted women were merely confused and distressed by the debate.

Throughout these two decades of domestic and international feminist activism, the NWP was led by a small group of articulate, energetic women who were committed to equality. The NWP activists were generally upper middle-class, but also included a number of wealthy and socially prominent women. They were well-educated and often had a background of settlement work, urban reform movements during the Progressive period, or unusual achievement in the professions. Many were related by birth or marriage, nearly all lived their adult lives in the northeastern United States, and most had been involved in the militant phase of the struggle for the Nineteenth Amendment. Mrs. O. H. P. Belmont and Alice Paul were perhaps the two leaders best known to the public.

Although the real position of power within the Party was the chairman of the national council, Mrs. O. H. P. Belmont retained the title of president of the NWP from 1921 until her death in 1933. After her scandalous divorce from William K. Vanderbilt in 1895, she had married Oliver Hazard Perry Belmont, who died in 1909. Mrs. Belmont had worked with the Women's Trade Union League and had received a great deal of publicity when she organized mass meetings to raise money for the shirtwaist strikers in New York. Her militancy led her to serve on the executive committee of the Congressional Union and Woman's Party, and she became president of the new National Woman's Party.

Inspired by Mrs. Pankhurst in England, Mrs. Belmont had advocated the use of similar tactics by the Congressional Union in the United States. The younger women were never too radical for her; in fact they sometimes had difficulty keeping up with her pace. She did not look with favor upon endless discussion and committee meetings, for "action, always action, was her guiding genius." Having developed her qualities of "initiative, independence and executive genius" in New

York society, Mrs. Belmont then put these qualities to use in further-ing feminist objectives. According to her co-workers, she displayed "a fine sense of dramatic values, a capacity for detail and a mastery of organization which has never deserted her."[11]

In 1920, Mrs. Belmont was sixty-seven years old, but her militancy was unabated. She believed that women were still a "subject class" in America, and urged all self-respecting women to fight for "their full heritage as human beings." She saw the Equal Rights Amendment as only a step toward women's freedom; the NWP's Declaration of Principles of 1922 demonstrates her belief in the necessity of changing the basis of women's relationships with men. Her faith in women was boundless, but her underlying distrust of men led her to insert a clause in the deed of the Washington headquarters she had purchased for the NWP providing that the property would revert to her if any man were ever permitted to hold an office or a paid position in the Party. In fact, she often intimidated others and was sometimes "misunder-stood by her own generation."[12] Her daughter, whose marriage to the Duke of Marlborough had been such a feather in Mrs. Belmont's cap until Consuelo divorced him to marry a French officer, was quite harsh in her evaluation of her mother's personality. As Consuelo described her mother:

> Her combative nature rejoiced in conquests. She loved a fight. A born dictator, she dominated events about her as thoroughly as she eventually dominated her husband and her children. If she admitted another point of view she never conceded it; we were pawns in her game to be moved as her wishes decreed.[13]

After 1923, Mrs. Belmont lived in France and occasionally made trips back to the United States. But she continued to take a lively in-terest in the NWP, especially in its international activities. She also demanded a personal accounting of the purposes for which her money was being used, and sometimes complained that she had not been con-sulted prior to the planning of the activities. Often Mrs. Belmont had her own ideas, and on one occasion suggested that the working women of the NWP needed something social, like a ball. "I could see her giving the money that we need so much for other purposes for a social affair for the industrial women," wrote NWP officer Jane Norman Smith, "and my heart sank." But the persuasive Smith was finally able to convince Belmont to contribute $5,000 for organizational purposes.[14]

Alice Paul has been described as the most charismatic leader produced by the American suffrage movement.[15] A Quaker from Moorestown, New Jersey, Paul earned her B.A. at Swarthmore and then her M.A. and Ph.D. in sociology at the University of Pennsylvania. In the twenties she received a Bachelor of Laws at Washington College of Law, and a Master of Laws and Doctor of Civil Laws at American University. While doing settlement work in Europe, Paul had met Mrs. Pankhurst and had begun working full time for woman suffrage in England. Returning to the University of Pennsylvania in 1912, she completed her doctoral work on the legal position of women in Pennsylvania. That same year, Alice Paul also became chairman of the congressional committee of NAWSA; by 1913 she had recruited many other suffragists and formed the Congressional Union. In 1916 she established the Woman's Party, which broke with NAWSA the following year over the question of militant tactics.

Alice Paul completely dominated and single handedly directed the activities of the Congressional Union and the Woman's Party during the militant phase of the suffrage struggle. The fact that the Woman's Party members confined their militancy to parades, picketing, watch-fires, and anti-Wilson speeches, however, did not spare them from arrest, prison sentences, and occasionally forced feeding. Alice Paul, like her counterpart Mrs. Pankhurst in England, was in the forefront of both the protests and punishments. After suffrage was attained, she took part in the reorganization of the NWP and the drafting of the Equal Rights Amendment, although she had publicly announced her intention to retire as head of the Party.

Paul never totally retired, serving on the national council for much of the period, or as vice-president or advisory chairman of the Party. She also directed the InterAmerican Commission on Women's research on nationality laws. During most of the 1930s, Alice Paul was in Europe. Having previously cultivated overseas contacts as allies for the NWP, she worked with the Equal Rights International, the Open

Door Council, and other women's groups lobbying at the International Labour Office and the League of Nations. By the late thirties, Paul was ready to pull together the disparate splinter elements of international feminism into a World Woman's Party under her leadership, with headquarters in Geneva. When war made her plans impossible to carry out, she returned to the United States, rested briefly at her home in Vermont, and resumed the chairmanship of the NWP in 1942.

No straightforward biographical account can explain the impact of Alice Paul's personality on her followers. Her many admirers were devoted and loyal, believing that she could not make a mistake in either politics or tactics. They were always ready to follow her lead, impressed by the way she drove herself and others for the good of the cause. Mabel Vernon, a fellow student at Swarthmore, remembered how Paul had forced herself to be good enough in athletics to make the team. While serving her 1917 prison sentence, Alice Paul absolutely refused to eat, and after three weeks she was hospitalized and examined by a psychologist. Such martyrdom for the cause was widely admired by many suffragists, although not everyone shared that opinion. Many of the inhabitants of Paul's hometown thought these English tactics "outrageous," and preferred the methods of Carrie Chapman Catt. While emphasizing her respect for the Paul family, one outspoken elderly woman criticized such "unseemly" behavior and told a reporter that "Alice has chosen to fly in the face of her religion, which bids us be meek, and of her country, which tells us to be law abiding."[16]

Alice Paul's appearance also impressed many of her admirers. She gave the impression of fragility, serenity, and quiet intelligence. Her eyes were always mentioned in any physical descriptions of her, "great earnest childlike eyes that seem to seize you and hold you to her purpose despite your own desires and intentions." Not even foreign observers were immune, and after Paul's visit with French feminists in 1925, Simone Tery wrote: "She speaks but little, laying on you the straight and thoughtful look of her big dark eyes. She knows what she wants and she doesn't need shouting."[17]

Both Crystal Eastman and Doris Stevens recognized the difficulties inherent in any attempt to describe Alice Paul's leadership. Stevens began to write, only to discover "how little we know about this laconic person, and yet how abundantly we feel her power, her will and her compelling leadership." In describing what had happened during the suffrage campaign, Stevens wrote that "in an instant and vivid reaction, I am either congealed or inspired; exhilarated or depressed; sometimes even exasperated, but always *moved*." Crystal Eastman thought the strength of Alice Paul's leadership was as a tactician and activist, rather than as an abstract thinker because "her joy is in the fight itself, in the specific drawn battle." Eastman argued that such terms as radical, liberal, or reactionary had no meaning when applied to such a feminist, and observed that Paul possessed a rare combination of "the shrewd calculating mind of a born political leader. . . with the ruthless driving force, sure judgement and phenonmenal grasp of detail that characterize a great entrepreneur."[18]

Paul seems to have had no close personal friends in the Party during this period and was usually able to keep herself above the factionalism from which the Party intermittently suffered. Inez Haynes Irwin very accurately described the membership's feelings about their leader when she wrote that "with one accord they say, 'She is the Party.'"[19] In the late 1920s when Paul was begining to concentrate her efforts on international feminism, there were rumors reported in the press that she would leave the NWP because of personality conflicts with other leaders. Denying these rumors vigorously and accusing the press of yellow journalism, *Equal Rights* editorialized:

> Alice Paul is, has been, and always will be the leader of the NWP. . . . The program for which we are working is her program; the amendment we are supporting is the child of her brain; our trail through the wilderness was blazed by her, and now what she tells us is, Proceed, build the broad road over which all American women can journey to emancipation.[20]

Jane Norman Smith said quite simply that Alice Paul had "done more to improve the status of women than any other individual," while Doris Stevens gave Paul full credit for the feminist advances at the League of Nations, stating that "women everywhere are her debtors." Although Paul had resigned temporarily from the national council and her position as advisory chairman, she told Smith it was because she "could not do any work for the present and could not bear to be on the Council and not work." Yet Paul never completely stopped advising the Party, even at the height of her involvement in the establishment of the World Woman's Party.[21] Although it was neither the most lyrical nor the most romantic of the many poems dedicated to Alice Paul during the era, Myrtle Patterson's was typical of the heartfelt admiration of the rank and file members. Alice Paul was a genius who transcended male opinion; in fact, she was "God's gift to women," Patterson wrote.[22]

In the two decades between 1920 and 1940, seven women served as national chairmen of the NWP's national council.[23] Miss Elsie Hill, chairman from 1921 to 1925, was a Congressman's daughter, Vassar graduate, and high school French teacher. She became involved in college suffrage work, although her dissatisfaction with NAWSA led her to join the Congressional Union at its inception in 1913. A militant demonstrator, Hill was sentenced to a D.C. jail for speaking at a Lafayette Square meeting in 1918, and was arrested for participating in the Boston demonstration of 1919. In 1921 she completed her first year of law school, married a law professor, and when her daughter Elsie Hill-Leavitt was born, enrolled the baby as a founder of the NWP.

Hill resigned her chairmanship in 1925, although she remained active in the Party and belonged to the national council for nearly twenty years. But she did not leave much trace of her personality upon the Party for several reasons. The NWP's reorganization was directed mainly by Alice Paul and Mrs. Belmont, while the opening skirmishes with the Consumers' League and the League of Women Voters over protective legislation took place in New York. Although the Equal Rights Amendment was introduced in Congress in 1923, the lobbying was directed by the NWP's veteran suffrage lobbyist, Maud Younger, and state equal rights campaigns were organized by local leaders.

Edith Houghton Hooker filled the remaining year and a half of Elsie Hill's unexpired term as chairman. Mrs. Hooker was a graduate of Byrn Mawr, had done graduate work in sociology in Berlin and in social hygiene at Johns Hopkins, and had written a book, *The Laws of Sex*, that was an examination of prostitution and venereal disease from the standpoint of the purity crusaders.[24] Mother of five children and foster mother to several more, she was married to Dr. Donald Hooker, who edited two physiological journals and was also concerned with social hygiene. Mrs. Hooker had been a member of the NWP council since 1914, and for many years was president of the Maryland branch of the NWP. She had edited a Maryland suffrage journal, and was the editor of the NWP organ, *Equal Rights*, from 1923 to 1934. Involved in the Party disagreement over reform, strategy, and priorities in the mid-thirties, Hooker no doubt would have been willing to serve as national chairman again, but she had alienated many council members with her continual attempts to broaden and democratize the NWP. Thus, although she remained active on the national council and later on the executive council, she did not serve again as chairman during this period.

The head of the NWP's national council from 1926 to 1929 was Jane Norman Smith. Perhaps the most effective of the national chairmen, Mrs. Smith's influence lasted long after she gave up the chairmanship for she served on the national council actively throughout the period. Her papers reveal how heavily successive chairmen relied on her, especially Mrs. Harvey Wiley and Mrs. Sarah Pell, and her advice was generally based on common sense combined with decisions made in the best interests of the Party. She was a capable administrator, and her special talent was to soothe hurt feelings and personal jealousies. Mrs. Smith had believed that after suffrage was attained women would get their legislation handed to them "on a silver platter." In fact, in 1921, she had turned down the legislative chairmanship for New York City, saying she was not conscious of any further discriminations against women and wanted to renew the study of law which she had dropped at the time of her marriage. But Smith soon became deeply involved in NWP activities, and since Alice Paul resigned from the national council during this period, Smith was left to make all the decisions. Smith also served for many years as a key member of the investment and endowment committee.[25]

Jane Norman Smith was very efficient, but occasionally even she complained that the travel, paper work, meetings, and lobbying were too much for her. In a letter to her good friend Mabel Vernon at NWP headquarters she wrote that "every once in a while I get thoroughly fed up with Woman's Party work, and I am that way just now." In

1928, when she was vacationing with her husband and two daughters on Long Island, she was asked to return to Washington to press Hoover for a commitment to the Equal Rights Amendment. After explaining that she had left her maid in New York City, had been working for the Party in upstate New York at Christmas, had been in Cuba for five weeks, had attended the political convention in Kansas City, and had spent two or three days in Washington every month, she apologized for not being able to make the trip. "If I were a person of some independent means or one earning her livelihood or even making some contribution by way of services in the home," she wrote, "I would be justified in going off and leaving my husband to sit around by himself weekends."[26]

Mrs. Harvey Wiley replaced Mrs. Smith and served as national chairman from 1929 to 1932, and again from 1939 to 1941. A general's daughter, she had worked at the Library of Congress and had joined the Congressional Union in 1913 after being called upon by Alice Paul. Wiley did lobbying, political work, and picketing during the suffrage campaign. Sentenced to fifteen days for picketing in 1917, she appealed her case and won. Her husband, who died in 1930 at the age of eighty-six, was a leader in the drive for pure food laws. Mrs. Wiley never wanted to be national chairman and accepted the responsibility very reluctantly through a sense of loyalty and duty to the Party. Her first chairmanship coincided with the stock market crash and the onslaught of the depression, and during this period she often turned to Jane Norman Smith for advice. Active in the General Federation of Women's Clubs, she became president of the District of Columbia Federation in 1932, and wrote to Mrs. Smith that this gave her a good excuse to resign as chairman of the national council. "The NWP, I fear," she explained, "wears out its members before they realize it."[27]

Wiley continued to serve on the national council, to work with a Washington citizens' group for home rule, and to represent the General Federation of Women's Clubs in Panama, Costa Rica, Cuba, and Mexico in the mid-thirties. Very hesitantly she resumed the chairmanship when Mrs. Sarah Pell died in 1939. A fervent admirer of Alice Paul, Mrs. Wiley was much more a follower than a leader. Mrs. Wiley's second chairmanship from 1939 to 1941 was much the same as her first. The ERA, which had won increasing support from orga-

nized women during the 1930s, was still not passed by Congress, state
equal rights activities were purely defensive, and the NWP primarily
struggled to retain the women's rights won earlier and to prevent setbacks in the field of economic opportunities.

The remaining three chairmen were Sarah Colvin, Florence Bayard
Hilles, and Sarah Pell. Mrs. Colvin was a Southerner who had trained
as a nurse at Johns Hopkins and served with the Red Cross during
World War I. Arrested in Washington after a watchfire suffrage demonstration in 1919, she moved to Minnesota with her husband, a former
Army surgeon, after the vote was attained. In 1933 she became chairman of the national council but served less than a year. Mrs. Colvin
was enthusiastic, outspoken, and frequently tactless. She had the additional disadvantage of living in the midwest when most of the Party
activities and all of its decision making took place in the east. Resigning
under pressure from the national council, she was succeeded by
Florence Bayard Hilles of Delaware.

Like many other NWP leaders, Mrs. Hilles came from a distinguished family. During World War I, Mrs. Hilles was a munitions
worker and she later did postwar reconstruction work in France. She
joined the Congressional Union in 1913, picketed the White House
in 1917, and did organizing work for the NWP throughout the twenties. Active in the Consumers' League and the Women's Trade Union
League, Hilles later broke with them over protective legislation. She
continued to work with business and professional women, however,
and her other activities included social welfare work, the American
Civil Liberties Union, the National Council for the Prevention of War,
the Birth Control League, and various cultural and country club
groups. Mrs. Hilles served continuously on the national council, as well
as on the budget committee of the NWP, and also participated in the
international work of the Party. Despite her many activities, Mrs.
Hilles was an able chairman of the NWP from 1933 until her resignation because of ill health in 1936. Although the Party schism occurred
during Mrs. Hilles' chairmanship, she retained the respect of both
sides. "She leads," wrote the editor of the renegade journal *Equal
Rights Independent Feminist Weekly* in 1936, "because people follow
her." Mrs. Hilles explained her own willingness to work for feminist
goals and especially for the ERA by insisting that "I should feel myself

a slacker if I were not in the ranks of those women who, today, the world over, are working for the liberty and freedom of their own sex."[28]

Florence Bayard Hilles was succeeded by the socialite Mrs. Stephen Pell of Fort Ticonderoga. Mrs. Pell had become interested in the suffrage movement when she met Mrs. Emmeline Pankhurst in England, but although she worked for suffrage she did not join the NWP until 1922. She was active on the national council throughout the 1920s and early 1930s. Selected chairman in 1936, she served until her death in 1939. Like Mrs. Wiley, Mrs. Pell relied heavily upon Jane Norman Smith for advice and upon the secretary and staff in Washington for the implementation of Party policies.

Of the seven national chairmen during these two decades, all but Jane Norman Smith and Sarah Pell were members of the Congressional Union and took part in the militant suffrage campaign. All of the women but Sarah Colvin lived in the east, and without exception these women were well-educated, with sufficient income to provide the leisure necessary for full time NWP work. All were married, and five of the women had children.[29] Probably the most effective and influential as chairmen and party workers were Jane Norman Smith and Florence Bayard Hilles.

Although at the highest level Party leadership remained relatively stable, the NWP lost members through death, marriage and involvement with other causes. But it also gained new members during this period, many of whom were professional or working women. The Party, like other women's groups, had little success in its efforts to recruit very young women during the twenties and thirties. Unlike other women's groups, however, the NWP was able to maintain a solid financial base throughout these two decades, and it remained committed to an active feminist program.

After the vote was attained, a number of women wished to give priority to their careers, such as attorney Sue White, author Inez Haynes Irwin, historian Mary Beard, politician Anne Martin, and civil service worker Jessie Dell. Some women were lost to the Party because of their postsuffrage involvement with other causes. Florence Kelley spent the remainder of her life trying to protect the special legislation for working women which had been won by the Consumers' League, while the peace movement absorbed the energies of such members as

Alice Park, Florence Brewer Boeckel, and Mary Winsor. Helena Hill Weed, one of the first pickets to be arrested during the militant campaign, divided her time among the American Civil Liberties Union, the League of Women Voters, and the American Association of University Women.

Still other women found that marriage and family responsibilities at least temporarily curtailed their NWP activities. Elsie Hill resigned as chairman after she married and had a child. Betty Gram Swing followed her radio commentator husband on his reassignment to England, Rebecca Hourwich went to live with her journalist husband and small child in an isolated New England town, Mrs. Amy Ransome relocated with her college professor husband to California, and Fanny Bunand-Sevastos married a foreign service officer and moved to Europe. Very few of the younger women were able to combine full time NWP work with their marriages. Three partial exceptions were Doris Stevens, Anita Pollitzer, and Muna Lee. But many of those women who had been diverted from NWP work because of their marriages, careers, or interest in other causes eventually rejoined or became active again in the Party.

Death also took its toll of the activists who had been among the original membership of the Woman's Party. During the 1920s the Party lost Crystal Eastman, Mrs. H. O. Havemeyer, Mrs. Lawrence Lewis, Sophie Meredith and many others. Among the important activists who died during the 1930s were Mrs. Belmont, Eunice Dana Brannan, Zona Gale, Mrs. Sarah Pell, Ella Riegel, Mrs. Richard Wainwright, and Maud Younger. Yet the NWP also gained a number of outstanding new members during these two decades. Most were career women or women who had been leaders in other organizations and had become converted to the equal rights program. Among these valuable new members were attorneys Laura Berrien, Burnita Shelton Matthews, and Rebecca Greathouse; college professors Helen Bitterman, Muna Lee, and Clara Snell Wolfe; author Alma Lutz; and politician Emma Guffy Miller. From the Brooklyn Rapid Transit System came organizer Mary Murray, and from the newly organized federal government workers, Edwina Avery. Sue Brobst and Lena Madesin Phillips had been leaders in the Business and Professional Women, Caroline Lexow Babcock in the League of Women Voters, and Lola Maverick

Lloyd in the Women's International League for Peace and Freedom. But the membership of the NWP had never been large, and Alma Lutz reported to the council about 1930 that "our 9000 members are a myth." The NWP did not like to admit this, and Mabel Vernon reminded Lutz that "at the present time we are considering the 9000 people we have on our lists as members, whether their dues are paid or not."[30]

Financially, the NWP was better off than many other women's groups during the 1920s. During the depression its membership dues, state branch contributions, and support from wealthy individuals all declined, but the Party's property and investments continued to give it a solid base. During the period from 1923 through 1929, the NWP's income averaged about $46,000 a year, although a pattern of declining revenue was apparent. Between 1930 and 1936, the last year for which full figures are available, the NWP's average yearly income was about $13,550. Of course, the Party's income included Mrs. Belmont's cash contributions, but these only averaged about $6,000 per year for the period 1923 through 1929, and $5,000 per year between 1930 and her death in 1933. Mrs. Belmont's greatest contribution was her gift of a headquarters building in Washington. The federal government instituted proceedings to acquire the property in the mid-twenties, conducting a series of hearings in which the NWP lawyers attempted first to stop the condemnation of the historic building, and then argued for and won a higher award than the government had originally offered. The Party used part of the condemnation award to purchase a new headquarters in the same neighborhood, set aside some of the money for renovation, and in 1929, invested the remaining $163,500.[31]

Wealthy individuals' contributions to the Party were undeniably important. Dr. and Mrs. Hooker, for example, contributed more than $20,000 toward the publication expenses of *Equal Rights* between 1925 and 1928. Various members of the Dupont family of Delaware gave a total of $5,000 to the NWP during the decade 1926 to 1936, while the Winsor family of Pennsylvania contributed over $4,000 between 1923 and 1928. Mrs. William Kent, wife of the former U.S. Senator from California, made contributions totalling more than $11,000 between 1923 and 1935, while the wealthy "widow of the sugar king," Mrs. H. O. Havemeyer, gave about $3,000 between 1923 and her death in early 1929.[32]

Other women contributed valuable antiques to furnish NWP head-quarters, gave shares of stock, or occasionally paid the salaries of the stenographers and typists hired by the Party. The dues from active and associate members were divided between the national organization and the state branches, but the national retained almost all the contri-butions of the founders, sustainers, life members, and endowers. This arrangement proved to be the source of considerable dissatisfaction. "Do you really mean to say $95 of it goes to Washington!" complained Mrs. Havemeyer about the $100 founder's fee. "It is hard to believe." After discovering that it was indeed true, she wrote to Jane Norman Smith that in the future she would give most of her contributions di-rectly to the New York City branch.[33]

The NWP also encouraged women to make provisions for the Party in their wills. Reminding women to use a lawyer and three witnesses to make certain the will would be valid in any state, the NWP asked that a copy be sent to Party headquarters. Maud Younger left her home adjacent to the national headquarters to the Party; M. Carey Thomas of Bryn Mawr left the NWP a bequest of $50,000 for investment pur-poses; and Mrs. O. H. P. Belmont's estate provided a $100,000 legacy. Early in the 1920s, a wealthy but inactive member from New Jersey willed her considerable property to the Party, which then worked steadily to prevent her from changing her mind. The Party's concern about the possibilities of losing some of its steady supporters was not entirely unfounded. After an unsuccessful attempt to obtain more con-tributions from long time Party activist Mary Winsor, Jane Norman Smith noted that "she is giving all of her cash to birth control and peace." To the dissappointment of the Party, Mrs. H. O. Havemeyer left her magnificent and very valuable art collection to the Metro-politan Museum of New York rather than to the NWP.[34]

The NWP managed its funds in two different ways. An autonomous endowment committee was created in 1925 to handle the stocks and bonds donated by members, and in late 1927, a small investment and endowment committee was chosen by Mrs. Belmont to direct the in-vestment of the large surplus from the government's condemnation award. This committee's membership remained quite stable, although a few new members were added during the 1930s. The largest original investment of $144,363 had been in utilities and railroad bonds. Later, U.S. Treasury bonds were added, and $89,047 of the 1934 Belmont legacy went into U.S. Government bonds. These investments were audited regularly and reports sent to the national council.[35]

But there was never any real agreement about the policy the investment and endowment committee should follow. Because of the very conservative nature of the investments the committee had made, the Party weathered the vagaries of the depression era stock market quite well. At the end of 1933, chairman Maud Younger was able to report that only two of the bonds held by the NWP had defaulted. She proposed at the biennial convention that year that the Belmont legacy be "conservatively invested," and that the Party spend only the income from the investment. Although her resolution was hotly debated, it was eventually adopted, but the principal was not restricted in the same manner as the headquarters fund. Beginning in 1938, the national council gradually appropriated the money until the legacy was finally exhausted in 1949.[36]

In addition to the investment and endowment committee which directed the use of the Party's capital, the NWP managed its other financial matters, such as dues and budgets, through its finance committee in cooperation with the national council. The major problem was to try to offset the decline in revenue from membership dues, state branches, and other sources so as to meet the Party's operating expenses. A strong *Equal Rights* editorial in 1926 decried those women who spent their money on material things which satisfied the ego, rather than on those things that indicated "a genuine intellectual interest or a thorough-going desire to bring order out of the present social chaos." According to this optimistic editorial, people needed only to be educated to realize what was important, and then they would support it financially. In fact, one could better be judged by one's checkbook than by one's words.[37]

The national headquarters continued to depend on the states to keep membership lists up to date, collect dues, and forward the national's share to Washington. Early attempts by the NWP to assign state revenue quotas were unsuccessful and were abandoned after 1924. The last published financial reports for receipts from dues covered the first six months of 1937, and the following year the national council voted to use money from the principal of the Belmont legacy. After the Hookers stopped underwriting *Equal Rights* in 1934, it also became more and more difficult for the Party to support its official organ. The journal limped along but survived, suspending publication for four months in 1940.[38]

NWP budgets reflected the heavy emphasis the Party placed on legal and field research, publication of literature, and activities involved with publicity and public relations. The amount of money provided for organizational work in the states and state legislative work was generally small and varied with the direction of the Party's commitment during any particular year. To some degree, the second national headquarters was an asset because its rooms were rented to visiting Party members and because its value increased with inflation. Headquarters was also a liability, however, since after the initial remodeling there were still maintenance costs as well as taxes to pay. In 1928, Mabel Vernon estimated the general operating expenses at $700 a month, of which only $160 was provided for by special pledges, and complained that it seemed impossible to make up the remainder from membership dues.[39]   Of course, the situation became much worse during the depression.

Many NWP pledges were earmarked for special purposes, separately administered, and thus usually could not be used for headquarters' needs, although in some instances "borrowing" from other funds did take place. During the depression, the budgets were much reduced; there were few paid national organizers and little money was available for state legislative work. The national work of the congressional committee for the ERA continued, but in 1936 it was budgeted at less than $2,000 from the $5,225 investment income. The *Equal Rights* deficit, a new furnace, office supplies, and clerical salaries used up the remainder of the investment income, while contributions and dues from the membership that year only totalled about $4,878.[40]

Having reorganized their Party by 1923, NWP members spent the rest of the 1920s and all of the 1930s working to achieve complete legal equality for women. Their chosen weapons were the Equal Rights Amendment, the Equal Rights Treaty, and the Equal Nationality Treaty—their battlefields were in the United States, Europe, and Latin America. As a result of their equalitarian offensive, they found themselves perpetually in conflict with social feminists who feared the destruction of protective laws and conventions for women. Even within their own Party, they suffered from a power struggle among their leaders, some fundamental disagreements over both the structue of the Party and the priorities that should be assigned to its goals, and constitutional revisions that upset rank and file members.

Yet there was never any doubt that the NWP was a committed feminist organization. Both sympathizers and enemies of the Party admitted that this was true, although the NWP's enemies criticized its uncompromising insistence on equality. Within the NWP itself, conservatives, moderates, and reformers all displayed a consistent concern about the meaning of feminism, and an unwavering belief in the need for feminist organizations. The NWP's commitment to equality during the interwar years forced many other people—antifeminists, social feminists, and nonfeminists alike—to think about women's status and needs. What, after all, was the meaning of feminism?

NOTES

1. Sochen, *The New Woman in Greenwich Village*, pp. 115–16.

2. *The Suffragist*, 8 (October 1920), 232–37.

3. Crystal Eastman, "Alice Paul's Convention," *The Liberator* 4 (April 1921), 9–10.

4. Florence Kelley, "The New Woman's Party," *Survey* 45 (March 5, 1921), 827–28.

5. Letter from Florence Kelley, *New York Times*, June 8, 1922, pp. 40; *New York Times*, 1922, April 12, p. 5; April 25, p. 3; May 16, p. 19; October 30, p. 17; November 5, II, p. 1; November 13, p. 14.

6. "Women Open Campaign for Equal Rights," *ER* 1 (July 28, 1923), 189; Editorial, "Why a Constitutional Amendment?" *ER* 1 (November 24, 1923), 324; Editorial, "The Lucretia Mott Amendment," *ER* (November 10, 1923), 308; Editorial, "March On," *ER* 1 (November 10, 1923), 308.

7. *Equal Rights: Weekly Bulletin of the National Woman's Party*, September 13, 1922, no page number; the complete list included actresses, architects, artists, authors, businesswomen, dentists, farmers, government workers, homemakers, journalists, labor, lawyers, librarians, ministers, musicians, nurses, osteopaths, physicians, play-

wrights, political, religious workers, scientists, sculptors, social workers, and teachers. Later, poets', students', and young women's councils were added.

8. Editorial, "Youth's Touchstone," *ER* 1 (May 19, 1923), 108; Hazel MacKaye, "Youth and Equal Rights," *ER* 1 (December 15, 1923), 349; "Meeting of the Inez Milholland Memorial Committee," *ER* 1 (December 8, 1923), 341.

9. "Intercollegiate Equal Rights Prize," *ER* 12 (April 11, 1925), 67; "Intercollegiate Equal Rights Prize," *ER* 12 (March 28, 1925), 53; Margaret Luers, "The Equal Rights Essay Contest," *ER* 18 (May 14, 1932), 115; Emilie Doetsch, "The Story of the NWP Conference," *ER* 19 (June 3, 1933), 143.

10. "An Apostle of Action," reprinted from *Time and Tide*, October 26, 1928 in *ER* 14 bis (November 17, 1928), 325.

11. Muna Lee, "Alva Belmont—Feminist," *ER* 16 (January 10, 1931), 391–92; Editorial, "We Must Not Fail Her," *ER* 19 (February 4, 1933), 2.

12. "Mrs. Belmont Gives A Resumé," *ER* 14 (April 9, 1927), 69; "Mrs. Belmont's Message," *ER* 14 (July 23, 1927), 189; Muna Lee, "Alva Belmont House," *ER* 16 (January 3, 1931), 379; Editorial, "A Woman of Action," *ER* 19 (February 18, 1933), 18.

13. Consuelo Balsan, *The Glitter and the Gold* (New York: Harper, 1952), p. 6.

14. Mrs. O. H. P. Belmont to Jane Norman Smith, February 14, 1929, Jane Norman Smith Papers, Box 5, f. 102, SL; Jane Norman Smith to Mabel Vernon, 1928, Jane Norman Smith Papers, Box 2, f. 65, SL.

15. O'Neill, *Everyone Was Brave*.

16. Irwin, *Story of the Woman's Party*, p. 8; Inez Haynes Irwin, *Angels and Amazons* (New York: Doubleday, 1933), p. 388; Anne Herendeen, "What the Hometown Thinks of Alice Paul," *Everybody's* 41 (October 1919), 45.

17. Crystal Eastman, "Striking Pen Picture of Alice Paul," *ER* 1 (August 18, 1923), 214; Simone Tery, "American Apostles to France," *ER* 12 (June 20, 1925), 150.

18. Stevens, *Jailed For Freedom*, pp. 10–11; Crystal Eastman, "Alice Paul's Convention," *The Liberator* 4 (April 1921), 10; Eastman,

"Striking Pen Pictures of Alice Paul," *ER* 1 (August 18, 1923), 214.

19. Irwin, *Story of the Woman's Party*, p. 15.

20. Editorial, "They Say," *ER* 14 (February 26, 1927), 20.

21. Notes for an interview, n. d., Jane Norman Smith Papers, Box 1, f. 18, SL; "Doris Stevens' Speech at the Conference," *ER* 17 (June 6, 1931), 142; Jane Norman Smith to Mabel Vernon, April 14, 1928, Jane Norman Smith Papers, Box 2, f. 65, SL; Mrs. Harvey Wiley to Alma Lutz, October 11, 1940, Alma Lutz Papers, Box 6, f. 100, SL.

22. Myrtle R. Patterson, "In Praise of Alice Paul," *ER* 20 (February 3, 1934), 8.

23. The following biographical information is from Stevens, *Jailed for Freedom*, and *Equal Rights*, the official journal of the NWP, unless otherwise cited.

24. Edith Houghton Hooker, *The Laws of Sex* (Boston: R. G. Badger, 1921); David Pivar, *Purity Crusade* (Westport, Conn.: Greenwood, 1973).

25. "Equal Rights Campaign—NWP," Jane Norman Smith Papers, Box 1, f. 65, SL.

26. Jane Norman Smith to Mabel Vernon, April 14, 1928; Jane Norman Smith to Laura Berrien, July 5, 1928, Jane Norman Smith Papers, Box 2, fs. 65, 67, SL.

27. Mrs. Harvey Wiley to Jane Norman Smith, July 26, 1932, Jane Norman Smith Papers, Box 3, f. 80, SL.

28. Editorial, "The Leader of the American Feminist Movement." *ERIFW* 2 (November 14, 1936), 291.

29. There is insufficient biographical information to determine whether Sarah Colvin had any children.

30. Mabel Vernon to Alma Lutz, 1930, Alma Lutz Papers, Box 3, f. 23, SL.

31. Jane Norman Smith Papers, Box 8, f. 153, SL.

32. *Equal Rights,* 1923–1941.

33. Mrs. O. H. Havemeyer to Jane Norman Smith, Jane Norman Smith Papers, Box 2, f. 60, SL.

34. "Remember the Woman's Party in Your Will," *ER*, 11 (November 29, 1924), 335; "Clause for a Gift by Will to the NWP," *ER* 15 (June 29, 1929), 168; "Woman's Party to Receive Munificent Bequest," *ER* 22 (April 15, 1936), 1; *ER* 21 (January 15, 1936), 2; Burnita

Shelton Matthews to Jane Norman Smith, October 3, 1927; Jane Norman Smith to Laura Berrien, July 5, 1928, Jane Norman Smith Papers, Box 2, fs. 64, 67, SL.

35. Jane Norman Smith Papers, Box 8, f. 153, SL; Alice Paul to Jane Norman Smith, March 29, 1931, Jane Norman Smith Papers, Box 6, f. 114, SL.

36. "Woman's Party Holds Greatest Biennial," *ER* 19 (November 11, 1933), 316; "Biennial Postscript," *ER* 19 (December 16, 1933), 360; "Statement From the Investment and Endowment Committee, NWP," October 17, 1952, Jane Norman Smith Papers, Box 8, f. 166, SL; Jane Norman Smith to Maud Younger, April 3, 1933; Jane Norman Smith to Burnita Shelton Matthews, January 11, 1935, Jane Norman Smith Papers, Box 4, fs. 82, 86, SL.

37. Editorial, "How Do You Spend Your Money," *ER*, 12 (January 2, 1926), 372.

38. E.g., the 1923 allocation ranged from New York, Pennsylvania, and Illinois assessed at $14,000 each, down to Wyoming and Nevada assessed at $400 each. *ER* 1 (March 31, 1923), 51; "Concerning Dues," *ER* 25 (March 1, 1939), 39; "Council Takes Action on Dues," *ER* 25 (May 1, 1939), 72.

39. Mabel Vernon to Jane Norman Smith, March 27, 1928, Jane Norman Smith Papers, Box 2, f. 65, SL.

40. An example of a separate fund would be the $10,442.89 pledged to the work of the InterAmerican Commission on Women, see "Inter-American Commission on Women Makes Financial Report," *ER* 15 (March 29, 1929), 62. "Borrowing" occurred when a $2,150 note at Riggs National Bank was paid off by money taken from the organization fund. See Mabel Vernon to Jane Norman Smith (1928), Jane Norman Smith Papers, Box 2, f. 65, SL; "Notes of the Council Meeting," *ER* 21 (December 15, 1935), 2. Total income for 1936 from reports in *ER* 22 (July 1, 1936), 4; (July 15, 1936), 3–4; (October 15, 1936), 4; *ER* 23 (June 1, 1937), 80.

2
WHAT DID FEMINISTS REALLY WANT?

Central to any study of the women's movement has always been the question, "What is feminism?" The definition of this term becomes even more important when some women, such as the NWP members, insist that they are the only "true" or "real" feminists during a particular time period. Historians have had little success in their struggle to define feminism; their reactions to the people about whom they are writing, their own frames of reference, and the differences in the connotations of words used in earlier time periods are all obstacles in this search for meaning. More importantly, feminism is a cluster of ideas rather than a single concept, and there may well be unresolved ideological inconsistencies contained within this philosophy or exhibited in the beliefs of those who call themselves feminists.

Yet to understand the women of the NWP, their sponsorship of the ERA, their international activities, and their views about women and men, it is essential to try to know what they meant by feminism. What did they say, to whom did they address their rhetoric, and what were they trying to do? Further consideration must be given to the intellectual climate of their times and the differences or similarities among the views of feminists, nonfeminists, and antifeminists.

Writing in the 1960s, William O'Neill argued that American feminists never developed a precise vocabulary. O'Neill identified two basic types of feminists: social feminists who worked for broad humanitarian reforms which were often related only peripherally to the advancement of women, and "hard core" feminists who refused to be diverted into other reforms until women had achieved equality. During the suffrage campaign the differences between social and hard core feminists were obscured, according to O'Neill, and were only recognized with the introduction of the ERA in the 1920s.[1] This division seems somewhat simplistic, since there were many areas of agreement between the two groups even after suffrage. Furthermore, it suggests that there was very little difference between humanitarian reformers and social feminists, when in fact some humanitarian reformers were nonfeminists or even antifeminists.

Also writing in the 1960s, Carl Degler suggested that feminism simply means that women should be considered as human beings entitled to the same opportunities as men, and he argued that there have been two phases of feminism, rather than two types of feminists. The first phase, culminating in the Nineteenth Amendment, was legal and political; the second phase, still continuing today, was the attempt to reconcile marriage and the family with work outside the home for women. Degler's premise was that since Americans have a national aversion to ideologies, American feminism was typical in its failure to develop a viable ideology. Therefore, he argued not very convincingly, those changes in women's status which have taken place have not aroused very much opposition.[2] In fact, phases of feminism cannot be so easily separated, certain themes run consistently through American feminism, and the opposition to women's changing status has been considerable.

More recently, Gerda Lerner has emphasized the need to define feminism more carefully. To Lerner, there is a distinction between the women's rights movement, which means essentially legal rights, and women's emancipation, which demands self-determination, autonomy, and freedom from oppressive sexual restrictions. Feminism, Lerner argues, must include all aspects of women's emancipation, "that is, any struggle designed to elevate their status, socially, politically, economically, and in regard to their self-concepts."[3] Lerner's definition, while perhaps quite useful to feminists today, is ahistorical, and could not be applied to women in the past without constituting a kind of test to determine whether they were or were not feminists. Few women would pass.

During the early twenties, those outside the National Woman's Party began to question the need for feminism. In general, public opinion was reluctant to accept the Party's contention that women had not achieved equality, and much of the equalitarian feminists' effort, therefore, took the form of a kind of consciousness raising directed toward educating women about the continuing legal discriminations against them. By the late twenties and during the thirties, circumstances had changed considerably. But the feminists were still on the defensive even though the repeated failure of nearly half the states to extend jury service and the increase in economic discriminations had demonstrated women's lack of equality more clearly. However, the attacks on feminism had also shifted, and in the thirties, antifeminists often denied that women had any right of equal economic opportunity or insisted that some kinds of equality were definitely harmful to feminine identity and fulfillment.

During these two decades, the NWP was consistent in its concern with the meaning of feminism and in its insistence that there was an urgent need for organized feminism. Neither O'Neill's, Degler's, nor Lerner's definition of feminism fits the NWP members very well. If feminism demands the opportunity for all women to develop their human potential to the fullest, then inherent in this demand is an insistence on equality between men and women. Whether that equality meant identical opportunities for men and women, as the NWP tended to argue, or whether men's and women's opportunities could be different but equal, as the social feminists insisted, was the crux of the argument over protective legislation. Underlying this failure to agree on the meaning of equality lay conflicting perceptions of the nature of men and women. Most social feminists were able to agree that the differences between men and women were more important than the similarities; equalitarian feminists like the NWP members, however, were ambivalent. The logic of the NWP members' insistence on the ERA led them to emphasize the similarities between men and women, but they also believed that the biological fact of motherhood made women possess very different values from men.

The NWP's concept of feminism frequently reflected the idea that women were not only different from men, but were in many ways superior to them. At times this came close to a total acceptance of the fundamental Victorian assumptions about woman's higher spiritual and moral characteristics that stemmed from her maternal functions. The NWP often argued that women had special gifts to bring to civilization, and that feminists simply wanted "to give the world back to its mother." Woman was described as "the friend of peace, the enemy of poverty and vice, the guardian of the home, the creator of civilization and its basic arts, in short, the devoted mother of mankind." This tended to establish a dichotomy between women and men, who resisted women's demands for equality because they possessed the opposite characteristics. Men were "the warrior sex," those who paid for prostitutes, and those who created an economy of scarcity rather than an economy of abundance.[4]

But NWP members were not all consistent in their beliefs about motherhood and the special characteristics of women, for just as often they stressed the similarities rather than the differences between men and women. Mrs. Harvey Wiley described one of the Party's major aims as the transformation of the social order so that women would be considered simply as human beings all the time. A 1929 *Equal Rights* editorial maintained that the real basis of feminism was psychological, and that "women do not cease to be human beings when they marry or become parents, any more than men cease to be human beings when they marry or become parents." Experience and a deep distrust of men, however, led to this bitter analogy: "The average man looks upon a woman as a white man looks upon a Negro. He would die sooner than change places."[5] It followed that only extraordinary men were capable of looking on women as equals.

Alma Lutz believed that men always resisted considering women as human beings because it was inconsistent with their strongly held faith in the right of male domination. "Their best weapon in the contest of the sexes," she wrote, "has been to make women believe they were men's spiritual superiors and their inspiration, that because they were on such a high plane they needed protection from the grossness of a man's world." Bitter reality showed women how such a myth restricted their opportunities, she concluded. NWP members found it possible both to glorify and to denigrate women's maternal role without recognizing any ideological inconsistencies. Motherhood was "a force to combat war, to minimize venereal disease and prostitution, to protect the racial stock and to insure social justice." On the other hand, "motherhood has been the rod held over the backs of women to drive them into submission; it has been the chain to hold them in dependence and to close-rivet them to a condition of slavery." Nonetheless, no woman would have sentenced two youths to six years in jail for stealing a watch, the NWP argued, although an all male jury did. "Her maternal instinct would have intervened," for unlike a man she valued life more than personal property rights.[6]

The NWP was perfectly willing to attribute higher and finer characteristics to all women because of their inherent maternity and to accuse men of not really appreciating these finer qualities. But the Party found its opponents in the struggle over protective legislation using these same arguments about motherhood to justify special labor laws for women only. Unable to deny that biologically all women were potential mothers or that motherhood was supremely important to civilization, the NWP did refuse to accept the contention that maternity made women weak and in need of protection. So-called protective legislation, the Party argued, restricted and hindered women in economic competition with men. Women were not "semi-invalids," stricken with the incurable "disease" of womanhood. The Party accused advocates of protective legislation of holding a pathological view of the female sex, and of believing that "maternity, of course, accentuates the malady, but even in the unmarried it is there, obstinately recurring as does the moon at regular intervals." When an NWP delegation called on Governor Alfred E. Smith in 1928 to try to convince him to oppose special legislation for women, he replied, "I believe in equality but I cannot nurse a baby." Smith's remark was widely quoted and Party feminists were furious, believing that the remark showed the governor's basic contempt for women. As *Equal Rights* pointed out, women were proud of their roles as mothers, but "if Governor Smith should wake up some morning and find after all that he could nurse a baby, the shock (to) his self-esteem would be so terrific he would never recover."[7]

The NWP resolutely claimed, however, that its members were not man-haters. The interests of humankind were identical, members argued, but men did not realize very well how to further these goals. The interests of men and women differed like those of capital and labor, the equalitarian feminists insisted, and since men currently had "the whip hand over women," it was extremely unlikely that they would give up any power "until it is wrested from their hands." NWP feminists also denied that they were trying to imitate men. "What a dull world, what a sterile, defunct, uninteresting place the planet would be if women were men," *Equal Rights* exclaimed, "a hideous calamity and one which Feminists more than all others would deplore."[8]

The Party saw itself as a "pioneer vanguard" whose members were completely devoted to an ideal. Advising feminists not to support too many other causes, a Party fund raiser urged NWP members to "leave other work to other women who do not yet feel the vital need of liberation." The NWP's reaction to nonfeminist women was generally sympathetic although often patronizing. Unthinking women who put other causes above feminism were foolish altruists, indulging in "moral cosmetics," argued Pennsylvania activist Mary Winsor, who believed that "the woman who gives no help in any way is a traitor to her own sex and her better self." But Alma Lutz recognized that "Feminism has a great work to do to clean house in women's minds, to sweep out the remnants of the myth," and believed that it would take at least another generation before there were any truly emancipated women. Lutz observed that generally "women have not yet learned to be themselves and still strive to be what men want them to be or what they think men want them to be."[9] Party members vacillated between earnest attempts to raise the consciousness of nonfeminist women so that they would become angry about discriminations against them, and smug satisfaction with their own position as enlightened, avant-garde, sensitive feminist women.

In 1927 the treasurer of the New Jersey branch wrote to *Equal Rights* about the "misleading term" feminism, asking whether it really meant equality or whether it meant women's domination of men. To explain, the Party had to fall back on *Webster's Collegiate Dictionary* for its definition: "the theory, cult, or practice of those who hold that present laws, conventions and conditions of society should admit of and further the free and full development of woman." NWP members never abandoned or modified this definition, although by the decade of the thirties they were increasingly defensive about feminism. "There is nothing to be ashamed of in Feminism," editorialized their journal. Feminism involved both the self-respect of women and the mutual respect between men and women, according to the Party. Alma Lutz vehemently denied that the goal of feminism was a matriarchy. "It is not a desire merely to follow in men's footsteps, to take over their ideals and their work," she wrote, "but a demand for the opportunity to act and develop as freely as men."[10] Perhaps the Party's most articulate statement of the meaning of feminism was contained in one of its many rejoinders to the critics of the Equal Rights Amendment. "It is liberty we seek, not repression. We wish to free women, not to restrain them. Our aim is to enable women to do what their own abilities and preferences and necessities urge them to do."[11] Yet Party members recognized that feminism had the power to antagonize men greatly and even reveal "in some women a slave complex for which they contend with almost fanatical zeal."[12]

The NWP's official objective was complete equality between men and women before the law and in all human relationships. In November 1922, the Party had adopted a list of immediate objectives to remove the remaining forms of women's subjection. Modeled on the original Declaration of Rights and Sentiments adopted at Seneca Falls in 1848, the NWP's Declaration listed twenty-nine goals. The economic objectives included equal opportunities in education, employment, and job promotion as well as equal pay for equal work. The equalitarian feminists also demanded a single moral standard, equal penalties for sex offenses, equal treatment for those suspected of having venereal diseases, and asked "that the exploitation of the sex of women shall no longer exist, but women shall have the same right to the control of their persons as men." Although this statement in modern context would probably include the right to abortion, in the context of the twenties it referred to access to birth control information. Significantly, the last fourteen principles specifically dealt with the rights of married women. For these women, the Party wanted the right to their own names, services, earnings, and property as well as equal rights with regard to grounds for divorce, control of their children, independent citizenship, and the right to make contracts. More generally the Party resolved that the wife should be able to retain her own identity and to contract with her husband about their marital relationship. The NWP also maintained that a wife should not be considered to be "supported" by her husband, but rather that their mutual contributions to the marriage and home should be recognized.[13]

NWP members believed that an important part of feminism was the friendship and appreciation which arose among women working together for a cause. Perhaps the greatest accomplishment of the NWP, *Equal Rights* editorialized, "is this fine and genuine spirit of comradeship among women." Women working together for a just cause such as equal rights would develop a "sex solidarity" which would cut across classes and break down artificial barriers among women. On the other hand, to take on the unfinished work of the feminist pioneers was "a thing of pain and toil, of sacrifice and suffering, of effort unrecognized and honor postponed or forgotten." A martyrdom theme dominated most of the Party rhetoric throughout the entire period. At times, NWP members likened feminism to religion, "a faith so deep that one loses one's self in it," at other times, they suggested that feminism was "a passion like love."[14]

Feminists were self-respecting individuals who only wanted women to have the opportunity to develop themselves fully, or as Alma Lutz averred, "Feminists today are keeping the world safe for women." Obviously, complete devotion to feminism meant the neglect of other aspects of one's self-development. "The things we have personally intended to do with our lives we cannot do—for this we must do instead," wrote an NWP member in the twenties. It did not matter that feminists were often made into scapegoats, for "they are used to giving up their own lives that other women may live more fully." Other reformers might become discouraged in time and lose faith, but NWP feminists rejoiced that their movement was free of such "burnt-out people."[15]

Judging from the reaction to the Congressional Union's role in the suffrage campaign, the NWP expected opposition to its fight for complete equality. "We know the difficulties ahead," Mrs. Belmont wrote, "we recognize the endless strife, the opposition to be met." Opposition was often a good sign, the NWP believed, because it indicated that the Party was making progress. The more rapidly progress took place, the more heated the controversy. "Precisely because the methods of the

Congressional Union contained within them the seeds of victory were they so hotly opposed," concluded Edith Houghton Hooker. Even the rather timid Mrs. Wiley had been impressed by what seemed to be the fruits of suffrage militancy. "What a glorious kind of warfare!" she exclaimed in her speech to NWP officials in 1923. "Let us go on carrying our banners with their inspiring messages, and singing our songs," she urged, "until we accomplish our mission."[16]

Why did women become feminists? Historians have frequently dealt with this question by isolating feminists from other kinds of reformers, or by examining one individual's career and motives in depth. A few have considered the feminists in the context of the abolitionists or Progressive reformers. Robert Riegel stressed the feminists' relationships with men, particularly their fathers, and also noted the desire for power and importance as a contributing factor, although he did not explore the possibility that militant feminism might have offered an alternative social role for women. Gerda Lerner, on the other hand, emphasized the shrinking opportunities for women throughout the nineteenth century and suggested that feminism might be a response to both actual and perceived status loss for educated white middle class women. The suffrage victory of 1920 was achieved basically because in the Progressive period "the interests of women of all classes briefly coincided," but also because by that time certain preconditions for the advancement of women such as easier divorce, access to birth control information, and greater mobility had been achieved. This approach tends to encourage the inclusion of feminists in the general classification of Progressive reformers, although the status loss concept is only one possible explanation. In his analysis of Progressive psychologists and psychiatrists, John Burnham has argued that all Progressive reformers accepted certain assumptions. Able, literate, optimistic, and righteous, the Progressives believed that most problems stemmed from the social environment and therefore could be solved.[17] The most significant difference between the psychiatrists and psychologists Burnham describes and the equalitarian feminists is in each group's identification of the causes and effects of social problems. The psychiatrists and psychologists tried to combat what they believed were the major causes of insanity by working primarily for eugenics, prohibition, and the elimination of prostitution. The NWP, however, believed that prostitution, intemperance, and the declining quality of the race were due to the inequality which prevented women from playing a full role in the world. Therefore, they made equal rights the primary goal.

Christopher Lasch has suggested that feminism was an alternative to the increasing idleness imposed on middle class women by the advance of industrialization. This discontented woman of leisure was frequently depicted in the fiction of the time as restless, selfish, materialistic, and destructive—a kind of female parasite. Other studies of the members of the two generations of middle class women in the late nineteenth and early twentieth century have stressed their sense of mission, their feeling that their knowledge and education should be used, and the lack of appropriate role models for these women. In describing the "woman problem" at the turn of the century, Jill Conway noted that the Puritan work ethic made urban leisured women feel uneasy about their wealth and education. "For women it was *unearned* wealth," argued Conway, "and carried with it guilt and feelings of obligation to society which must be reconciled."[18]

The NWP members exhibited all these reasons and more for becoming feminists. They consistently deplored "parasitism," and, of course, the core of their own group consisted of upper middle class and wealthy women. Jane Norman Smith believed that feminism gave life meaning, and wrote to a friend after the death of Mrs. H. O. Havemeyer that "I have always felt that the Woman's Party gave her something in life which all her wealth could not supply, and I feel the same way about Mrs. Belmont." It did give meaning to many women's lives to work for what they believed to be a supremely important cause. Mrs. Harvey Wiley often spoke of the self-sacrifice and courage it required to work for equal rights, maintaining that "one must lose himself in some worthwhile cause to find real contentment." Feminists were very fortunate women because of their enlightened leaders, *Equal Rights* pointed out, for "through them, our own lives have derived force, direction, and dignity."[19]

Women who had struggled to achieve success in nontraditional roles, such as pilot Amelia Earhart, often joined the Party. As Helena Rubenstein, wealthy and powerful head of her own cosmetics corporation, explained: "Freedom and Equality of opportunity for women is a cause that has always been close to my heart." Some NWP members had achieved success against heavy odds only to find that they were still not fully accepted in a male field. Journalist Rheta Childe Dorr's autobiography, written during her convalescence from a nervous breakdown in the early twenties, revealed how she was considered exceptional by her colleagues and yet always referred to as a "good girl." Even the male reviewer of Dorr's book commented that "her victory, complete as it is, is as sad a victory as courage and talent ever won."[20] There were actually several sides to careerism as an impetus for becoming a feminist. Women who were successful in careers, especially professionals such as doctors, dentists, and lawyers, often became feminists, as well as women who found success disillusioning like Dorr, or women whose careers and advancement were blocked by remaining discriminations, such as married women teachers, government workers, and waitresses.

Some women joined the NWP because it had a positive, rather than a negative, attitude toward women's abilities, and encouraged women to develop to their full capacity. The NWP argued that it was very understandable that women suffered from inferiority feelings because society considered all real virtues "manly," while negative qualities were labeled womanly or effeminate. Other women joined because they felt isolated and needed support in their beliefs about women's rights. As the Party saw it, the isolation of women was both typical and tragic. "Lonely women," *Equal Rights* summed up, "thousands of them, millions of them, true in their faith, strong in their idealism, but helpless and alone." Many women claimed to have become feminists because of contact with woman suffrage leaders. Most feminists had been inspired by some great woman leader, Mrs. Hooker believed, "whose high ideals and ennobling life roused in us a sense of personal responsibility to our time and generation." Author Inez Haynes Irwin gave credit to her aunt, the Reverend Lorenza Haynes, for converting her to feminism when she was thirteen years old, while among those NWP activists who had personal contacts with the Pankhursts, for example, were Alice Paul, Mrs. O. H. P. Belmont, Rheta Childe Dorr, Marie Moore Forrest, Dora Ogle, Mrs. Sarah Pell, and Doris Stevens.[21] Many other NWP members became feminists after they were recruited by Alice Paul for the militant suffrage campaign.

Yet the "new women" of the twenties showed very little interest in feminism or in any other organized women's activities, and both contemporaries and historians have tried to explain this "death" of feminism. In 1923, Charlotte Perkins Gilman tried to analyze why the younger women were not living up to the feminists' expectations, and concluded both that the changes had been too rapid and that women themselves were partly to blame. Women were showing distinct tendencies to imitate men's vices, she observed, for both sexes were abusing and mishandling birth control information. Moral relaxation and lowered standards were universal phenomena, she noted, and the Germans had contributed the worst feature, "the solemn philosophical sexmania of Sigmund Freud, now widely poisoning the world." Yet Gilman also believed that although old standards were breaking down, new standards that were not yet clear were developing. Elizabeth Cady Stanton's daughter, Harriot Stanton Blatch, was equally outspoken in her 1940 autobiography. Modern women were "resting on their oars," were still flattered by protection, and did not realize how difficult it had been to win the rights women currently enjoyed. If they had, she argued, "they would be less indifferent to the back-to-the-home movement which is sweeping the world." Women had to have vision and courage, dare to think independently and be themselves; then they could unite to protest their rights.[22]

Historians have offered several explanations of the "death" of feminism. Aileen Kraditor suggested that the shift from justice and human rights to expediency in rationalizing the vote laid the groundwork for later disillusionment with feminism, and William O'Neill argued that the suffragists not only oversold the vote, but in so doing betrayed the incipient radicalism of their own nineteenth century movement. J. Stanley Lemons implied that the social feminism of such groups as the League of Women Voters was diverted and finally exhausted by the struggle against the NWP and its Equal Rights Amendment, while William Chafe emphasized the post–World War II social and psychological reinforcement of ideas about "woman's place." Leftist historian Sheila Rowbotham has offered still another explanation of why the feminists could no longer recruit younger women after World War I. Writing about both British and American feminists, she argued that they were isolated from the younger generation in the confusion after the vote was won, and compromised their earlier feminist vision of collective sisterhood by confining feminism to a series of isolated liberal reforms. Class differences and the new sexual climate were brushed aside by older feminists, while younger women grew up despising the feminist movement. Thus, feminism gradually became "a sentimental attachment of older women," and because the majority of women could not focus their discontent, they became apathetic.[23]

There were also contemporary critics of the NWP's feminism within its own camp. First to raise a question concerning the Party's rather dogmatic claim to a monopoly on "true" feminism was Sue White, a former picketer and national council member who returned to her native Tennessee in the twenties to practice law and work in Democratic politics. When the Party criticized the practice of passing on the positions of deceased men to their widows, calling it "a stupid reversion from feminism," White disagreed completely. "I see progress in it," she wrote, "perhaps it is because I still hold a cheerful philosophy even while assuming to be something of a feminist." In a more serious vein she asked: "Do pure feminists stand only for women who think as they do or for all women including those less conscious of their feminism?"[24] Sue White's question was never answered, her dissatisfaction with the NWP increased, and eventually she broke with the Party.

Historian Mary Beard's criticisms went more deeply into the NWP's philosophy and goals. Beard had been a member of the Congressional Union executive committee from 1913 to 1916, although her reservations about the impact of the proposed ERA on protective legislation for women kept her on the fringes of the Party throughout this period. She never completely severed her ties with the NWP, was a frequent speaker at its conferences, and called on the Party for support in her attempts to encourage women's history. Disassociating herself from the power struggle between the social feminists and the NWP, she nevertheless seriously questioned the Party's interpretation of feminism. In a 1932 article for *Current History*, Beard pointed out that one of the worst consequences of the depression was "the disaster which has overtaken American feminism." Until the 1930s, she believed, American women had been making regular progress, responding to the impact of industrialism on the family with a kind of "rugged feminism." Women had gained administrative experience, a worldwide outlook, and a sense of sex consciousness as well as some solid achievements.[25]

But Beard noted that there were flaws in the demand for the kind of rigid equality which led feminists to praise women achievers indiscriminately, to work for army rank for nurses while at the same time working for peace, and to place high values on certain occupations simply because men valued them. Circumstances had changed greatly since nineteenth century feminists formulated their aims, while feminist ideology had remained fixed. Beard thought that equality and laissez-faire economic philosophy were inextricably tied together, and that women, even feminists, had blindly followed the lead of men.[26] Although she did not suggest any specific alternatives for American feminists, Beard came to these disheartening conclusions about past feminist achievements:

> They rejoiced to receive institutional education just at the time when it had lost its momentum and become hopelessly formalized; they got the vote when it had become least effective, owing to the power of the so-called invisible government; they entered remunerative positions at the period when big business was dropping into a deep air-pocket; they made their main intellectual drive on masculine knowledge at the very stage of man's intellectual collapse.[27]

The Party's response to Beard's challenge was to characterize her as somewhat disillusioned with equality. At a Party banquet the next year, Beard insisted she was still a feminist. "I don't want women to go back to sheer domesticity," she argued, but insisted once again that the "women of 1848 could not have done all our thinking for us." Gail Laughlin, answering for the NWP, denied that the circumstances demanded a new feminist ideology. "We have the same old conditions they had in 1848," she maintained, "the only difference is that they are more widespread now, more oppressive, because there are more women who want jobs." Laughlin expressed the sentiments of the majority of the NWP when she closed with the ringing declaration: "We have enlisted for the war and will carry on until the victory is won!" But Beard again directly raised the question of ideololgy with the Party in 1935, maintaining that feminists must return to the eighteenth century concept of human rights in order to resist the trend toward fascism. She also emphasized the need to work toward transforming an economy of want into an economy of plenty, as well as the need to abandon the concept of equal rights as "the be-all and end-all of effort."[28]

Still another challenge to the NWP's kind of feminism came from Party member and journalist Vee Terrys Perlman in the mid-thirties. Unlike Beard, Perlman did not challenge the ideology but rather the image of the Party, urging that the name of the NWP be changed. "In a long period of years I have met with but one clearcut reaction to the name of our organization," she began, "and that is instinctive antagonism." The major drawbacks of the name were that it lacked educational value, she thought, and, in fact, created a false and unpopular impression of the Party's aims. According to Perlman, people believed that the NWP wanted to reverse the positions of men and women, "to obtain preferment, advantages and glory for women at the expense of men." "Naturally," Perlman concluded, "men resent it and women fear it."[29]

Few people were aware of the Party's existence, even fewer understood the need to work for equal rights, and feminists were perceived as man-haters, Perlman had insisted. She correctly anticipated opposition from the old guard because of the traditions which had grown up around the Party, but Perlman believed that the advantages of a new name would outweigh the disadvantages. Her suggestion was hotly debated and the overwhelming majority of members were against any change of name, even a compromise proposal, the NWP for Equal Rights.[30] An open letter to the Party journal from a member in California expressed all the militancy and fervor of the former picket days. Protesting that any change of name would destroy the Party's identity and all it ever stood for and accomplished, Bernice Dryer wrote:

> I like the NWP just as it is—with all its belligerent history, past and present. . . . Its faithful members have fought, bled and died for the purple, white and gold, and a new name at this critical stage in its history seems like a surrender to the enemy in time of war.[31]

Vee Terrys Perlman had recognized and spoken about the growing hostility to feminism present in the late twenties that reached a peak during the depression. Although women as well as men were anti-feminist, John Macy's article in 1926 about the "myth" of women's equality with men was typical in its range of arguments against femi-ism. Macy believed that women basically did not like each other, and he accused feminists of being completely misguided in their refusal to admit women's biological inferiority and need for protection. Women, he wrote, "are handicapped by the maternal function and by periodic illnesses associated with that function." Feminist leaders were the worst of all possible zealots, doing harm to everyone. Character-izing most feminists as "hard-favored vinegar-faced shrews who have it in for the men," he accused them of ruining the happiness of "other more comely women."[32] To prove his point, Macy quoted at length from Dr. H. W. Frink's study, *Morbid Fears and Compulsions*.

> A certain proportion of at least the most militant suffragists are neurotics who in some instances are compensating for masochistic trends, in others are more or less successfully sub-limating sadistic and homosexual ones (which usually are unconscious). I hope this statement may not be construed as an effort on my part to throw mud on woman suffrage, for one the whole I am very much in favor of it.[33]

Such women "should be spanked and put to bed," Macy concluded, and the rest of the women should recognize that their proper place was in the home, intelligently raising the next generation.

Macy might be dismissed as an old-fashioned misogynist whose arguments were bolstered by popularized Freudianism, but the same could hardly be said of Gina Lombrose Ferrero. The daughter of a well-known criminologist and the wife of a historian, she was the author of the highly controversial study, *The Soul of Woman*. Ferrero's basic thesis was that feminism had destroyed women's chances for happiness by encouraging them to imitate men. Men needed glory, wealth, and independence, she argued, but women needed only love. The more women became like men, the less chance they had of being loved on any higher plane than the purely sexual. Men, since they were autonomous, could be themselves. But even if "what man loves in a woman is a mirage; yet if woman wishes to be loved she must incarnate that mirage." Woman, then, "must continually strive to reproduce in actual life what man desires her to be." This kind of analysis written by a woman of achievements compelled the NWP to answer directly. The Ferrero article should be preserved in a museum as a "period piece," the NWP respondent wrote, for "it is incredible to find such a specimen intact today." Objecting to the definition of happiness as one man's love, she accused Ferrero of confusing happy marriages with "the power to endure."[34]

Other women, less influenced by popular Freudianism, simply argued that the need for feminism has passed. Sarah Schuyler Butler, daughter of the president of Columbia University and the vice-president of the New York Republican Women's Committee, told women that if they wanted political influence they should "drop feministic and sex-conscious ideas and get down to work." Former NWP member Mary Austin, writing in *Nation*, accused nineteenth century feminists of using claims of injustice merely as an excuse to obtain the opportunity to develop their executive and organizing skills and to participate in public affairs. The result, she wrote, was the sexual antagonism between men and women of the suffrage generation and the sexual revolt of the next generation. Dorothy Bromley described the old-fashioned feminists as antagonistic women wearing flat heels and masculine dress, who disliked men, were publicity seekers, and "rant about equality when they might better prove their ability." The "new" feminists, she wrote, would lead full lives because they would combine careers with marriage and children.[35] Yet her description of these "new" women was far from acceptable to feminists like the NWP members.

> Feminist-New Style professes no loyalty to women *en masse* although she staunchly believes in individual women. Surveying her sex as a whole, she finds their actions petty, their range of interests narrow, their talk trivial and repetitious.[36]

In 1931, Albert Pillsbury left a bequest of $25,000 each to Harvard, Princeton, Yale and Columbia Universities to be used to combat feminism. Feminism, Pillsbury believed, took women out of the home and impaired "the family as the basis of civilization and its advance." That same year, the book of essays, *Woman's Coming of Age*, was published. In the introduction, the editors declared that feminism had no more to offer because "it has practically fulfilled its mission." Contributor Mary Ross, in her essay on the status of American women, agreed. "The very word feminist," she wrote, "has come to seem a trifle archaic." "What More Do Women Want?" queried Creighton Peet in his 1931 article in *Outlook*. Arguing that women now dominated every field except business, Peet asked his readers: "Who wants to run a silly old steel corporation when you can influence the emotional, intellectual and artistic life of a nation?"[37]

As the only admittedly American feminist organization during the twenties and thirties, the NWP bore the brunt of this growing hostility. Its natural allies, the social feminists, had been so alienated by the suffrage campaign, the fight over the ERA, and the power struggle in the international women's movement that they could not bring themselves to defend feminism if it meant defending the NWP at the same time. Yet a few voices sympathetic to the feminist purpose and convinced of the continuing need for feminism spoke out during the 1920s. The thirties brought even more support because of the threat to women implicit in the spread of fascism and the greatly increased attacks on marrried women's right to work.

A 1923 editorial in *Nation* suggested that "it is not what men do *to* women but what they do *for* them, that keeps women in a state of rebellious subordination." Since this was the basis of chivalry, women should give up all these special privileges, including alimony. Women should become ruthlessly independent, "letting masculine vanity shrivel and droop as it will," the editorial concluded, and then women would be truly emancipated. Freda Kirchwey explained feminism to the readers of *World Tomorrow* as "a state of mind and a state of heart," arguing that since discrimination existed everywhere, feminism must begin at home with very young children. A few of the feminist sympathizers of the twenties hindered more than they helped the cause. Havelock Ellis saw equal rights as a paradox because there was no real equality in nature, but approved of the feminist drive for equality of opportunity. But Ellis believed that men and women were basically different in most ways and should complement one another. Women must not stray too far from motherhood, he warned, because this would be the major occupation of most women. Emancipation had provided alternatives, however, for "those women who, physically or mentally, are not adapted for motherhood."[38] Ellis wrote this not as a conservative defending woman's traditional sphere, but as a highly regarded liberal spokesman for modern sexuality.

In 1927, the feminist author Mildred Adams attempted an objective analysis of what had happened to feminism during the twenties. She concluded that the loss of unanimity among women stemmed from disillusionment with suffrage as a means to power. She too believed that the vote had been oversold so that "it became a symbol of all the balked desires, the aspirations, the withheld masculine rights, the incoherent longings, and the chaotic clutchings of women." Former suffrage leaders were understandably disappointed and irritated by the new generation, Adams wrote, yet they must share some of the blame. The younger women found the older women illogical because they had fought for freedom for women and then were shocked by the dress and behavior of the younger generation. Unlike most critics of feminist ideology, Adams made some constructive suggestions. As an alternative to being judged by men's standards, feminists should set up their own standards of accomplishment as the first step toward the development of a new feminist culture and philosophy. Women, after all, were free to experiment even if it meant risking mistakes, even if it meant that women "must try to find out how masculine freedom feels before they can set up a clear-eyed satisfactory code of feminine freedom."[39]

Vera Brittain, who belonged to the militant English Six Point Group, took a predictably hard line in defense of the NWP's concept of feminism. Nothing that might happen, she insisted in 1926, "should be permitted by the true Feminist to deflect her from the pursuit of absolute equality between men and women." Brittain believed that feminism needed more fanatics who were uncompromising idealists, and she deplored the fact that most women of the new generation seemed to be afraid of what men would think. In 1928, Brittain was still firm in her belief, although she recognized that feminism had become an unpopular cause which "bores rather than enthralls," and which was treated by the media either with open contempt or patronizing humor. However, modern women must not lose faith, Brittain pleaded.[40]

During the thirties, concern about the need for feminism increased among women for several reasons. Chase Going Woodhouse evaluated the status of women in 1930 for the *American Journal of Sociology*, and found that women moving into the labor field were concentrated in certain limited occupations which rapidly became "feminized." Surveying women college teachers, she observed "a feeling of despair and resentment concerning their situation in regard to salary and promotion." Yet Woodhouse's overall evaluation was optimistic, for she believed that the long range tendency was toward equality of opportunity for women. Mabel Lee, writing in the same year, did not find the prospects so promising. Addressing herself particularly to "The Dilemma of the Educated Woman," she argued that woman's relatively rapid movement into education and careers had unsettled the average male, who had reacted by trying to push her firmly back into the biological role of wife and mother. In other words, Lee observed, women were still forced to choose between a career and a marriage with children, and this placed them under a tremendous handicap. College educated women became restless, discontented, confused and generally unable to adjust to the old ideas about marriage, she concluded.[41]

Emily Blair, a social feminist long active in Democratic politics, called herself a "discouraged feminist" in 1931. All the feminists had wanted to achieve was a world where men and women could work competitively and where the best individual would win, but it had not been achieved. "The best man continued to win," she wrote, "and women, even the best, worked for and under him." Blair did not believe that equality with men meant identity with them, although she concluded that the only way a woman could be accepted as an equal in a man's world was to duplicate his financial success. Placing her hopes in the new generation of college women, she maintained that since these women had been educated to equality, they would be shocked into action by the discriminations they encountered.[42]

In a thoughtful analysis written in 1932, Beatrice Hinkle located the crux of the woman problem not in economics but in psychology. Women were still dependent upon men, and intelligent well-educated women still accepted a masculine point of view about themselves. Even women achievers believed themselves inferior to men because of their reproductive functions, she discovered. Hinkle insisted that women must struggle to achieve a sense of selfhood, although "psychoanalysis in the hands of many of its men exponents condemns all efforts or achievement of women in an intellectual or a nonbiological line as masculine or away from women's 'normal sphere.'" Women, Hinkle advised, should try to conceive of themselves as distinct personalities, apart from their biological functions, and independent of men. They must develop an inner sense of personal worth as well as good loyal relationships with other women, although she warned that men might attack these relationships as evidence of homosexuality.[43]

There definitely was a woman problem, Winifred Holtby insisted in her 1935 book, *Women in a Changing Civilisation*. Previously feminists had acted to remove injustices in a climate of rationalism, individualism, and democracy; however, the current age was one of mysticism, community, and authority. Women were still considered in relation to men; lacking self-confidence women were unwilling to be ruthless and young girls had no appropriate models to pattern themselves after. Men were supposed to support their wives, she wrote, and "dependence, slightly shameful in a man, is, under this tradition, pleasing in a woman." Her conclusion was that the necessary conditions for women's emancipation must include the use of reason and a rational philosophy, free access to birth control knowledge, rejection of military values, and more flexibility in political, economic, and social systems. Olga Knopf agreed that there was a serious woman problem, but in her book, *Women on Their Own*, she maintained that the woman problem was inseparable from the current problems of society. Arguing that organized feminist activity only created more antagonism and invited repressive measures, Knopf suggested that feminists concentrate on education as a means for social change. Although the NWP recommended Knopf's book to its members, it was with the reservation that "no submerged group can win rights for itself except by organized activity."[44]

Other women also recognized the lessons of the times. "Is Feminism Dead?" asked Genevieve Pankhust in 1935. She was concerned because although the depression had made some setbacks inevitable, women had suffered "in undue proportion" with respect to job opportunities, pay, and eligibility for New Deal programs. Feminists were supposed to be their sisters' keepers, she charged, but they had failed to help working women or to warn women adequately against the rise of fascism. When M. Cary Thomas bequeathed money for the NWP equal rights work, she explained that the depression proved that "women can no longer be supported by men." Pearl Buck, returning to the United States from China at the end of the decade, found women unhappy and dissatisfied. In her brief book, *Of Men and Women*, Buck maintained that "the average American woman is the weakest link in American democracy, and by her weakness she drags at the man and hampers the child." Explaining why she had written this particular kind of study, she insisted that women everywhere were threatened by the spread of fascism. "To delay," she warned, "might mean to be compelled to silence."[45]

Actually, organized feminists like the NWP were among the first to protest against the rise of fascism. In the twenties Mussolini gave women the right to vote in municipal elections, and then abolished those same elections. But an NWP editorial warned American women not to be surprised that Italian women submitted so quietly, when in the United States their own civil and economic rights were also being subverted. A decade later the Party was even more alarmed by manifestations of what seemed to be American fascism, such as the attacks on married women's right to work, Governor Curley's speech to Boston Italian-Americans praising Mussolini, and Lawrence Dennis' book, *The Coming of American Fascism*. "Fascism," editorialized *Equal Rights*, "spells doom for women."[46]

The NWP believed that German women failed to prevent the rise of Nazism because they had had little experience in the development of strong feminist organizations prior to the Weimar Republic. Speaking at the NWP Eastern Regional Conference in 1935, Mary Beard characterized fascism as "the neurosis of the patriarchal age," and expressed her concern about the economic crisis and the ensuing movement against women's jobs. "We read that the woman power of the nation has been computed for war work," she told her audience, "and we await the word that we in our turn are to be ordered back to the kitchen and the nursery." Although they believed fascism was restricting women's opportunities all over the world, NWP members could still see "one ray of sunshine." More women were beginning to complain, to rebel, "to realize that in their own right they are human beings." Disdaining male chivalry, women were fighting for their jobs.

As a result, *Equal Rights* reported, "in greater and greater numbers women are being driven into the Feminist camp by stark necessity."[47]

The NWP, then, had its own definition of feminism based on the assumption that although women, like men, were human beings, women did have special characteristics and values. Women were cooperative, spiritual, and peaceful; they valued human life because they gave birth to it. Party members believed that a male-dominated society was often mistaken in its goals and maintained that society would be better balanced and better able to serve humanity when women could participate fully in the affairs of the world. Equality before the law was an essential prerequisite for women to have this opportunity to develop fully their special potential. Feminism itself could further this development, the NWP insisted, because it cut across class lines, fostered a sense of sex solidarity, and strengthened women's character through work for a good and just cause. The NWP attracted women who had experienced discrimination and been unable to overcome it by themselves, as well as women who had been successful but wished to make such a struggle unnecessary for future generations. Some members became feminists through their participation in other reforms, some as a means of utilizing their talents, and some because they had been inspired by some woman leader, usually during the suffrage campaign. Many women in the Party felt that feminism gave meaning and direction to their lives, and they were convinced that their work would help create a better world.

NWP feminists were concerned about the apparent lack of interest and participation of the newer generation of women, as well as about the rise of fascism with its obviously regressive effects upon women's status. The Party did not advocate its kind of feminism in a vacuum, however. There were outspoken feminist sympathizers outside the Party in the twenties and even more supporters in the thirties. Criticism of feminism, its basic assumptions, its goals, and its effects also increased during the period. Yet the NWP's insistence on equal rights and the Equal Rights Amendment as the primary goals of all "true" feminists made it impossible for other feminists to cooperate with them. Even well-meaning critics close to the Party, like Mary Beard, or within the NWP ranks, like Sue White or Vee Terrys Perlman, were unable to convince the Party to modify its narrow and rather exclusive kind of feminism. Furthermore, the tactics the NWP relied upon to implement its goals often alienated both the social feminists and the general public. As a result, the NWP remained an articulate but small group of feminists who were unable to develop a viable alternative program acceptable to other feminists concerned with the trends of these two decades.

NOTES

1. William O'Neill, "Feminism as a Radical Ideology," in *Dissent: Explorations in the History of American Radicalism*, edited by Alfred E. Young (DeKalb, Ill.: Northern Illinois University Press, 1968).

2. Carl Degler, "Revolution Without Ideology: The Changing Place of Women in America," in *The Woman in America*, edited by Robert Jay Lifton (Boston: Beacon Press, 1964).

3. Gerda Lerner, "Women's Rights and American Feminism," *American Scholar* 40 (Spring 1971), 236–37.

4. Editorial, "What Is Feminism?" *ERIFW* 1 (March 2, 1935), 66; Editorial, "Accept No Substitute," *ERIFW* 1 (July 6, 1935), 138.

5. "Greetings From Mrs. Harvey Wiley," *ER* 1 (December 1, 1923), 333; Editorial, "For Economic Freedom" *ER* 15 (July 20, 1929), 186; Editorial, "What Is Feminism?" *ERIFW* 1 (March 2, 1935), 66.

6. Alma Lutz, "That Much-Maligned Feminism," *ERIFW* 1 (August 3, 1935), 171; Editorial, "The Cost of Subordination," *ER* 1 (July 14, 1923), 252; Editorial, "Standardizing Service," *ER* 1 (July 14, 1923), 172; Edith Houghton Hooker, "Utilizing the Maternal Instinct," *ER* 11 (July 5, 1924), 166.

7. Editorial, "Invalids?" *ER* 11 (June 7, 1924), 132; Editorial, "Are Women a Sub-Human Species?" *ER* 14 bis (October 13, 1928), 282.

8. Editorial, "Men Vs. Women," *ER* 1 (November 10, 1923), 308; Editorial, "Heaven Forbid!" *ER* 14 bis (January 19, 1929), 394.

9. Bernice Marks Stearns, "An Appeal for Funds," *ER* 11 (February 16, 1924), 8; Mary Winsor, "The Freedom of Equality," *ER* 1 (February 24, 1923), 12–13; Alma Lutz, "That Much Maligned Feminism," *ERIFW* 1 (August 3, 1935), 172; Alma Lutz, "A Feminist Thinks It Over," *ER* 23 (December 15, 1937), 182.

10. Editorial, "What Is Feminism," *ER* 14 (May 14, 1927), 180; Editorial, "Elizabeth Cady Stanton," *ER* 20 (November 10, 1934),

322; Editorial, "What Is Feminism," *ERIFW* 1 (March 2, 1935), 66; Alma Lutz, "That Much-Maligned Feminism," *ERIFW* 1 (August 3, 1935), 171.

11. Editorial, "Boosting Liberty," *ER* 14 bis (August 11, 1928), 212.

12. Alma Lutz, "That Much-Maligned Feminism," *ERIFW* 1 (August 3, 1935), 171.

13. "Declaration of Principles," *ER* 1 (February 17, 1923), 5.

14. Editorial, "Comrades," *ER* 1 (November 24, 1923), 324; Lavinia Egan, "Women See Need of Organization," *ER* 1 (September 29, 1923), 259; Editorial, "The Comradeship," *ER* 11 (April 26, 1924), 84; Editorial, "The Mantle of the Pioneers," ER 1 (June 30, 1923), 156; Editorial, "The Religion of Feminism," *ER* 15 (March 29, 1929), 58; Editorial, "What Is Feminism," *ERIFW* 1 (March 2, 1935), 66.

15. Alma Lutz, "A Feminist Thinks It Over," *ER* 23 (December 15, 1937), 182; "Business Conference," *ER* 1 (November 24, 1923), 326; Editorial, "Accept No Substitute," *ERIFW* 1 (July 6, 1935), 138; Editorial, "Is It Any Wonder," *ER* 16 (October 25, 1930), 298.

16. Mrs. O. H. P. Belmont, "The Need for the Woman's Party," *ER* 1 (March 10, 1923), 26; Edith Houghton Hooker, "The Woman with Gifts to Bring," *ER* 1 (April 28, 1923), 85; "Greetings from Mrs. Harvey Wiley," *ER* 1 (December 1, 1923), 333.

17. Robert Riegel, *American Feminists* (Lawrence, Kan.: University of Kansas Press, 1963), pp. 188–89, 194, 200; Gerda Lerner, "Women's Rights and American Feminism," *American Scholar* 40 (Spring 1971), 239, 246–47; John Burnham, "Psychiatry, Psychology, and the Progressive Movement," *American Quarterly* 12 (1960), 457–58.

18. Christopher Lasch, *The New Radicalism in America, 1889-1963* (New York: Alfred Knopf, 1965), pp. 38–39, 47; Jill Conway, "Jane Addams: An American Heroine," in *The Woman in America*, edited by Robert Jay Lifton (Boston: Beacon Press, 1964), pp. 247–48, 259.

19. Jane Norman Smith to Mary Gertrude Fendall, January 7, 1929, Jane Norman Smith Papers, Box 3, f. 72, SL; "Report of the National Chairman," *ER* 17 (December 12, 1931), 358; Editorial, "Our Fortunate Selves," *ER* 20 (November 3, 1934), 314.

20. "Beauty and Freedom Go Hand in Hand," *ER* 20 (December 22, 1934), 373; John Mitchell, review of *A Woman of Fifty*, by Rheta Childe Door, in *ER* 12 (April 25, 1925), 85–86.

21. Editorial, "The Inferiority Complex," *ER* 1 (March 3, 1923), 24; Editorial, "Lonely? Join Us," *ER* 13 (May 22, 1926), 116; Editorial, "Our Fortunate Selves," *ER* 20; (November 3, 1934), 314; Inez Haynes Irwin, "Adventures of Yesterday," unpublished autobiography in Inez Haynes Irwin Papers, Box 3, f. 12, SL, 450.

22. Charlotte Perkins Gilman, "The New Generation of Women," *Current History* 18 (August 1923), 731–36; Alma Lutz and Harriot Stanton Blatch, *Challenging Years* (New York: G. P. Putnam's Sons, 1940), p. 335.

23. Kraditor, *The Ideas of the Woman Suffrage Movement*; O'Neill, *Everyone Was Brave;* Lemons, *The Woman Citizen*; Chafe, *The American Woman*; Sheila Rowbotham, *Hidden From History* (London: Pluto Press, 1973), pp. 162–93.

24. Sue S. White, "What Is Feminism?" *ER* 11 (January 3, 1925), 274.

25. Mary R. Beard, "Test for the Modern Woman," *Current History* 37 (November 1932), 181–82.

26. *Ibid.*

27. *Ibid.*, p. 183.

28. "Banquet Attracts Brilliant Assemblage," *ER* 19 (November 11, 1933), 319; Mary R. Beard, "A New Task for Social Democracy," *ERIFW* 1 (July 6, 1935), 139–41.

29. Vee Terrys Perlman, "Shall the Name of the Woman's Party Be Changed," *ER* 19 (June 10, 1933), 150.

30. *Ibid.*, p. 151.

31. Open Letter from Bernice A. Dryer, "Let the Name Stand," *ER* 19 (June 24, 1933), 168.

32. John Macy, "Equality of Women with Men: A Myth," *Harper's* 153 (November 1926), 709.

33. *Ibid.*, pp. 710–11.

34. Gina Lombroso Ferrero, "Feminism Destructive of Woman's Happiness," *Current History* 25 (January 1927), 487, 492; Martha Bensley Bruere, "Highway to Woman's Happiness," *Current History*, 27 (October 1927), 26–28.

35. Editorial, "Not Dead or Even Sleeping," *ER* 13 (January 8, 1927), 380; Mary Austin, "The Forward Turn," *Nation* 125 (July 20, 1927), 57–58; Dorothy Bromley, "Feminist New Style," *Harper's* 155 (October 1927), 552.

36. Bromley, "Feminist New Style," p. 556.

37. "Universities Reject Anti-Feminist Fund," *ER* 17, (February 7, 1931), 7; S. D. Schmalhausen and V. F. Calverton, eds., *Woman's Coming of Age* (New York: H. Liveright, 1931) pp. xvi, 545; Creighton Peet, "What More Do Women Want?" *Outlook* 158 (August 5, 1931), 433.

38. Editorial, "New Program for Women," *Nation* 107 (September 19, 1923), 285–86; Freda Kirchwey, "Are You A Feminist?" *World Tomorrow* 6 (December 1923), 361–62; Havelock Ellis, "Equal Rights: A Paradox," *Pictorial Review* 26 (November 1924), 5, 121, 122.

39. Mildred Adams, "Did They Know What They Wanted?" *Outlook* 147 (December 28, 1927), 528, 529, 544.

40. Vera Brittain, "Feminism Divided—The American Example," *ER* 13 (October 23, 1926), 291; Vera Brittain, "Why Feminism Lives," *ER* 14 bis (May 19, 1928), 115.

41. Chase Going Woodhouse, "The Status of Women," *American Journal of Sociology* 35 (May 1930), 1096; Mabel B. Lee, "The Dilemma of the Educated Woman," *Atlantic* 146 (November 1930), 590–95.

42. Emily N. Blair, "Discouraged Feminists," *Outlook* 158 (July 8, 1931), 303, 318.

43. Beatrice Hinkle, "Women's Dependence Upon Men," *Harper's* 164 (January 1932), 193–205.

44. Winifred Holtby, *Women in a Changing Civilisation* (New York: Longman's Green, 1935), pp. 7, 100, 104, 107, 188–90; Olga Knopf, *Women On Their Own* (Boston: Little, Brown, 1935), pp. 287–89; "A Study of Women's Problems," review of *Women On Their Own* by Olga Knopf, in *ERIFW* 1 (April 13, 1935), 47.

45. Genevieve Parkhurst, "Is Feminism Dead?" *Harper's* 170 (May 1935), 735; "Woman's Party To Receive Munificent Bequest," *ER* 22 (April 1, 1936), 1; Pearl Buck, *Of Men and Women* (New York: John Day and Company, 1941), pp. 40, vii.

46. Editorial, "See Saw Margery Daw," *ER* 13 (November 6, 1926), 308; Editorial, "The Menace of Fascism," *ERIFW* 1 (February 8, 1936), 386.

47. Editorial, "In Time of Comparative Peace," *ERIFW* 1 (September 21, 1935), 226; Mary Beard, "A New Task for Social Democracy," *ERIFW* 1 (July 6, 1935), 140; Editorial, "The Sun Is Still There," *ERIFW* 1 (February 29, 1936), 410.

3
MORE THAN A GOOD PROPAGANDA TECHNIQUE

Even NWP feminists who shared a common base of ideas and goals were unable to arrive at a consensus on how to achieve these aims. They agreed that the ideal would be to incorporate the Equal Rights Amendment into the Constitution, but differed about how much and what kind of state work was necessary to accomplish congressional passage of the Amendment. Participation in international work was even more controversial. The national officers urged a continuation of the NWP's suffrage policy of holding the party in power responsible, but this policy was questioned in the twenties and abandoned in the thirties. The Party never altered its uncompromising stand for complete equality for women, but during the 1930s suffered a serious schism between its old guard and reform factions.

The militant actions which had characterized the Party during the final years of the suffrage campaign were often invoked nostalgically, but were not repeated in the domestic equal rights campaign. In the international campaign, a few confrontations and arrests occurred, but were the exceptions rather than the rule. An integral part of the NWP's equality campaign was the support of women for both elective and appointive positions in the government. The Party also consistently stressed the importance of publicity as an educational device, including radio talks, newspaper coverage and distribution of literature. Whenever possible, and particularly during the twenties, it made use of dramatic pageants such as those staged at Seneca Falls, New York, and the Garden of the Gods, Colorado. NWP members had a strong sense of participation in the making of history and tradition, cooperating with all efforts to encourage the preservation, publication, and study of women's history. They also tended to ascribe the status of heroines to outstanding women achievers of both the past and their own time.

From the beginning of the equality campaign, members disagreed over the balance and relative importance of state and national work. Although in 1923 *Equal Rights* alleged that it was immaterial whether discriminations were removed by state legislation, state constitutional amendment, or federal amendment, the national officers always favored the federal amendment method. To demonstrate the insecurity of state equal rights legislation they used the example of North Dakota, where in 1916 the mother of an illegitimate child was its only legal parent, in 1917 both the mother and father were legal parents, and in 1923 again only the mother was a legal parent. Based on their suffrage experience, they reminded members of the great cost, labor, and disappointments involved in the referenda campaigns often necessary to amend state constitutions. Every unsuccessful campaign for equal rights legislation drained money and strength that could be better used working for the federal amendment, they argued. In 1923, the Connecticut legislature rejected twenty-six specific equal rights measures, New York twenty-five, Rhode Island twenty, Ohio fourteen, Oklahoma nine, and Michigan five. Blanket equal rights bills which would have removed many discriminations at once were defeated in Massachusetts, Illinois, and Minnesota. Although not all of these bills had been sponsored by the NWP, the message seemed clear that the Party would do better to concentrate on the federal amendment.[1]

Women needed the Equal Rights Amendment in the same way that men needed the Declaration of Independence, argued former nurses' settlement worker Lavinia Dock. The long struggle for the vote had been "mainly that we might alter the whole position of women and enable them to come forward in all the affairs of life, nationally and internationally, to the full extent of their competence." But in the twenties not all the former Party members were convinced of the need for another federal amendment. Harriot Stanton Blatch, who later rejoined the NWP, raised two fundamental questions: what does sex equality mean, and can it be legislated? The ERA seemed to her to be either meaningless words, or else something which would be open to court interpretation for generations. " 'Tis a strange illusion," she wrote, "much like the cure-all theory of patent medicine." Anne Martin also questioned whether equality laws really equalized. "Are they not taking the shadow for the substance?" she asked, and never rejoined the Party. Elizabeth Green Kalb, who dropped out of the NWP for most of the twenties, confessed that she too had been skeptical about legislating equality. Speaking to the Hawaiian League of Women Voters in 1931, she said: "I was one of those who believed that the work of the NWP was ended." But ten years of futile work for such reforms as the extension of jury service to women, as well as the increasing discriminations against working women, had convinced her of the need for the Equal Rights Amendment.[2]

Another question which arose in connection with the need for the ERA was the existence of the Fourteenth Amendment, the first section of which guarantees equal protection of the laws to all persons. Until the 1970s, however, this clause was never interpreted to include women. On at least two occasions, the NWP participated in and financed test cases based on the application of Constitutional protections to women, with disappointing results. In 1931, the Massachusetts branch financed the case of Genevieve Welosky, charged with keeping and selling liquor, and challenged the all-male jury system as denying her a jury of her peers. The Massachusetts League of Women Voters had submitted an amicae curiae brief, and jury service for women had widespread public support. The jury statute, reenacted after the Nineteenth Amendment, read: "A person qualified to vote for representatives to the General Court shall be liable to serve as a juror." Yet the Court's tortuous reasoning was that the word "person" did not include women because the Nineteenth Amendment had created a new class of human beings. In the words of the Court:

> It did not extend the right to vote to members of an existing classification thereto disqualified, but created a new class.

It added to qualified voters those who did not fall within the meaning of the word "person" in the jury statutes.[3]

A similar case occurred in 1935. Virginia, like Massachusetts, did not permit women to serve on juries. In this instance, however, the trial contained irregularities, and a first degree murder conviction had been brought in against the defendant, a schoolteacher accused of killing her father. As in the Welosky case, the NWP arranged for finances and a lawyer, who moved for a new trial. The basic contention again was that because the defendant was not tried by a jury of her peers, she had been denied equal protection of the laws. As *Equal Rights Independent Feminist Weekly* described the potential of the case, "it is the opportunity of the ages for the Feminist movement!"[4] Unfortunately, although the case dragged on through several appeals, the equal protection argument was thrown out and the conviction upheld.

The NWP's answer to the question of whether or not equality could be legislated was to point out that if a man were discriminated against in job opportunities, wages, hours, jury service, parenthood, and had to take his wife's name as well, he would be severely handicapped. The Party hoped to accomplish a number of important goals through the ERA, Crystal Eastman explained. It was a way to remove all common law barriers to women's equality, as well as a bill of rights against future discriminations; moreover, it would separate women from children in the field of industrial legislation.[5]

Although disagreements about the relative importance of state and national work continued throughout the twenties, the Party regularly lobbied Congress and the national political conventions and sent deputations of prominent women to call on the president on behalf of the ERA. One hundred women visited President Harding in 1921, and in 1923, Coolidge was deputized by a group which included such prominent Republican NWP speakers as Maud Younger, Mrs. Victor DuPont, and Mrs. Stephen Pell. Party members visited Coolidge again in early 1927, this time demanding a presidential endorsement of the ERA, industrial equality with men, and more appointments of women to high government positions. Mrs. Harvey Wiley and Anita Pollitzer took Amelia Earhart with them when they called on President Hoover, for whom the NWP had campaigned. By this time, opposition to the

ERA had focused on its potential destruction of protective legislation for women, and Earhart told the president that even her career had been hampered by sex discrimination.[6]

The NWP finally ran into insuperable obstacles, however, in Franklin and Eleanor Roosevelt. Not only were the Roosevelts connected with those same "welfare workers" who were unalterably opposed to the ERA, but also the New York branch of the Party had angered Franklin Roosevelt by its obstructionist tactics when, as governor, he had attempted to obtain legislation for women and children. Repeated attempts to make an appointment with the president were unsuccessful, and the NWP plans for a deputation had to be cancelled. After Roosevelt's reelection, Alice Paul wrote to Party congressional chairman Helen Hunt West, who had been the first registered women voter in Florida, had run for Democratic committeewoman in that state, and had represented the NWP at Democratic conventions. Referring to Eleanor Roosevelt, Paul noted that "as one observes her work in the White House one cannot but feel that she belongs with us and not against us," and asked West "whether, since you have more access to those in authority in the Democratic Party than most of us, you could not have a real discussion of the equality program with Mrs. Roosevelt." Nothing came of this suggestion, and during the 1940 Democratic convention Laura Berrien wrote to NWP representative Caroline Lexow Babcock that "the Roosevelts own the Democratic party and there is no chance to get anything they don't want."[7]

The thirties seemed to provide a more encouraging climate for the passage of the Amendment because of the economic discriminations and the discouragements of the past ten years with regard to state legislation. Congressmen generally did not care about the ERA, the National Woman's Party believed, but they did care about what their constituents thought. The Party's job would be to stir up these constituents and this period marked the beginning of the Party reformers' stress on a mass organization and democratization. "The task today is therefore not so much to convince women that they need Equal Rights," wrote Mrs. Hooker, "as to organize the already existing sentiment in support of a definite program of action." Mass organization would aid the passage of the Amendment, she explained, because the majority of Congressmen were responsive only to votes. "We must work. . . as though we expected to win tomorrow," Anita Pollitzer advised the Maryland branch in a speech in 1933.[8]

The rationale behind the treaty method for achieving equal rights internationally was the same as that which was used to justify the federal amendment method. Referring to the approval of the Equal Rights Treaty by four Latin American nations, Doris Stevens insisted that "it was primarily *the method used* which brightened not only our hearts, but the hearts of many enlightened jurists as well." Yet the Party's international work diverted time, money, and effort from both state and national campaigns, and there were some members who believed that the Party ought not to engage in international activities until American women had achieved equality. "As you know, I cannot understand how the question of amendment versus treaty ever originated," Doris Stevens wrote to Jane Norman Smith in 1934. "Certainly I have never heard anyone advocate working for one to the exclusion of the other."[9] But the Party's resources were limited, and money budgeted to international work meant even less could be used for national and state campaigns.

The strongest advocates of state equal rights work were those who wished to reform the Party. In 1927, the reformers described state gains as fundamental to the national work because they were educational and provided an "entering wedge" for the ERA. Local women in isolated groups must be brought into contact with each other through state federations, and reinspired through more frequent meetings and conferences, Mrs. Hooker declared. It was a mistake to believe that the passage of the Amendment could be achieved by lobbying in Washington, the reformers argued, for the majority of the NWP work must be in the field. By 1935, disagreements between advocates of state and national work were intense. In her call to the convention, Florence Bayard Hilles emphasized the increasing outside attacks on the principles of equality and maintained that "the passage of the Equal Rights Amendment, and methods for our struggle to attain it must be thoroughly discussed and, in its far reaching importance, better understood."[10]

But the impatience of the old guard with specific state equal rights legislation had increased throughout the twenties. Both Alice Paul and Jane Norman Smith believed that eleven years of state work had educated the public sufficiently and that the time was ripe to concentrate on the ERA. In spite of some objections from its members, the New York state branch had decided late in 1931 to concentrate on the passage of the federal amendment. Although Mrs. Hooker and the reformers strongly urged the expansion of state work, the national council in 1932 voted to concentrate on the ERA. This first council vote did not mention, and thus did not preclude, state work, but in 1935, the council recommended that the NWP state branches work only for the federal amendment and the international equality treaties. The reformers, however, ascribed the failure to obtain the passage of the Amendment to the concentration on national lobbying at the expense of state work. "The utter hopelessness of such procedure," they stated, "is evidenced by the results."[11]

During the Party's postsuffrage reorganization, the NWP leadership had provided a temporary constitution, and no significant changes were incorporated into the 1927 by-laws. Officers served for two years, but their duties were only vaguely described. The national council consisted of the officers and the twenty-four members at large who were also elected at the biennial convention. The council was empowered to appoint an executive secretary, all standing and special committees, the chairs of occupational councils, and to fill any vacancies resulting from death or resignation. Between conventions, the duty of the national council was to direct the affairs and policy of the Party.[12]

In actual practice, this arrangement concentrated power in the hands of a small group of women. Mrs. Belmont was president until her death; she was never replaced and eventually the office was eliminated. The advisory chairman was a position specifically intended for Alice Paul, whose use of her power to "suggest" varied throughout the period. Her major influences on the Party's domestic policies between 1925 and 1940 were her intervention on behalf on endorsing Hoover for president in 1928, her support of the Party's old guard in the 1934 revision of the constitution, and her assistance in the compromises of late 1936 that helped reunite the Party.

Only seven standing committees were created by the 1927 constitution, although the national council could create other committees

if necessary. Occupational councils were to work against discriminations in their special fields, and an international advisory council was
established for foreign feminists who might wish to affiliate with the
NWP. The constitution set the national council quorum requirement
at less than one-fourth of the council members, while the quorum for
a national convention was fixed at a majority of the voting members
present. A state branch could determine its own organizational form,
set its own dues, and direct its own activities so long as state actions
did not conflict with national policies.[13] The entire system was open to
manipulation by the national council, whose members not only had
individual votes and extensive appointive power, but who could also
determine the date and place of the convention.

Declining membership and the NWP's increasing failure to secure
equality legislation during the 1920s led to pressures for democratization of the Party throughout the period, culminating in constitutional
revisions in 1934 and 1938. In 1934 the reformers, led by Edith
Houghton Hooker and the Maryland branch, failed to win passage
of any of their proposed amendments. In fact, the constitution was
amended in such a way as to make further challenges to the leadership
even more difficult, and this led to a temporary division of the Party
into two separate factions, publishing two separate journals during
1935 and 1936. In 1937 the schism was healed, and the 1938 constitutional revisions reflected a compromise with some of the reformers'
demands.

Prior to the 1934 convention the reformers had met in their Eastern
Regional Conference at Richmond and Edith Houghton Hooker had
received an ovation when she insisted that no one could give freedom
to another person because freeing women would require a great social
movement. Her conclusion that "the great social movements of the
world do not arise because of the whimsies of a few individuals" was
a direct challenge to the NWP leadership. In 1934, Mrs. Hooker's
group proposed a reorganization of the officers who would constitute
an executive committee in charge of Party affairs and policies between
conventions, which would be held annually. The reformers also proposed to reduce the national council's power to appoint and to increase
the council's required quorum. The voting body of the Party would
be enlarged, and the amendment procedure would be made easier.

None of the reformers' proposals passed. Instead, Party leaders tightened their control through a series of amendments of their own. One of the most important of these established the investment and endowment committee. Through this amendment, financial control of the Party's major assets was firmly vested in a small, self-perpetuating appointive group of the old guard membership. Another revision made a two-thirds vote necessary to amend the constitution, rather than the majority vote required by the 1927 by-laws.[14]

Members continued to take sides in the struggle to control the Party, despite Mrs. Harvey Wiley's plea for unity and solidarity as the convention business meeting opened. However, Sarah Colvin along with four council members resigned at the meeting, and two months later the break was symbolized by Edith Houghton Hooker's publication of the first issue *Equal Rights Independent Feminist Weekly*. The dissidents never completely broke with the Party, for there was no other "true" feminist alternative as they saw it. Most of them were loyal to the Party in their own way and had no wish to form a rival organization. The old guard was not above pettiness, however, as the minutes of the national council in January 1935 showed. The Party refused to allow the Eastern Conference to display the NWP banners because "the Conference is not an official gathering of the NWP, not having been approved by the Council."[15]

The position of neutrals who were active and committed Party members was particularly difficult during this period. Feminist author Alma Lutz had joined the Massachusetts branch in the twenties. Secretary of her branch for several years, she served the national Party as organization chairman, contributing editor to *Equal Rights*, chairman of the literature committee, and member of the national council. When the reformers invited Lutz to join a strategy meeting in 1935, she replied that she would like to serve as literature chairman if there were no conflict with her other NWP offices, but that she could not be active in organization work. Although she believed that feminists must stop fighting one another, Lutz did admit that there was organizational and educational work the NWP did not care to undertake. Agreeing that there was room for a new group, she wrote in a conciliatory manner to Mrs. Hooker that "some temperaments cannot work together, but can do good work toward the same goal when separated."[16]

The key to the 1935 schism in the NWP may be found in the internal disagreement over three fundamental issues: structure, priorities, and leadership. The only issue publicly discussed by both sides was that of structure. The old guard view was that a small group like the original Constitutional Union could best provide leadership in the struggle for equal rights. The conservatives saw themselves as the vanguard of the largely inarticulate and unorganized masses of women, who nonetheless would support the Party because of the basic justice of the cause. This firmly held belief in the small elite vanguard of leadership stemmed from the old guard's analysis of the role that the NWP had played in the final few years of the struggle for the Nineteenth Amendment. The fallacy in their analysis, of course, was that they badly underestimated NAWSA's tremendous educational and organizational work in convincing more than two million women of the need for suffrage.

Mrs. Hooker and the reformers believed in mass organization with more direct membership representation than the NWP provided. The reformers admitted that their Eastern Regional Conference had caused an "organization within an organization" to develop, but saw nothing wrong with that. Pointing out that the conferences were financially self-supporting and were actually increasing the NWP membership, the reformers recommended a "duplex" form of Party, geographical within states and occupational across state lines. Their most revolutionary proposal was a provision for the affiliation of other organizations endorsing the object of the NWP, and they wished to allow such organizations one voting delegate for each fifty members.[17]

The advantages of regional meetings, according to Mrs. Hooker, were that they strengthened the subsidiary organizations, resulted in good publicity, sparked new equality campaigns, and discovered and developed new local feminist leaders. But the old guard was not yet ready to compromise. As congressional committee member Helen Hunt West explained, the Party had never accepted just anyone as a member. "It has not always been an easy matter to be a member of the Woman's Party," she concluded. "It has taken what men have been pleased to term politically 'intestinal stamina.'" Meanwhile, the reformers continued their organizing efforts, turning their attention to the midwest which they described as "an almost untapped gold mine so far as the Feminist movement is concerned." According to Mrs. Hooker, midwestern women already recognized the economic discrimination against them and very little "converting" was necessary.[18]

The neutrals actively worked for reconciliation between the old guard and the reformers. Alma Lutz continued to serve on the editorial boards of both journals, writing to another neutral and long time Party member Betty Gram Swing that "I too have refused to take part in the controversy and feel that we can do more by keeping calm than by fanning the flames and driving Mrs. Hooker out of the Party." The Party's loss of good workers in the past had proven detrimental to the cause of feminism, Lutz explained, "and I am doing all I can now to avert another such blunder."[19]

By 1936, Mrs. Hooker and national council chairman Florence Bayard Hilles were meeting to work out the details for consolidating the two factions and journals. The national Party agreed to support organizational work in the field and the development of regional conferences, to improve headquarters' efficiency and budget planning, and to stop trying to channel and control the activities of state and occupational branches. Speaking for the reformers, Mrs. Hooker agreed to a semimonthly *Equal Rights*, and did not insist on being editor because she knew that "some members of the Council would be antagonistic to any such arrangement on personal grounds."[20]

The reformers considered the two year schism a good experience for all concerned, much like the splits between the National and the American Woman Suffrage Associations, or between the Congressional Union and NAWSA. As Mrs. Hooker explained, "the NWP may have its faults, since everything human has, but its virtues and its visions make it a veritable fortress for women." She believed that any differences of opinion which could not be ironed out should be forgotten so that women with the same goal could work toward it together. "Every Feminist is a friend and every anti-Feminist is an enemy," she wrote, "and upon this basis the fight must be waged."[21]

The merger was concluded in January, 1937, and the compromises were included in the 1938 constitutional revisions. The reformers did not gain everything that they had hoped for, but the revisions passed by the NWP convention in the fall of 1938 made some important concessions to them. The number of officers was reduced, the national council was enlarged, and the control of Party affairs between conventions was vested in an executive council. The amount of dues and the proportion payable to the national Party would be determined by the national council, and the Belmont legacy was freed from the restrictions against spending its capital funds.[22]

No changes were made in the voting representation at the conventions, however, which meant that the large occupational councils like the industrial workers and government workers still had only one vote. The old guard was also able to resist the reformers' demand for annual conventions and the affiliation of members only with the branches of their domicile. Actually, the changes in the 1938 constitution did not really democratize the Party nor make it less hierarchical. The revisions merely gave the reformers more opportunity to share the leadership with the old guard, and clarified the officers' and executive council's duties and responsibilities. More importantly for the future of the Party, the reforms touched only one of the three areas of internal Party disagreement, that of organization.

The two other serious areas of disagreement within the NWP, priorities and the personal leadership of Alice Paul, were not openly faced by either side during these two decades. Priorities were troublesome because equality for women was never really a "single issue" as the Party maintained. One could work for the ERA by concentrating on lobbying Congress, or work for the Amendment by emphasizing educational and organizational work in the states. Another option was to stress specific state equal rights bills rather than the federal amendment. There was also the whole question of international work, and whether the Party should divert any resources to the international movement before equality for American women had been achieved.

Although some reformers, some newer members, and some younger members tended to bring up the social and pyschological aspects of women's position from time to time, they never made much impact on the majority of NWP membership. In fact, one of the major failures of the Party was that it neglected to follow through the ideological ramifications of equality on the relationships among men, women, and children. The majority of Party members remained rather narrowly legalistic in outlook, and only extended their vision to include economics when the recessions of the 1920s and particularly the depression of the 1930s made job discrimination against women an immediate concern. The real issue, then, was whether to emphasize the federal amendment, state equal rights work, or international work. Much of the dispute over organization merely reflected the old guard's preference for national lobbying for the ERA combined with international pressure for equal rights treaties, as opposed to the reformers' desire for grass roots strength that would work for both the federal amendment and state equal rights measures simultaneously.

Both Alice Paul and Mrs. O. H. P. Belmont strongly supported national lobbying for the ERA from the first, and they increasingly advocated international work. Since finances and membership were noticeably declining by 1929, there were those who felt more effort should be put into work for the federal amendment even if it were at the expense of state work. "This past winter we have merely been dragging anchor, with people falling away," congressional chairman Maud Younger reported to Jane Norman Smith. "I was horrified to see the small list of people who could be telephoned to come to our condemnation hearing—" she continued, "I had no idea we had dwindled so." On the other hand, in 1930 the first Eastern Regional Conference decided that work to prevent economic discrimination against women during the unemployment crisis should have top priority. At first this generally meant state work, although it eventually included pressure for the repeal of the married persons clause of the federal Economy Act and lobbying for equal pay scales in the National Recovery Act codes as well as for federal relief projects for women. A questionnaire Alma Lutz sent to state chairmen in 1930 showed that the overwhelming majority favored state work, rather than national or international work.[23]

At the 1936 Party conference, Clara Snell Wolfe used Ohio as an example to prove the worth of state work. Before active organizational work, the Ohio branch had held no meetings, gained no endorsements of the ERA, done little publicity work, and had been unable to prevent passage of a minimum wage law for women only. There were only about a dozen Party members, and any legislative work was financed directly through the personal efforts of the state chairman. After organizational work by the reformers, the Ohio branch hosted a Party conference, deputized all its Congressmen on behalf of the ERA, carried on publicity and educational campaigns against the women's minimum wage law, and helped defeat a bill to prevent both husband and wife from holding state civil service jobs. State membership had increased to more than two hundred active members, in addition to several founders and life members. Mrs. Wolfe concluded that although NWP efforts would eventually culminate in congressional work, "success in Congressional work is largely dependent on organization in the States."[24]

The reformers did not believe the need for the Party would disappear after the passage of the ERA any more than the need for feminist activity had disappeared after the passage of the Nineteenth Amendment. Yet they understood the appeal of a second federal women's rights amendment, particularly to women who had worked in the suffrage campaign, "when the objective of the Feminist movement was clear to all thinking women and when solidarity, all be it of a transient kind, bound women together in a common sisterhood." But reformers warned that those women who believed the ERA could be substituted for the suffrage amendment as a means of recapturing feminist solidarity were mistaken. The ERA did not have the potential of the Nineteenth Amendment, they argued. Furthermore, they pointed out, "the Fourteenth Amendment has not conferred equality upon all men, neither will the Equal Rights Amendment confer equality upon all men and women." Even after the merger of the two factions had been agreed upon, the reformers were not convinced that work for the ERA should have priority. "Tactics, the phraseology of the Amendment, the point of least resistance, the next step," wrote Mrs. Hooker, "are all more or less debatable."[25]

Actually very little was debatable in the NWP because of a continuing power struggle among the leaders. This was the most important source of the lingering disagreements, and an issue that was never squarely faced until the series of law suits for control of the Party which erupted in the mid-1940s. A certain amount of personality conflict might be expected in any group which primarily attracted highly accomplished, activist, committed reformers, and the NWP also included a number of wealthy women whose experience in working with others on a give-and-take basis was somewhat limited. During the Party's reorganization period, for example, Jane Norman Smith had served both as acting state chairman and legislative chairman of the New York branch. Criticized for this by a socially prominent member from upstate New York, Smith had enough common sense to take this in her stride. "It is a good thing that I have a sense of humor," she wrote to former organizer Rebecca Hourwich, "and that I am not anxious to be State Chairman." Hourwich, much less philosophical about being patronized, replied vehemently: "I am fed up with wealth and social position!"[26]

Difficult as these personality clashes were, their effect probably could have been minimized by a talented administrator such as Smith or Hilles had it not been for the omnipresence of Alice Paul's influence. In his survey of American women, William Chafe lays many of the NWP's faults at Paul's doorstep. According to Chafe, Alice Paul was an authoritarian personality who inspired some but alienated many others, especially other women leaders.[27] The real problem was that nearly all of the NWP's goals, tactics, and even the Party's image were closely identified with Alice Paul and the precedents she had set during the suffrage campaign. Her leadership during the twenties and thirties was erratic for in many ways she had withdrawn both physically and intellectually from the day-to-day operations of the Party, yet she still retained the ultimate authority in the eyes of her devoted followers. This meant that the old guard considered any attempt to change the Party or to redirect its activities as a personal challenge to Alice Paul and the betrayal of all that the NWP had ever represented. Paul's own personality further complicated the situation, for to some she seemed aloof to the point of coldness, selfless to the point of martyrdom, and nearly fanatic in her devotion to feminism. Many old guard members, however, considered Paul a genius because of her achievements and academic degrees.

Genuine challenges to Alice Paul's leadership did develop during this period from both Mrs. Colvin and Mrs. Hooker. During the late 1920s when Paul was spending most of her time on international work, criticism of her became more open. In 1929, Maud Younger reported on the NWP convention to Mrs. Smith who had been unable to attend because of illness. Although the convention went smoothly, Younger wrote that "to our surprise, we found a vicious undercurrent—a whispering campaign so to speak against Alice Paul, and also Doris

(Stevens) less." Mrs. Smith was very distressed and insisted that "the NWP ought to get down on its knees and thank God it has a genius upon whom it can call for advice. Where would the Party be otherwise?" When a minor disagreement arose the next year which led Mabel Vernon and the headquarters staff to resign, Anna Kelton Wiley's interpretation was that "really the whole situation is this, shall we follow Miss Paul's leadership or Miss Vernon?" In reply, Mrs. Stephen Pell wrote that "it makes no difference how many lesser lights go so long as Miss Paul remains."[28] Into a situation increasingly hostile to any reform came the new chairman, Sarah Colvin, in 1933.

The tactless Mrs. Colvin was only chairman for about a year, because she challenged and alienated the old guard by everything she did. In January, 1933, she shocked the New York City branch by criticizing the Party's activities at the Pan American Conference and maintaining that the NWP would have been unable to accomplish anything without the League of Women Voters' assistance. Colvin further asserted that she would never be a figurehead chairman, nor would she raise money because funds should be provided by the wealthy states like New York. Jane Norman Smith described how upset the veteran suffragist Elizabeth Selden Rogers became at these remarks. Although Rogers had frequently criticized Smith, "bless her heart, when an outsider does it, she bristles with anger and defends everything I've done!" Smith wrote. In Mrs. Colvin's statement of Party aims, she listed in order: equal pay for equal work, especially in the NRA codes; the right of all women to work under protective legislation which applied to both men and women; the Equal Rights Amendment; and a membership drive for fifty thousand new members. The international objectives for which Alice Paul and the old guard had been working were not mentioned at all. Colvin's final transgression was to criticize headquarters as an economic burden, the old guard's other investments as even worse, and to insist that most women were interested mainly in bread-and-butter issues. "And if you want to meet a profoundly reactionary attitude towards economic freedom for women and men," concluded Colvin, "just talk to Miss Paul."[29]

Mrs. Colvin was not an ally of Mrs. Hooker, and in fact, had once said that Mrs. Hooker made her "so angry she feels like knocking her over the head with a stick of wood." Yet in many ways they were advocating the same goals for the NWP. As a result, Colvin's resignation from the chairmanship in 1934 combined with the reformers' continuing attempts to amend the constitution put the old guard very much on the defensive and contributed to the Party schism. Mrs. Hooker represented much more of a threat to Alice Paul's leadership than Sarah Colvin ever did. Hooker's social credentials were excellent, she was not an "outsider," and her record of Party work and financial support was unimpeachable. "Either Mrs. Hooker, with the aid of the new Philadelphia members and those from Maryland, will get control of the Party," warned Mrs. Smith after New York withdrew from the Eastern Conference in 1933, "or those of us who disagree with her ideas in every respect will control it." Maud Younger believed that the Party had experienced a "narrow escape" in 1933, and thought that Hooker was especially dangerous because of "the desire of the lady for a personal machine and control of the NWP and the unscrupulous methods to which she stoops to secure them." When the old guard enlisted Alice Paul's aid in formulating the 1934 constitutional revisions, their avowed purpose was to prevent Mrs. Hooker and her followers from gaining power.[30]

Mrs. Hooker's open protest against the Party leadership had begun with the complaint that the leaders, although courageous, able, committed, and disinterested, were not responsive to the membership because they were not democratically elected. One of the reasons why the reformers advocated a federated organization was because "it permits the development of leaders and avoids conflict by not crowding too many leaders into one group." Organizations based on a single personality tended to disintegrate, Hooker argued, and the immediate goal of the current leaders should be to develop feminist organizations which could continue to grow without the same leadership.[31]

The reformers were not blind to the dangers of their challenge to the status quo. In 1934, Sara Cummings reminded the delegates at the Eastern Regional Conference that it was difficult to keep people organized. "They are prone to put personalities above issues;" she warned, "to submerge reason for united action under whims and prejudices; to weaken and even desert when the need for strength is most urgent." Yet an organization without debate and even dissension, Cummings argued, was a decaying organization. After the two factions were reconciled in late 1936, Mrs. Hooker editorialized that "genuine dyed-in-the-wool Feminists are above the trivial personalities that ordinarily act to fragment human organizations."[32] Unfortunately this was a case of wishful thinking on Mrs. Hooker's part, for the whole power struggle erupted again a decade later and involved an even more bitter division of loyalties among NWP members.

Although the NWP was troubled internally during the thirties by the increasing division of its members into old guard and reform factions, common areas of agreement remained. Party structure, leadership, and priorities were questioned by the reformers, yet the goal—civil equality for women—was agreed upon by both factions. They also utilized similar tactics, even during the schism. One tactic favored by both the reformers and the old guard was the NWP's decision to work for endorsements of the ERA by other women's organizations. In the late twenties Jane Norman Smith had attempted to get endorsements from such groups as the California Business and Professional Women, and the reformers tried to persuade individual clubs within the General Federation of Women's Clubs to support the ERA. In 1935, Mrs. Hilles announced that three national organizations had endorsed the Amendment, four had placed it on their study programs, and thirteen international organizations had approved the same principle as contained within the Equal Rights Treaty. By 1937, Helen Hill Weed noted that nine national women's organizations as well as over one hundred state and local groups had endorsed the ERA.[33]

Thus the NWP never abandoned its primary reliance on the federal amendment method to remove remaining legal discriminations against women, even in the face of opposition from within its own ranks. Another tactic the Party had used during the suffrage campaign was to hold the political party in power responsible for the failure to give women the vote. Borrowed directly from the militant English suffragettes, this strategy did not adapt well to American politics since the president could not be brought down by a vote of no confidence, and his own party might not even control the majority of votes in Congress. Nevertheless, the militants had obtained spectacular publicity as a result of their confrontations with Wilson during and immediately following World War I, and they were convinced that the method was workable. After suffrage, according to Mrs. Belmont, the NWP could become a kind of third party to hold the other two parties accountable to higher standards in government.[34]

The NWP had at first interpreted Coolidge's 1923 comment that Congress would pass the ERA if that were what American women really wanted as a Republican policy decision. As the Party began to encounter more opposition and failed to get either political party to adopt an equal rights plank, its members became less certain. In 1924, Alice Paul pointed out that there was nothing to be gained in holding the party in power responsible, "for there is no party in power this year." Instead, Paul suggested that the ERA might be made a political issue through the development of a congressional woman's bloc, similar to the farm and labor blocs. But after the election, which resulted in a Republican president and Republican majorities in both houses of Congress, the NWP reverted to its old policy of party responsibility. The 1927 delegation to Coolidge, however, found him noncommittal and evasive.[35] Some Party members were already disillusioned with the idea of party responsibility. From Mississippi state chairman Ellen Phelps Crump, isolated in Nitta Yuma, a small town with neither household help nor restaurants, came this complaint in 1927.

> I was a very true and loyal friend to Governor-elect Bilbo. . . .
> I was warned some time ago that he, Bilbo, had double-crossed me in my Equal Rights work, and he used the equal rights plank to help get himself elected this time.[36]

In the presidential election of 1928, the NWP departed from its previous nonpartisan policies and endorsed the Hoover-Curtis ticket. There were a number of reasons for this policy change, and partisanship was perhaps the least important. Many of the national officers were Republicans, but there were also prominent NWP members who were active Democrats. More important was the fact that the Democratic candidate was Alfred Smith, who by this time had come out strongly for protective legislation for women and children. In contrast, Hoover stressed equal opportunity for all Americans, and the Republican candidate for vice-president was Senator Charles Curtis, who had sponsored the introduction of the ERA. Alice Paul favored Hoover, and believed that he could be convinced to support the Amendment.

The endorsement turned out to be a serious mistake in strategy, however, for the NWP's own Democrats were enraged and the few feminist sympathizers outside the Party accused the NWP of political partisanship.

Before the political conventions in 1928, the members of the national council had discussed how they might aid Senator Curtis in his bid for the vice-presidential nomination. Action of this sort was consistent with the Party's previous policy of supporting anyone who had clearly endorsed the ERA. The more politically astute NWP Republicans suggested that "we not have such a flourish of banners at Kansas City if it would injure Senator Curtis' chances of getting the nomination," but Alice Paul was upset by the suggestion that the NWP should stay in the background. Still, as Maud Younger wrote to Jane Norman Smith later, "the things we have been doing in his behalf had been done quietly—which is the only possible way they could have been done."[37]

Equal Rights began its attack on Smith prior to the convention, calling him a "presidential impossibility," and maintaining that even if he won the Democratic nomination he had no chance of election. Sue White, one of the NWP's leading Democrats, was unimpressed with either party platform, describing the Democratic protective legislation plank as "equality and inequality side by side under a classification of 'women and children.'" But as *Equal Rights* continued to criticize Smith, objections began to come in from other Democratic members. Helen Caldwell, a New Jersey branch officer, protested directly to editor Edith Houghton Hooker. "This is very poor policy," Caldwell wrote, "it is most embarrassing to every Democratic member of the Party," and she then announced her intention to campaign for Smith because of his good political record. Sue White was contacted by Eleanor Roosevelt and asked to work for Smith in Tennessee; White agreed to cooperate with local Democratic officials although she stressed her reservations about the protective legislation plank. But in September, 1928, the NWP announced that by a four to one vote the national council had decided to support the Republican presidential ticket and make equal rights for women a campaign issue.[38]

Congressional chairman Maud Younger was put in charge of the Party strategy, which was to concentrate on speaking campaigns in the East, while Mabel Vernon tried to anwser the growing criticism by explaining that women must be independent voters who put their own feminist interest before party affiliation. Vernon insisted that the Party's record had been consistently nonpartisan, since in 1916 the NWP had campaigned against the Democrats, in 1920 had picketed the Republican convention, and in 1924 had supported five women congressional candidates who were all running against Republicans. The ERA would have a much better chance with Hoover than with Smith, and by voting Republican, feminists could show their gratitude to Senator Curtis. This would be a test of sincerity for NWP members, like being pacifists in time of war, because they must not only vote Republican but must work actively for the ticket.[39]

That same month, Sue White wrote to Jane Norman Smith that although she trusted the Party leaders she could not follow them blindly when Hoover had not endorsed the ERA. Denying that she had any "political axe to grind," White explained that "I expect little from the Democratic party for myself and little from it in this generation for the cause of women." After the election, Sue White wrote to NWP officers and members, further justifying her work for Smith and her agreement with Democratic vice-chairman Molly Dewson that if Hoover came out for the ERA, White would immediately resign from Smith's campaign. But White's independence and actions contrary to NWP election policy had made her a traitor, "too dangerous a person to be entrusted with anything in writing."[40] White resigned from the NWP and made her career in Democratic politics.

Sue White was only one of the NWP members unhappy with the endorsement of the Republican ticket, and reluctant or unwilling to follow the Party's leadership. Grace Kay Long of Albany wrote Mrs. Smith that only a clearcut approval of the Amendment by Hoover would convince her, warning that the Party could do nothing if he later decided not to support the ERA. *Nation*, one of the few periodicals even slightly sympathetic to the Party, was disappointed that "the uncompromising NWP has compromised," by supporting a candidate who had not endorsed the Equal Rights Amendment. Despite the growing criticism, the Party did not change its policy. Admitting that both she and Maud Younger had favored the endorsement, Laura Berrien noted that Alice Paul supported Hoover very strongly and "she thinks that if we withdraw now we will utterly infuriate the Republicans and 'never have any influence with anybody.' "[41]

Lavinia Dock was representative of the old nonpartisan members of the NWP. "The Democrats are just another wing of the Republican party," she wrote, "imperialism abroad—stealing the public wealth at home—oppressive to civil liberty—and liars generally." Stressing the need for independent voting in order to make the parties accountable to women, Dock confessed that she thought Smith might make a better President than Hoover, yet admitted "the Party is in a pickle because of Curtis." Branches had not been consulted in the decision, and Ruby Black reported that the entire Nebraska branch had unanimously refused to support the council's endorsement of Hoover and Curtis. Other members were convinced that the action was based on Republican partisanship. Olive Cate, an avid Democratic NWP member active in organizing Smith For President leagues among New York business and professional women, wrote protesting the NWP's endorsement of Hoover. "Whenever the NWP decides to stick to its original purpose and conducts its efforts along non-partisan lines, it can expect me to work in its interest," she concluded, "and until then, so far as I am concerned, the NWP does not even exist."[42]

Party members tried to salvage what they could from their policy. Governor Smith's reply to their appeal for industrial equality had been that "before I would subscribe to any theory of this kind I would see the cornerstone of the Capital at Albany crumble into dust beneath my feet," and they compared his position with Hoover's speeches on equal opportunity for every American boy and girl. But NWP speakers campaigning for Hoover were attacked by a Democratic mob in New York's City Hall Park, and the Party's request that Mayor Walker investigate the failure of police protection resulted only in adverse publicity for the women. After the Republican election victory, NWP members congratulated themselves on their role in the campaign, but Hoover failed to endorse the ERA. Although Party officers sent out a lengthy postelection memorandum on how to hold the Republicans responsible for the Amendment, the doctrine of party responsibility had been thoroughly discredited. In 1930, *Equal Rights* noted the increased attempts of the Democratic party to encourage women's political participation, but expressed doubt that either party was really interested in women. In 1936, the NWP described the Democratic platform as slightly better than the Republican, but concluded that there was very little actual difference between the two parties.[43]

Militancy was another policy basic to the NWP campaign for the Nineteenth Amendment which was abandoned during the ERA campaign. Older members continued to call for more militancy, yet only a few of the international actions could be described as militant. Crystal Eastman recognized that militancy had functioned to enliven the workers and give them the faith of crusaders, while at the same time stimulating the more conservative suffragists. But that had been at a time when there was fundamental agreement among women's organizations on the goal of suffrage, and during the twenties and thirties this militant heritage and the antagonisms it had aroused became a hindrance to the NWP. The Party liked to think of itself as impatient, and thus different from other women's organizations. Since Party members believed that the greatest problem in winning the vote had been the indifference of women, the NWP always found it difficult to take a passive position. Members rejoiced that during the 1925 hearings on a New York state forty-eight hour bill for women and children "for the first time in three years the Woman's Party was the aggressor, and the proponents of the bill were markedly on the defensive." "It is magnificent to think," declared veteran NWP campaigner Margaret Whittemore, "but it is more magnificent to do."[44] Older NWP members insisted that they were, and always would be, a party of action, but militancy never really became a basic element in the NWP activities during these two decades. A militant tone was always part of the Party rhetoric, but even it was much diluted and generally took the form of calling for feminist conferences and praising the expressions of sex solidarity which resulted from such meetings.

> A crowd and a good rousing speech is excellent medicine for a flagging spirit. It stiffens the neck, renews the courage, and makes one realize that one's efforts are perhaps less futile than, all alone, they appear to be.[45]

As opposition to equal rights for women increased, NWP feminists continued to compare the situation with the suffrage campaign. According to their interpretation, no real progress was made until the militant phase of the campaign. "Was sixty-nine years long enough to appeal to the male intelligence before becoming a Feminist nuisance?" asked *Equal Rights*. Harriot Stanton Blatch expressed all the old time militancy in her eightieth birthday dinner speech: "America loves to be against someone. Attack your enemies." But both the reform faction and younger conservative members of the NWP questioned the role of militancy in the context of the twenties. The feminist movement had "grown up," Mrs. Hooker concluded in 1930, and "this shift of circumstances demands a corresponding shift in tactics." Mrs. Hooker believed that by using their votes American women could obtain the Amendment in an orderly manner. "We need conservative planning and democratic control," she insisted, "and we do not need agitation."[46]

Along with its reputation for militancy, the Party entered the postwar era with a reputation for being uncompromising. NWP members were devoted to a cause that "involves a complete disregard for popularity, a standard of values based upon actualities and not upon appearances, and an almost ruthless zeal in the prosecution of work." The Party's image sometimes weighed heavily on its members, for to live up to their reputation they felt they could not accept any half-way measures or fail to follow through on their policies. For example, the NWP was openly critical of the Wisconsin equal rights law because it contained a clause exempting protective legislation and special privileges. "We either believe in Equal Rights or we do not," insisted the Party journal.[47] Not all members grasped the significance of the NWP's insistence on complete equality, however. In the mid-thirties the Arkansas branch's legislative chairman wrote suggesting that if the ERA included clauses exempting women from military service and protecting special legislation it would be passed.

> Would not the help and cooperation of all women's clubs be worth adding those two clauses to our Amendment? I say we are foolish not to add them, since that is exactly what we are working for anyway.[48]

But the Party answered that women must be equal to men in every way, and thus legislation should apply to both sexes or to neither sex.

Otherwise, it was "merely a polite euphemism for covert discrimination." Pragmatic principles such as those held by political parties were not worth a feminist's effort and devotion, the Party consistently maintained. Why compromise on something so perfectly designed to prevent discrimination as the ERA?[49]

NWP members were uncompromising in the sense that they refused to abandon or modify their Amendment. But this did not mean that they never cooperated with less dogmatic women's organizations, nor that they imagined that they would always be isolated because of the purity of their feminist principles. Early in 1923, Alice Paul had instructed all NWP state officers to support any equal rights legislation. In practice, this frequently meant working for state measures such as jury service bills sponsored by the League of Women Voters. The Party believed that the advantages of the ERA would eventually win it supporters from other women's organizations, although in the meantime the Party was prepared to stand alone. By the early thirties, NWP speakers were urging cooperation on the problems of married working women, and later in the decade these efforts were rewarded by increasing endorsements of the Amendment.[50]

A new strategy developed by the NWP during the 1920s and continued into the 1930s was the promotion of women for important elective and appointive offices. Urging the election of women, Paul wrote in 1924 that "we must make the woman's vote in the United States count." The vote had been only a symbol and a means to achieve a better position for women, according to *Equal Rights*, and this campaign to elect women would make the participation of women in national government a public issue. Paul believed that more women might be elected gradually to Congress, but insisted that it would take a very long time. She resolved, therefore, that regardless of party affiliation the NWP should support all women nominees "who seem qualified to sit in Congress and who will support the Equal Rights Amendment and a general feminist program."[51]

The Party's position was strengthened by the fact that in September, when all but one state had held primaries, women had been nominated for Congress in only six states. A total of ten women had been nominated, five in Pennsylvania and one each in Illinois, Ohio, Tennessee, Kansas, and New Jersey. The Republican woman nominee lived in the South, four of the five Democratic women had been nominated for Republican districts, and the other four women had been chosen by the Socialist and Prohibition parties. The NWP decided to support all ten nominees but to concentrate their efforts in Pennsylvania where all five candidates were avowed feminists. The situation was complicated by the presence of the LaFollette party, which had endorsed four of the five Pennsylvania women and which had also offered Maryland and Delwaware nominations to two top NWP officers who declined. This again raised the question of partisanship which the NWP angrily denied, explaining that the Women For Congress campaign was a logical outcome of the need for solidarity in order to achieve equality. The NWP also brushed aside any suggestion that women should begin their political careers on the state level, arguing that it was Congress which dealt with all the really important problems like peace and war, the League of Nations, the World Court, national prohibition, and maternity laws.[52]

NWP organizers and officers sent into Pennsylvania to campaign for the five women nominees found they had to carry on a slow door-to-door educational campaign to arouse women, most of whom were apathetic. The Party also raised money for the five candidates, who were Mrs. Elizabeth Culbertson, Mrs. Jessie Collett, Mrs. Jennie Dornblum, Mrs. Daisy Detterline, and Miss Anna Van Skite. From an objective viewpoint, the results were disappointing; only one woman, Mary T. Norton of New Jersey, was elected to Congress in 1924, and she had been endorsed by the local machine and did not advocate women's causes. Candidate Jessie Collett's analysis of the election results included the usual complaints about padded poll books and Republican control of the wards, but she also recognized the significance of the Coolidge landslide and the presence of the LaFollette party. Anna Van Skite called the campaign "the most worthwhile work that I have ever done in my whole life," and believed that it had advanced the cause of equal rights and prepared the way for the future election of women to Congress. However, Mrs. Gifford Pinchot, wife of the governor of Pennsylvania, lashed out at the men who dominated public life. Although feminists would prefer to eliminate sex from politics, she insisted, "other things being equal, we demand that women as women shall be preferred to men until their number is equal." But NWP officer Mabel Vernon was optimistic in summarizing the election results, reminding members that the slogan for the Women For Congress campaign had been: "Whether we win or lose, we win."[53]

There were also some postelection criticisms. Mary Winsor, a long-time NWP activist and national council member, totally disagreed with the Women For Congress policy. The NWP, argued Winsor, had alienated many business and financial interests because "the name of LaFollette was like hundreds of red flags to thousands of bulls." Worst of all, she concluded, the Party had lost its standing as a non-partisan group and "the effect on the NWP in Pennsylvania was disastrous." Anne Martin also criticized the campaign. Martin had run twice for national office and had drawn strong support, but was passed over for the 1924 LaFollette campaign manager job. The position went to her former Socialist opponent, proving to Martin that even La-Follette "evidently prefers demonstrated male mediocrity and weakness to demonstrated female ability and strength." Her bitter political experience made her advocate feminist parties as the only hope for women, although she thought the women's bloc campaign began too late and failed to register women effectively. Martin did approve of the NWP's support of women candidates, however, and suggested that a common denominator for submerging the differences between the NWP and the League of Women Voters might be the support of qualified women for office.[54]

Although the Party never again mounted a campaign as extensive as its 1924 Women For Congress effort, it was not because members believed the strategy unworkable. Throughout the twenties and thirties they continued their efforts to gain elective and appointive positions for women, especially on the national level. But the decline in their membership and finances as well as their increased activities in the international field and on behalf of married women's right to work limited the amount of time and effort they could devote to promoting women for office. The internal Party schism of the mid-thirties and the growing support for the Equal Rights Amendment in the later thirties also diverted their attention.

The NWP experienced one notable success, however, during the Coolidge administration. It had been reported that the president was opposed to appointing women to positions not previously held by women, but this he denied, promising to make appointments only on the basis of merit. The first major job opportunity came through the death of the woman already in the position, so the question of opening new appointments to women was not involved. With the death of Helen H. Gardner, the first woman member of the Civil Service Commission, women's groups immediately began suggesting women to replace her. Coolidge agreed to appoint a woman who, under the law requiring a politically balanced Commission, would have to be either a Democrat or an independent, and Alice Paul on behalf of the NWP suggested that "a woman who has herself served under the Civil Service and knows intimately its problems would fill the position with particular ability."[55] It was a position high in both pay and prestige, and the NWP had one of its own members in mind for the appointment.

Jessie Dell was the NWP candidate for Civil Service Commissioner. Born and educated in Georgia, she had worked briefly as a railroad auditor and had read law in her father's law office. In addition to her twenty-five years' service in the U.S. War Department, she was a charter member and office holder in the National Federation of Federal Employees. Although she had not taken part in the NWP's wartime picketing, she had belonged to the Party since its inception and had headed the government worker's council. The confirmation of her appointment as Civil Service Commissioner, however, was delayed because the Senate was petitioned by the Woman Patriot Publishing Company. According to the NWP, this organization was a direct descendant of the National Association Opposed to Suffrage; in the 1920s its letterhead proclaimed it was "Opposed to Feminism and Communism."[56] Until this time, the Party had not been as seriously affected by the sort of red scare smear tactics that worried other more respectable and popular women's organizations like the League of Women Voters.

Characterizing the NWP as "an un-American organization with a concealed design to establish a tyranny of women in the guise of equality," the Woman Patriot charged that the Party used "sinister pressure" to get Dell appointed. The petition likened the NWP to the Socialist Party, with its international objectives, its "dictatorship of women," its twenty-four occupational councils, and its small but loyal membership. Miss Dell was described as a government clerk with no particular qualifications for Commissioner, a woman who was not aggressive herself but had become "a creature of this international Feminist lobby."[57] The Senate was not convinced, however, and Dell's appointment was unanimously confirmed.

The NWP was fairly successful in obtaining other positions for its own members. In the twenties Marie Moore Forrest, Party pageant director, won endorsement for District of Columbia Commissioner; Rebecca Greathouse, the niece of Dwight Morrow and an NPW attorney, was appointed Assistant U.S. District Attorney in 1925. Doris Stevens was selected to chair the Pan American Union's InterAmerican Commission of Women, and Emma Wold, NWP attorney, became technical advisor to the Hague Codification Conference in 1930. The NWP instructed all its branches to watch for opportunities to promote women for public office, although the Party often had to work in the background because of its unpopularity. In 1926, Sue White wrote Jane Norman Smith asking her to get endorsements for Forrest's candidacy, adding: "Please let me know what you can do, but be careful that nothing reaches the press." But when Democrat Helen Caldwell was nominated for Congress, the New Jersey branch proudly reported that although she had been advised not to identify herself with the NWP, Caldwell had persisted "in referring to herself as a 'loyal member of the National Woman's Party and Democratic Party.' " Inquiring about the opening for Assistant Attorney General in 1929, however, Burnita Shelton Matthews was warned that it would be better if the Women's Bar Association or the D.C. Republican Women's organization proposed her name. "The Woman's Party, *without publicity,* could then work as hard as it could for you," promised Jane Norman Smith.[58]

The NWP did not limit its efforts to its own members, for in 1925, it joined other women's organizations in urging Mrs. Robert LaFollette to run for the U.S. Senate after her husband died. In 1928, the Party supported the Democratic nomination of Ruth Bryan Owens for a Florida congressional seat and sympathized with Bertha K. Landes when she was defeated in her bid for a second term as mayor of Seattle. On the other hand, the NWP opposed the election of Republican congressional nominee Ruth Hanna McCormick who had been outspoken in her criticism of the NWP, and the Party temporarily abandoned its policy of supporting women in 1930 when the New York branch endorsed both the Socialist candidate Heywood Broun and the Democratic candidate Louis Brodsky while withholding support from incumbent Republican Ruth Baker Pratt. Heywood Broun was married to NWP activist Ruth Hale, founder of the Lucy Stone League, and he was considered a better feminist than many women. Brodsky was also sympathetic to equal rights for women, while Pratt actively opposed the ERA.[59]

The endorsement of Broun and Brodsky was the only time during these two decades when the NWP supported men rather than their female opponents. When Party members were criticized for "putting sex into politics," they agreed that in theory their critics were right. But they stood by their practice, pointing out that in reality men totally dominated politics, and thus continued to urge "the selection of qualified women, *just because they are women,* to make the balance true, to offset the latent dominant prejudice." Women had also been criticized for not having used the vote effectively, and the Party believed that electing women to office was one way to accomplish feminist goals. As sex solidarity increased, it would convince political parties that women candidates would be an asset to their tickets. Furthermore, since the Party believed women were more concerned with the quality of human life, their viewpoint was urgently needed in Congress.[60]

In the early thirties, the NWP again requested its branches to determine which state, county, and municipal offices were open to women, as well as how many were held by women, and to report the results at the Party conference. NWP members were encouraged by signs of increasing dissatisfaction among both Republican and Democratic women, who were pressing for greater representation on the national committees and at national conventions. In 1933, the NWP concluded that the major parties were still "man-made and man-owned," and that despite their efforts women remained "rank outsiders." The Party had consistently offered membership to active Republican and Democratic women, with only the qualification that they place equal rights above party affiliation.[61] Of course, the NWP never really understood the importance of party loyalty for those women ambitious for advancement within the major parties, nor how absolute that loyalty had to be.

The Party had always valued good publicity and public relations. Whenever possible, the equalitarian feminists dramatized their activities in order to get the widest possible media coverage. The 1923 Seneca Falls conference was filmed, for the NWP had always emphasized the importance of reaching out to the average woman to demonstrate the need for equal rights in every day life. Party members were convinced that they had used advertising and "the new science of mass education" intuitively during the suffrage campaign, and openly admitted that their methods had always included the greatest amount of publicity for the least money. "Never let the people forget," their publicists admonished, "don't use words, use plays, pageants, and parades." Anything the least bit spectacular that the NWP carried out, wrote Minnie Karr from New Jersey, got good coverage in the local press. At the 1931 Party conference, speakers emphasized the necessity of endless publicity and of constantly scanning the local papers for discriminations against which the NWP could protest; several journalists instructed members in writing short, snappy, action-oriented press releases tied in with public interest and local angles.[62]

The NWP was not alone in thinking that it generally made good use of publicity. Reporting on the Seneca Falls conference, *Nation* wrote that the NWP's "boldness and sense of dramatic values never fail it." *Nation* was not quite so enthusiastic about the Women For Congress campaign, which it termed good publicity but poor politics, yet the editorial admitted grudgingly that "with a sure instinct, the NWP invariably challenges public attention and climbs to the top of the first page of the newspapers." By the mid-thirties, however, the Party itself was becoming somewhat discouraged. In fact, *Equal Rights Independent Feminist Weekly* conceded that it would take much more than a good "propaganda technique" to pass the ERA.[63]

The reformers' emphasis on the need to educate the public stemmed partly from the growing disregard of Prohibition laws. Realizing that public opinion was important in both the interpretation and enforcement of any legislation, Party members argued that feminists must "write the meaning of Equal Rights into the minds of the American people so that our Amendment will signify something in practical life when it is written into the Constitution." As part of this educational campaign, the NWP distributed free and low cost literature such as Doris Stevens' book on the Party, Burnita Shelton Matthew's articles on jury service for women, answers to anti-ERA arguments designed for use with club women, summaries of state laws discriminating against women, and copies of *Equal Rights*. The NWP also never traveled anywhere without fanfare. Delegates to the Seneca Falls conference rode in motorcades decked with the Party's purple, white and gold banners, stopping to speak along the way. When it was too cold to speak during Coolidge's inaugural, feminists acted as "voiceless speakers" with placards. The 1927 motor caravan to Coolidge's summer home in the Black Hills included a band and a chorus singing women's songs. In the early thirties, the Party journal reiterated that "the problem of Equal Rights is a problem in mass education," and the NWP members were urged to focus the attention of the country on their coming convention by traveling to it on foot, in an airplane, or in an oxcart.[64] No one actually carried out these suggestions, but the Party continued its devotion to the dramatic publicity gesture.

The NWP considered itself very modern in its approach to publicity techniques. Hazel MacKaye, a Party pageant director, pointed out in the twenties that "everything, whether merchandise or ideas, has to be 'sold' to the Public." Only a few women could be inspired by abstract ideals, she argued, so the NWP must reach the others through their desire for the spectacular. Ideas like human justice and freedom through equality could be "sold" by pageants like those staged by the Party at Seneca Falls or the Garden of the Gods. The Party was also quick to realize the significance of the radio for spreading their equality message. Nina Allender, the NWP editorial cartoonist, had once remarked that "people instinctively believe what they hear over the radio," and as early as 1925, the Party sponsored radio talks in nine major cities. State branches were urged to take advantage of the educational opportunities offered by radio talks; the national Party broadcast debates on the ERA as well as such special events as the dedication of their new national headquarters and the formation of the World Woman's Party over nationwide networks.[65]

The Seneca Falls conference in 1923 was perhaps the most successful example of the way the NWP dramatized events with a combination of tradition and pageantry. The conference was called to celebrate the seventy-fifth anniversary of the 1848 Women's Rights Conference and to introduce the Equal Rights Amendment. The Party carefully prepared the way by obtaining the participation of local girls, women, and city officials in both Rochester and Seneca Falls. The main events included a processional of five hundred girls dressed in white and carrying NWP banners with slogans from the picketing days, a still life pageant representing the original 1848 conference, and a choir concert while the Party's Declaration of Principles was being flashed on a large screen. The local press estimated that almost two thousand people participated in the procession to Susan B. Anthony's grave the following day, and all the major Eastern papers covered the conference.[66]

The Seneca Falls conference was so successful that the Party decided to repeat it in autumn at the Garden of the Gods in Colorado, where a western touch was added by an NWP car drawn by four white horses with mounted women bearing a huge scroll demanding the ERA. The pageant also represented Colorado women who were pioneer feminists and suffragists. The crowd at this event was estimated by the police at between fifteen and twenty thousand, and tremendous traffic jams developed both before and after the pageant. The final ceremony of the seventy-fifth anniversary year was held in the crypt of the Capitol at the foot of the statue of the suffrage pioneers which the Party had given to the nation in 1921, and poet Edna St. Vincent Millay, an associate editor of *Equal Rights* during the twenties, wrote a special poem for the occasion. Even during the thirties, the Party retained its faith in the power dramatic pageantry to get good publicity, and also as a "technique of popular enlightenment." Mrs. Belmont's feminist funeral received a great deal of coverage, and later that year a mass rally at Washington Monument was staged by the Party to honor Mrs. Belmont and other feminists who had died, including a special tribute to the "Unknown Woman."[67]

Party members had always had a distinct sense of being part of the making of history, and this continued throughout both these decades. Frequently emphasizing the similarities between the suffrage movement in 1913 and the equal rights movement, NWP feminists believed their contribution had been to focus on Congress and the federal amendment, and applied this historical analysis to the passage of the Equal Rights Amendment. Activist Party members believed they had participated in the actual shaping of history, much like those Americans who were present at events such as the Boston Tea Party.[68] Such events also became part of one's "permanent mental furniture," according to Mrs. Hooker. Reminiscing about Party history, she wrote:

> Certain occasions created by the NWP, such as the great Suf-
> frage Parade, the march around the White House in the rain,
> and the Seneca Falls convention, remain forever in the minds
> of the participants after the manner of a genuine emotional
> experience.[69]

The Party's sense of making history naturally led to an interest in women's history in general. Feminists were concerned that important dates such as the anniversary of the 1848 convention, Susan B. Anthony's birthday, and the date when suffrage was ratified were rarely commemorated. The NWP held celebrations on these and other occasions, urging its members to publicize the important dates of women's history. In the mid-thirties, several women's groups cooperated in the successful effort to get a Susan B. Anthony postage stamp issued. But when the New Deal Federal Theater Project produced Maud Wood Park's chronicle play, *Lucy Stone*, Alma Lutz reported that "the reaction of the audience and their gasps of astonishment showed plainly how little women know of their history."[70] The NWP continued to urge its members to call the attention of their alma maters, their children's colleges, and their local schools to books which stressed women's historical contributions.

In the thirties it was Mary Beard who sounded the call for the preservation of materials dealing with women's history, and for more writing and teaching of women's history. In 1933 she published *America Through Women's Eyes*, and NWP members praised her for compiling such an important record. Party members believed she had slighted the organized women's rights movement, however, which they considered "one of the most powerful influences in changing public opinion and developing our democratic institutions." The Party recognized that women's history and the success of feminist goals were intertwined. "Among our own members are many who do not realize how long women have struggled," editorialized *Equal Rights*. "But there are also many others outside the ranks who are not aware of their degradation or their ignorance."[71]

Beard's efforts on behalf of women's history continued throughout the thirties, and she wrote a series of articles for the journal of the Business and Professional Women in an attempt to break down what she considered ignorance of women's contributions to civilization. Beard urged women to learn their own history, and suggested that women alumnae and contributors to colleges demand women's history courses. Everyone, agreed the NWP members, should be a better "publicity agent" for her own sex, and ensure that the younger generation did not grow up ignorant of women's history. They wholeheartedly supported by Mary Beard's attempt to found a Woman's Archives, and Jane Norman Smith represented the NWP at the organizational meeting in New York City in 1935. Beard believed that the Archives would increase the importance of women by showing how indispensable to all aspects of public life they had been in the past. "We need some new way to dramatize our value after dramatizing our rights, do we not?" she asked. "Or rather, while we are driving for our rights, I should say."[72]

The NWP as well as other feminists of the era had a tendency to interpret women's history as the lives of great women of the past. Alma Lutz acted as sympathetic biographer for a number of feminists, including Emma Willard and Harriot Stanton Blatch, while Mary Beard characterized Susan B. Anthony as the "Heroine of a Democracy." Humanity was reflected by its heroes, Beard wrote, and "the kind of leaders it reveres and follows indicate its mind, its civilization, its temper and its ethics." Heroes of men's history had always been warriors, she argued, but Anthony could serve as a prototype of a heroine who changed the mind and politics of a nation peacefully.[73] The NWP also admired Anthony, especially for her insistence on the single issue of suffrage, her clear logical mind, her militancy, and her perseverance in the face of discouragement.

In announcing the Seneca Falls conference, the Party described it as a chance for women to pay homage to women as men did to men. "Let us learn that in honoring our great women," wrote Mrs. Hooker, "we honor ourselves and build up a new sex consciousness, a firmer solidarity." The NWP described its anniversary year ceremonies in the Capitol as a carefully planned "ritual" which would pay tribute to feminist leaders. But the Party did not restrict its admiration of heroines to great women of the distant past. Bernhardt was characterized as having "elements of the superwoman." Action was essential to her existence, noted the Party journal, and "work was the fountain of her youth." In 1926, the Party successfully supported the young actress and NWP founder, Eva LeGallienne, for *Pictorial Review*'s $5,000 prize for outstanding women's achievement. When Mary Cassatt, who had chaired the NWP artists' council, died in Paris that same year, *Equal Rights* reminded its readers that Cassatt was not merely a sentimental painter of children, but rather a woman who had always "lived and worked as an individualist." Upon the death of Mrs. Emmeline Pankhurst, the NWP described her militant suffrage activities as those of "a conventional women breaking her conventional shackles," and characterized her as "One of the Immortals."[74]

Member Amelia Earhart was honored with a life membership by her admirers in the Party in 1933, and commercial pilot Elizabeth Morrill Phillips also became the kind of modern heroine the Party admired after she flew from New York to the District of Columbia to deliver equality resolutions. NWP members, unlike many other American women, continued throughout these two decades to respect and admire Charlotte Perkins Gilman. "Charlotte Perkins Stetson Gilman probably made more Feminists among the generation now around forty years old than any other person," claimed Mrs. Hooker. Trying to come to terms with Gilman's suicide, Hooker concluded that "however one may disagree with the idea that a person has a right to end his own life, no one can deny that Mrs. Gilman died in glory and in clarity, as she had lived." Three years after her death, *Equal Rights* published a birthday tribute to Gilman in which her friend Harriet Howe described her as an "awakener." "She was building a new world," wrote Howe, "by teaching women what this world might be when women had their share in building it."[75]

The NWP members' faith in the dramatic publicity gesture, their support for women's achievements, and their attempts to act as a pressure group for equality were all carried over into both their domestic and international activities. Yet the growing division between the NWP and social feminists at home and abroad made these tactics less effective than they might have been if a feminist consensus on the issue of protective legislation had been reached. It was this issue, more than any personality clashes or differences of tactics, that came close to halting any further feminist advances during the twenties and thirties, and that made it impossible for social feminists to support the ERA.

NOTES

1. Editorial, "Equal Rights, Not the Method of Gaining Equal Rights, Is the Goal," *ER* 1 (December 8, 1923), 340; Editorial, "A National Amendment Is the Permanent Way of Establishing Equal Rights," *ER* 1 (December 15, 1923), 348; Burnita Shelton Matthews, "A Federal Amendment Avoids Referendum Campaigns," *ER* 1 (December 29, 1923), 365; Editorial, "An Argument for a Federal Amendment," *ER* 1 (December 29, 1923), 364.

2. Lavinia Dock, "Sub-Caste," *ER* 11 (May 31, 1924); Harriot Stanton Blatch, "Can Sex Equality Be Legislated?" *The Independent* 3 (December 22, 1923), 301; Anne Martin, "Equality Laws Vs. Women in Government," *Nation* 115 (August 16, 1922), 165; Elizabeth Green Kalb, "Equal Rights By Federal Amendment," *ER* 17 (May 2, 1931), 100.

3. Burnita Shelton Matthews, "Massachusetts Rules Against Women as Jurors," *ER* 17 (October 3, 1931), 276.

4. Editorial, "Are Feminists Practical?" *ERIFW* 1 (November 30, 1935), 306.

5. Editorial, "Putting on the Reverse," *ER* 13 (December 4, 1926), 340; "Letter from Crystal Eastman," reprinted from *New Republic* in *ER* 11 (November 29, 1924), 336.

6. Lavinia Egan, "One President Passes; Another Enters," *ER* 1 (August 11, 1923), 204; "Equal Rights Demand Is Taken To President Coolidge," *ER* 1 (November 24, 1923), 322; "President Coolidge Receives Deputation," *ER* 14 (February 26, 1927), 21; Editorial, "Amelia Earhart," *ER* 18 (October 1, 1932), 274.

7. "Woman's Party Asks Appointment with the President," *ER* 19 (August 19, 1933), 228–29; Alice Paul to Helen Hunt West, May 9, 1936, Helen Hunt West Papers, Box 1, f. 9, SL; Laura Berrien to Caroline Lexow Babcock, July 17, 1940, Caroline Lexow Babcock-Olive Hurburt Papers, Box 2, f. 24, SL.

8. Editorial, "Sell Your Idea," *ER* 16 (January 24, 1931), 402; Editorial, "The Present Problem," *ER* 17 (June 27, 1931), 162; Editorial, "Plan Your Work," *ER* 17 (October 3, 1931), 274; "Maryland Branch Hears Anita Pollitzer," *ER* 19 (October 7, 1933), 284.

9. "Treaty Method Best of Wiping Out Inferiority Stigma," *ER* 20 (June 16, 1934), 159–60; Doris Stevens to Jane Norman Smith, October 31, 1934, Jane Norman Smith Papers, Box 6, f. 126, SL.

10. "The Winter Campaign," *ER* 14 (November 5, 1927), 309; Editorial, "Use This Opportunity," *ER* 17 (November 13, 1931), 322; Editorial "Join the Chorus," *ER* 18 (March 12, 1932), 42; Florence Bayard Hilles, "Call To Biennial Conference," *ER* 21 (October 1, 1935), 1.

11. Editorial, "Methods and Results," *ER* 15 (March 30, 1929), 58; Muna Lee to Jane Norman Smith, December 9, 1931; Jane Norman Smith to Grace Kay Long, December 13, 1931; Jane Norman Smith to Maud Younger, January 4, 1932; Maud Younger to Jane Norman Smith, January 18, 1932, Jane Norman Smith Papers, Box 3, fs. 78, 79, SL; Editorial, "Concerning State Campaigns," *ERIFW* 2 (May 2, 1936), 66.

12. "Proposed Changes in the Party Constitution," *ER* 20 (October 27, 1934), 309.

13. *Ibid.*

14. *Ibid.*

15. Minutes of the National Council, January 19, 1935, Alma Lutz Papers, Box 1, f. 67, SL.

16. Edith Houghton Hooker to Alma Lutz, March 13, 1935; Alma Lutz to Edith Houghton Hooker, March 19, 1935, Alma Lutz Papers, Box 5, f. 67, SL.

17. Editorial, "We Believe. . . . " *ERIFW* 1 (June 29, 1935), 130; "Report of the Conference Committee on By-Laws," *ERIFW* 1 (July 6, 1935), 141–42.

18. Helen Hunt West, "The Significance of the Conference," *ER* 21 (November 15, 1935), 1; Editorial, "Thank God You Can Give" *ERIFW* 2 (May 9, 1936), 74.

19. Alma Lutz to Betty Gram Swing, 1936, Alma Lutz Papers, Box 3, f. 29, SL.

20. Edith Houghton Hooker to Alma Lutz, September 17, 1936, Alma Lutz Papers, Box 5, f. 68, SL.

21. Editorial, "In the Name of Justice," *ERIFW* 2 (December 26, 1936), 338.

22. "Proposed Amendments to the Constitution and By-Laws of the NWP," *ER* 24 (August 15, 1938), 310; "Amendments to the Constitution," *ER* 24 (November 15, 1938), 362.

23. Maud Younger to Jane Norman Smith, June 9, 1929, Jane Norman Smith Papers, Box 2, f. 66, SL; "Eastern Regional Conference Program," *ER* 16 (November 8, 1930), 315; "Report of Alma Lutz, Chairman of Organization," 1930, Alma Lutz Papers, Box 3, f. 23, SL.

24. Clara Snell Wolfe, "The Necessity of Organization," *ERIFW* 2 (November 28, 1936), 307.

25. "Annual Meetings to Replace Biennals," *ER* 19 (November 11, 1933), 316; Editorial, "Let's Prove It," *ERIFW* 1 (March 9, 1935), 2; Editorial, "In the Name of Justice," *ERIFW* 2 (December 26, 1936), 338.

26. Jane Norman Smith to Rebecca Hourwich, June 25, 1923; Rebecca Hourwich to Jane Norman Smith, June 27, 1923, Jane Norman Smith Papers, Box 2, f. 60, SL.

27. William Chafe, *The American Woman: Her Changing Social, Economic and Political Roles, 1920–1970* (New York: Oxford, 1972), p. 114.

28. Maud Younger to Jane Norman Smith, December 22, 1929; Jane Norman Smith to Maud Younger, December 24, 1929; Anna Kelton Wiley to Jane Norman Smith, March 24, 1930; Jane Norman Smith to Anna Kelton Wiley, March 26, 1930, Jane Norman Smith Papers, Box 3, fs. 73, 75, SL.

29. Jane Norman Smith to Maud Younger, January 6, 1933, Jane Norman Smith Papers, Box 4, f. 82, SL; "New Chairman Defines Party Aims," *ER* 19 (November 25, 1933), 333; Sarah T. Colvin to Jane Norman Smith, December 16, 1933, Jane Norman Smith Papers, Box 4, f. 83, SL.

30. Jane Norman Smith to Maud Younger, January 6, 1933; Maud Younger to Jane Norman Smith, June 29, 1934; Elizabeth Selden Rogers to Jane Norman Smith, June 29, 1934, Jane Norman Smith Papers, Box 4, fs. 83, 85, SL.

31. Editorial, "A Step Forward," *ER* 19 (November 11, 1933), 314; Editorial, "Design for Organizing," *ERIFW* 1 (April 20, 1935), 50.

32. "Organization for Equal Rights," *ER* 20 (June 30, 1934), 174; Editorial, "In the Name of Justice," *ERIFW* 2 (December 26, 1936), 338.

33. Editorial, "The Result of Feminist Schooling," *ER* 15 (May 25, 1929), 122; Jane Norman Smith to Maud Younger, January 4, 1932, Jane Norman Smith Papers, Box 3, f. 79, SL; Editorial, "Join the Chorus," *ER* 18 (March 12, 1932), 42; Florence Bayard Hilles, "Call to Biennial Convention," *ER* 21 (October 1, 1935), 1; Helena Hill Weed, "National News for Women," *ER* 23 (July 1, 1937), 95.

34. *Equal Rights: Weekly Bulletin of the NWP*, October 4, 1922, no page number; Alva E. Belmont, "What the Woman's Party Wants," *Collier's* 70 (December 23, 1922), 6.

35. Editorial, "The President's Attitude," *ER* 1 (November 24, 1923), 324; Edith Houghton Hooker, "A Test of Faith," *ER* 11 (June 21, 1924), 151; Alice Paul, "Women For Congress," *ER* 11 (August 30, 1924), 229; Editorial, "Republican Responsibility," *ER* 12 (December 26, 1925), 364; Editorial, "Challenge and Evasion," *ER* 14 (July 23, 1927), 188.

36. Ellen Phelps Crump to Jane Norman Smith, December 2, 1927, Jane Norman Smith Papers, Box 2, f. 64, SL.

37. Laura Berrien to Jane Norman Smith, July 1, 1928; Maud Younger to Jane Norman Smith, April 7, 1928, Jane Norman Smith Papers, Box 2, fs. 67, 65, SL.

38. Editorial, "A Presidential Impossibility," *ER* 14 bis (June 9, 1928), 140; Sue S. White, "Observations of a Democrat," *ER* 14 bis (July 14, 1928), 81; "Pre-Convention Work of Woman's Party Branches," *ER* 14 bis (July 21, 1928), 190–91; Eleanor Roosevelt to Sue White, September 7, 1928; Sue White to Eleanor Roosevelt, September 13, 1928, Sue White Papers, Box 3, SL; Editorial, "Equal Rights A Campaign Issue," *ER* 14 bis (September 22, 1928), 258.

39. "Equal Rights and Campaign Plans," *ER* 14 bis (September 29, 1928), 269; Editorial, "Let's Make Virtue Pay," *ER* 14 bis (September 29, 1928), 266; Editorial, "The Test of Sincerity," *ER* 14 bis (October 6, 1928), 274; Amelia Hines Walker to Jane Norman Smith, 1928, Jane Norman Smith Papers, Box 3, f. 70, SL; Editorial, "Judged By His Record," *ER* 14 bis (October 20, 1928), 290.

40. Sue White to Jane Norman Smith, September 15, 1928, Jane Norman Smith Papers, Box 3, f. 69, SL; Mrs. Myers Gillentine to

Sue White, September 18, 1928; Sue White to Mrs. Myers Gillentine, n.d., Sue White Papers, Box 3, SL; Sue White to Jane Norman Smith, December 8, 1928; Jane Norman Smith to Mabel Vernon, December 17, 1928; Jane Norman Smith to Mrs. Harvey Wiley, March 26, 1930, Jane Norman Smith Papers, Box 3, fs. 71, 75, SL.

41. Grace Kay Long to Jane Norman Smith, October 2, 1923, Jane Norman Smith Papers, Box 3, f. 70, SL; Editorial, "The Woman's Party and Mr. Hoover," *Nation* 127 (October 3, 1928), 312; Laura Berrien to Jane Norman Smith, October 30, 1928, Jane Norman Smith Papers, Box 3, f. 70, SL.

42. Lavinia Dock to Jane Norman Smith, n.d.; Ruby A. Black to Jane Norman Smith, November 7, 1928; Olive Cate to Jane Norman Smith, November 2, 1928, Jane Norman Smith Papers, Box 3, fs. 74, 70, SL.

43. "In Striking Contrast," *ER* 14 bis (Nobember 10, 1928), 315–16; "Woman's Party Speakers Attacked by Mob," *ER* 14 bis (November 10, 1928), 315; Editorial, "Coming Into Their Own," *ER* 14 bis (November 17, 1928), 322; Mimeograph to NWP members, November 20, 1928, Jane Norman Smith Papers, Box 3, f. 70, SL; "Party Seeks Women's Votes," *ER* 16 (October 11, 1930), 285–86; Editorial, "Betwixt the Devil and the Deep Blue Sea," *ERIFW* 2 (July 4, 1936), 138.

44. Crystal Eastman, "Striking Pen Picture of Alice Paul," *ER* 1 (August 18, 1923), 214; "Patience," *ER* 1 (August 18, 1923), 212; Editorial, "Bread and Butter Mindedness," *ER* 1 (September 8, 1923), 236; "Statement by Mrs. Belmont," *ER* 11 (May 31, 1924), 123; Editorial, "Don't Be A Cipher," *ER* 11 (January 17, 1925), 388; "Industrial Hearings At Albany," *ER* 12 (March 14, 1925), 38; Grace Hoffman White, "From Our Correspondents," *ER* 13 (August 21, 1926), 224.

45. Editorial, "Heart Warming," *ER* 12 (May 30, 1925), 124.

46. Editorial, "How To Win," *ER* 16 (August 30, 1930), 234; "Mrs. Blatch Addresses Host of Admirers," *ERIFW* 1 (January 25, 1936), 371–72; Editorial, "The End and the Beginning," *ER* 14 bis (June 2, 1928), 132; Editorial, "Growing Up," *ER* 16 (December 27, 1930), 370; Editorial, "Twelve Years of Age," *ER* 18 (September 3, 1932), 242.

47. Editorial, "The New Religion," *ER* 1 (June 16, 1923), 140;

Editorial, "The Bogeyman Argument," *ER* 11 (May 24, 1924), 116.

48. "News From the Field—Equality—No Less," *ER* 20 (November 3, 1934), 320.

49. Editorial, "Beware of Political Parties," *ER* 15 (May 18, 1929), 114; Editorial, "No Compromise With Right," *ER* 23 (January 15, 1937), 2.

50. Editorial, "The Opposition," *ER* 1 (December 22, 1923), 356; "Proceedings of the Conference," *ER* 17 (June 6, 1931), 139–40.

51. Alice Paul, "Women For Congress," *ER* 11 (August 30, 1924), 229.

52. Editorial, "The Election Campaign," *ER* 11 (September 27, 1924), 260; "Final News of the Election Conference," *ER* 11 (August 16, 1924), 211; Editorial, "The Campaign Is Non-Partisan," *ER* 11 (October 25, 1924), 300; Editorial, "Legislatures or Congress," *ER* 11 (September 13, 1924), 244.

53. "News of the Campaign," *ER* 11 (October 11, 1924), 275; "News of the Campaign," *ER* 11 (September 13, 1924), 243; Editorial, "The Election Results," *ER* 11 (November 15, 1924), 316; Jessie Collett, "An Analysis of the Election Results," *ER* 11 (November 22, 1924), 326–27; Anna Van Skite, "Some Results of the Campaign," *ER* 11 (November 29, 1924), 333; Editorial, "Taking Sex Out of Politics," *ER* 12 (March 21, 1925), 44; Mabel Vernon, "Reflections on the Campaign," *ER* 11 (November 22, 1924), 325.

54. Mary Winsor, "Women For Congress: A Campaign of the NWP in Pennsylvania in 1924: A Criticism of its folly and mistaken tactics," Mary Winsor Papers, SL; Anne Martin, "Feminists and Future Political Action," *Nation* 120; (February 18, 1925), 185–86.

55. "Feminist Notes," *ER* 12 (April 4, 1925), 58; Editorial, "The Same Right to Authority," *ER* 12 (August 15, 1925), 212; "A Woman Civil Service Commissioner," *ER* 12 (August 8, 1925), 205.

56. "Jessie Dell Confirmed by Senate," *ER* 12 (January 16, 1926), 389; O'Neill, *Everyone Was Brave*, pp. 228–30; "Petition Submitted By The Woman Patriot Against Miss Dell," *ER* 13 (March 6, 1926), 30.

57. "Petition Submitted By The Woman Patriot Against Miss Dell," *ER* 13 (March 6, 1926), 30–31; "Petition Submitted By The Woman Patriot Against Miss Dell, Part II," *ER* 13 (March 13, 1926), 38–39.

58. Sue White to Jane Norman Smith, August 24, 1926; Minnie Karr to Jane Norman Smith, July 11, 1928, Jane Norman Smith Papers, Box 2, fs. 63, 67, SL; Jane Norman Smith to Burnita Shelton Matthews, June 22, 1929, Jane Norman Smith Papers, Box 3, f. 72, SL.

59. "Mrs. LaFollette Urged to Enter Senate," *ER* 12 (July 25, 1925), 190; "Ruth Bryan Owens Nominated," *ER* 14 bis (June 16, 1928), 147; Julia N. Budlong, "What Happened in Seattle," *ER* 14 bis (September 15, 1928), 254–56; "NWP Supports Men as Better Feminists," *ER* 16 (November 8, 1930), 318.

60. Editorial, "Making the Balance True," *ER* 12 (October 24, 1925), 292; Editorial, "The Fruit of the Loom," *ER* 12 (December 12, 1925), 348; Editorial, "The Road to Victory," *ER* 13 (February 27, 1926), 20; Ernestine Parsons, "Why We Should Campaign For Women," *ER* 14 (August 16, 1927), 215.

61. Editorial, "Conference Offers Feminist Opportunity," *ER* 17 (April 8, 1931), 82; "Proceedings of the Conference," *ER* 17 (June 6, 1931), 139; Editorial, "A Word to the Politicians," *ER* 17 (January 16, 1932), 394; Editorial, "A Universal Need," *ER* 19 (May 27, 1933), 130.

62. "Seneca Falls Conference," *ER* 1 (August 4, 1923), 199; "Fellowship," *ER* 1 (September 1, 1923), 228; Editorial, "Woman's Party Methods," *ER* 14 bis (February 18, 1928), 12; Minnie Karr to Jane Norman Smith, July 11, 1928, Jane Norman Smith Papers, Box 2, f. 67, SL; "Proceedings of the Conference," *ER* 17 (June 6, 1931), 140.

63. "Comments of the Press," *ER* 1 (September 8, 1923), 246; Editorial, "The Pen Is Still Mightier," *ERIFW* 2 (September 5, 1936), 210.

64. Editorial, "Make the Amendment Mean Something," *ER* 1 (September 15, 1923), 244; Editorial, "Here Is Your Opportunity," *ER* 19 (June 10, 1033), 146.

65. Hazel MacKaye, "Campaigning With Pageantry," *ER* 1 (November 10, 1923), 309; "Equal Rights In the Air—Applause By Mail," *ER* 12 (May 2, 1925), 91; "Listen In On The Radio," *ER* 12 (November 28, 1925), 336.

66. "Plans for Seneca Falls and Rochester," *ER* 1 (June 23, 1923),

150; "Pilgrimage to the Grave of Susan B. Anthony," *ER* 1 (June 16, 1923), 139; "News From Seneca Falls and Rochester," *ER* 1 (July 14, 1923), 173; "Women of All States Have Representation in Tribute," *ER* 1 (July 28, 1923), 190; Lavinia Egan, "The Seneca Falls Conference," *ER* 1 (August 4, 1923), 195.

67. "The Colorado Pageant," *ER* 1 (September 1, 1923), 299; "Colorado Pageant Inspires Multitude," *ER* 1 (October 6, 1923), 269; "Memorial Pageant in the Garden of the Gods," *ER* 1 (September 8, 1923), 237–38; "75th Anniversary Year Closes," *ER* 1 (November 24, 1923), 327; "Party Renews Its Faith at Belmont Bier," *ER* 19 (February 18, 1933), 19–20; "Great and Good Women Honored in Impressive Pageant," *ER* 19 (July 15, 1933), 187.

68. Lavinia Egan, "The Seneca Falls Conference," *ER* 1 (August 4, 1923), 195; Editorial, "The Parallel Between the Suffrage and the Equal Rights Campaign," *ER* 1 (November 17, 1923), 316; Editorial, "The Boston Tea Party," *ER* 17 (March 7, 1931), 34.

69. Editorial, "Don't Miss It," *ER* 15 (April 16, 1929), 66.

70. Editorial, "Make July 20 A Red Letter Day," *ER* 1 (June 9, 1923), 132; "Woman's Emancipation Day, August 26," *ER* 22 (August 1, 1936), 2; Alma Lutz, "A Feminist Thinks It Over," *ER* 25 (June 1939), 82.

71. "Mary Beard Revalues Women," *ER* 19 (November 25, 1933), 330; Editorial, "We Must Follow Where They Led," *ER* 20 (June 23, 1934), 162.

72. Editorial, "Woman Has A History," *ER* 20 (December 22, 1934), 370; "Women's Archives Center Is Launched," *ER* 21 (November 1, 1935), 2.

73. Mary R. Beard, "Susan B. Anthony, Heroine of A Democracy," *ER* 23 (February 15, 1937), 20.

74. Editorial, "Seneca Falls Conference, 75 Years Later," *ER* 1 (May 5, 1923), 92; "The Anniversary Meeting in the Crypt of the Capitol," *ER* 1 (October 27, 1923), 291; "Bernhardt As One of the Remarkable Women of the Ages," *ER* 1 (April 14, 1923), 67; "Eva LeGallienne Wins Award," *ER* 14 (October 22, 1927), 293; Nina Allender, "Mary Cassatt, Feminist," *ER* 13 (September 11, 1926), 243; Editorial, "One of the Immortals," *ER* 14 bis (June 23, 1928), 156; Helen A. Archdale, "Mrs. Pankhurst," *ER* 14 bis (July 28, 1928), 195.

75. Editorial, "Charlotte Perkins Gilman," *ERIFW* 1 (August 31, 1935), 202; Harriet Howe, "A Tribute to Charlotte Perkins Gilman," *ER* 24 (July 1, 1938), 286.

4

EQUALITY BEGINS AT HOME

The NWP's primary domestic activities were to work for the federal Equal Rights Amendment and to sponsor either specific or "blanket" state equality bills. Although these political activities to eliminate the remaining legal discriminations against women took priority in the Party's planning, the economic issues of the times dominated and directed all the feminists' activities. It began with the objection of other women's organizations to the potential effect of the ERA on protective legislation for women, combined with the Party's early ambivalence toward such special legislation. However, the NWP soon concluded that protective legislation was both degrading to women and restrictive of their employment opportunities, so there was a clear cut division between the two groups on the question. The general public did not accept married women's "right" to paid employment, and as a result these women suffered even during the relatively minor economic dislocations of the twenties. During the depression, the pressure to remove married women from the work force increased immensely and those women's organizations favoring protective legislation and opposed to the Equal Rights Amendment were forced to recognize the severity of the problem. Social feminist organizations, along with the NWP, protested the married person's clause of the Government

Economy Act (which in practice applied mainly to women), the lower minimum wages for women embodied in many of the National Recovery Act codes, and the lack of relief projects for women. Unlike the NWP, however, they were not opposed to interstate compacts which established minimum wages for women and children only.

The NWP had attempted to come to some agreement with other women's organizations about the wording of the proposed Equal Rights Amendment during 1921, and had delayed its introduction into Congress until late 1923. Early drafts of the Amendment varied, and some contained a clause exempting protective legislation for women, very similar to the "blanket" equal rights bill passed in Wisconsin. But those organizations committed to special labor legislation for women were very reluctant to endorse any sort of sweeping equality amendment, even with a safeguarding clause. In December 1921, the NWP held a conference in Washington with representatives of the League of Women Voters, the General Federation of Women's Clubs, the Women's Christian Temperance Union, the Women's Trade Union League, and the National Consumers' League. Since the final version of the ERA contained no safeguarding clause and Alice Paul refused to state any official Party stand on protective legislation, no compromise was reached. Yet the NWP continued to correspond with the National Consumers' League about the possibility of reaching some agreement after the conference, and did not officially introduce the Amendment to its membership until the Seneca Falls conference in 1923.[1] On December 10, 1923, Senator Charles Curtis introduced the Amendment into the Senate, and three days later Representative Daniel R. Anthony, a distant relative of Susan B. Anthony, introduced it into the House.

The NWP developed its arguments in favor of the Amendment throughout the two decades, shifting focus somewhat to meet the objections of other women's organizations. Early in 1922, Elsie Hill and Florence Kelley published a debate in *Nation* on the question: "Shall Women Be Equal Before the Law?" While Kelley stressed the biological differences between men and women that she believed led to the need for different laws, Hill emphasized the legal discriminations that still remained. The Party was dedicated to removing all forms of the subjection of women, Hill wrote, and removing the legal discriminations would be the necessary first step. Hill admitted that the Party was considering the federal amendment, but insisted that it was the removal of discriminations rather than the method which was more important. In the meantime, the Party continued its state work, whenever possible trying to gain passage of blanket bills. Author and Party officer Zona Gale of Wisconsin maintained that the blanket equality bill had given the women of her state a kind of general bill of rights on which to depend, but pointed out that no equality law could do everything.[2] The Party began actively promoting the ERA in the summer of 1923.

Laws were too uncertain, argued the Party, because they could be repealed or altered later. It was the Constitution which defined human relationships, but the Constitution did not contain a clear statement of the equality of men and women. The courts had invariably interpreted the equal protection clause of the Fourteenth Amendment to mean only male persons, the NWP noted. "If women are 'persons' they deserve the protection of the 14th Amendment;" editorialized *Equal Rights*, "if they are not 'persons,' then in Heaven's name, what are they?" Party members believed that the ERA, with its unequivocal use of the phrase "men and women," could not possibly be subject to as much misinterpretation as the Fourteenth Amendment, although they did not claim the Amendment would do more than remove legal discriminations. Just as the Fourteenth Amendment "did not make colored men white," the ERA would not make women equal, but it would write a fundamental principle into law and give women a means with which to fight for their independence as citizens. To those critics like the Women's Trade Union League speakers who said women should not limit themselves to equality, meaning that they had certain privileges men did not have, the Party replied: "Let us be practical. Let us *reach* equality!"[3]

Another argument against the ERA was that since women had accomplished little or nothing with the vote, the Amendment would not increase their contributions either. This kind of argument was particularly abhorrent to all who had ever worked for or believed in woman suffrage. NWP member Ruby Black pointed out that women voters were not much more apathetic than men, and suggested that a lack of issues significant to women might explain their seeming indifference to some political campaigns. Mrs. Hooker, as usual, was more outspoken. Women, like men, often did not vote or if they did, voted unwisely. Replying to the criticism that women had accomplished nothing with the vote, she claimed that few people had really expected some sort of millenium. "They fling what they choose to regard as our glowing prophesies in our teeth," she wrote, "and clamor for the redeeming of pledges we never made." It was impertinent even to ask what women had accomplished with the vote, added Mrs. Wiley. Voting was a human right, "the key to the house of life," and besides, the real question should be: What had the vote done for women? Women had a new outlook, more job opportunity, and at least the chance to vote intelligently, she concluded, because "it has broadened their interests, made them courageous, made them straight shooters." Wiley did admit, however, that perhaps women voters were not as conscientious about voting as men, immediately adding that women had only been voting for ten years while men had been enfranchised for 150 years.[4]

The struggle begun in 1848 had not yet been completed, the NWP insisted, for the only substantial gain had been suffrage. The ERA would make a better world for future generations of women, Party members believed, even though the struggle for its passage might be extremely difficult. The Amendment was not only a way to achieve justice for women, but once women were free they would release a new "civilizing power that would strike at the roots of war, immorality, economic injustice, social neglect, intemperance and every other evil." Liberal reformer Judge Ben Lindsey agreed with this view of women's special contributions and supported the ERA; Rabbi Stephen S. Wise also thought that women's greater participation in the world would be beneficial to civilization because "women have a genius for service rather than a passion for gain." The NWP often quoted Elizabeth Cady Stanton's advice: "Take down every barrier in woman's way and let her find her own sphere." Any idea other than total freedom for women was antifeminist, according to the Party. After the 1929 hearings on the Amendment, *Equal Rights* reported that the opposition seemed to fear competition with women, and noted that this was a "man's point of view." Until the Amendment passed, the Party insisted, women were doomed to perpetual insecurity and lived in the modern world only on the sufferance of men.[5]

The League of Women Voters had obtained a number of opinions from prominent jurists who thought that the ERA would be subject to endless court interpretation, but the NWP brushed aside these objections by arguing that the courts would not have to deal with such cases if the state laws were brought into harmony with the Amendment. In the Party's opinion, state legislatures would probably extend certain men's privileges to women, such as jury duty. Both parents would share responsibility for illegitimate children, while the problem of equalizing the grounds for divorce could be met in any way the state desired. But Party members did not worry much about the details of applying the Amendment, for they believed that "the establishing of a righteous principle will certainly bring only good results." The Amendment would also have the side effect of helping to free women from their sense of ingrained inferiority, the NWP maintained.[6]

The NWP always justified its efforts on behalf of equality on the basis that no other women's organization had offered such a comparably sweeping program in 1921. Party members countered objections to the effects of the Amendment in what they thought was a logical manner, disdaining all special privileges women possessed as "sops" which they received in exchange for their freedom. Groups opposed to the Amendment should work instead for protection for all workers, encourage the unionization of industrial women, promote the establishment of an economic status for housewives, and work for adequate health standards for everyone, maintained Mrs. Anna Whittic in her 1924 defense of the ERA to the League of Women Voters. In her debate that same year with Dr. Alice Hamilton, Doris Stevens added that the ERA was based on the Party's view of women as important, intelligent, creative, independent units of society.[7]

Besides the major objection about the destruction of protective legislation, there were two recurring arguments which the NWP had to meet. One concerned the effect of the Amendment on maternity legislation and mothers' pensions, or what today would be called aid to dependent children. The Party argued that mothers were a special class of people, like disabled veterans, and insisted that maternity legislation such as the Sheppard-Towner Act would not be invalidated by the Amendment. Both motherhood and fatherhood were important to the race, wrote Lavinia Dock, but mothers' pensions were really aid to the child, not to the mother. Perhaps if such pensions were regarded as the right of all children in need, she suggested, more children would be aided and the stigma of accepting such aid would be removed. The argument that it was "more important for women to bear and rear children than to type letters in some man's office," however, was unacceptable to the Party, for the NWP consistently denied that women had to choose between jobs and families.[8]

Another argument which arose frequently, especially during the twenties, was that the ERA would make women eligible for conscription into the armed services. The NWP's answer was that the Amendment would simply give recognition to the patriotic services women had always rendered during wartime. The Party thought it was unlikely that women would be asked to serve in the trenches, but rather suggested that they would be placed in positions such as munitions factories, hospitals, and ambulance units. In the late twenties, when the pacifist feminist Rosika Schwimmer was denied U.S. citizenship, ostensibly because she refused to say she would kill in defense of her country, equalitarian feminists were outraged. It would be a tremendous injustice to conscript women who did not have the full rights of citizens, the Party journal maintained, even though other countries might have done so.[9]

In 1930, Mrs. Belmont predicted that "with sufficient determination on the part of American women, [equal rights] can be achieved before the next ten years have rolled by . . . so far, at least as it can be won by law." Her prediction did not come true, and in effect, the NWP and its social feminist opponents fought each other to an impasse over the Equal Rights Amendment. In a 1938 analysis of the equality question, *New Republic* praised the sincerity of the ERA proponents. Equalitarian feminists had not convinced the editors of the correctness of their arguments, but neither had the opposition; the editors therefore suggested that the Amendment hearings should continue. Three years later, two substitute equality amendments were introduced in the Senate. One provided that no person would be disqualified from office, barred from any profession or employment, or exempted from jury service on the basis of sex or marriage. The other amendment read: "No state shall make of enforce any law which shall discriminate between the rights of men and women, and no law making such discriminations shall be enacted by the Congress." Groups such as the

Business and Professional Women hoped that perhaps these substitutes might not encounter the same objections as the Party's ERA and gave them their tentative approval. But neither substitute amendment, nor the reworded Equal Rights Amendment proposed later in the forties, met with the approval of social feminist groups opposed to the original Amendment.[10]

The NWP did not consistently work with the same intensity for the ERA during these two decades. During the first two or three years after the introduction of the Amendment, the Party's efforts were relatively sustained. In 1925, Burnita Shelton Matthews noted that the House was most interested in the legal ramifications of the Amendment, while the Senate was more concerned with its effect on protective legislation. In the late twenties the Party's attention turned to international issues. "We let it rest while we worked on nationality," said Maud Younger in 1930, "but we are prepared now to start action in earnest."[11] But in the mid-thirties the Party's internal schism prevented effective concentration on the Amendment, and the major activities of the reformers centered on the attempt to counteract the threat to married women's right to earn. By the late thirties, the Amendment's prospects seemed to brighten with the increasing endorsements by women's organizations and the growing acceptance of the New Deal concept of protective legislation for all workers.

Although the Equal Rights Amendment came up before the subcommittee of the Senate and House Judiciary Committees in 1924, 1925, 1929, 1931, 1932, and 1933, it was not reported out until 1936, when the subcommittee of the House Judiciary reported it favorably to the full committee. In 1937 both House and Senate subcommittees reported the Amendment favorably, and in 1938 the full Judiciary Committee reported it out favorably to the Senate, followed by a similar report in the House in 1939. The 1940 Republican platform contained a plank advocating the submission of the Amendment to the states. Committee hearings and favorable reports followed in 1941, 1942, and 1943.[12] But the opposition of such an influential organization as the League of Women Voters was sufficient to prompt the movement for rewording the Amendment, although this still did not meet some of their objections. An Equal Rights Amendment was finally submitted to the states in 1972.

The NWP was not particularly effective in its political lobbying, and much of the change of Congressional heart in the late 1930s was due to pressure for the Amendment from other organized women, especially working women. NWP members had hoped that its 1924 Women For Congress campaign would convince men of the political expediency of the ERA, and they were even more optimistic about the prospects of their Amendment in 1928, after the Hoover landslide. By the thirties, however, the NWP was quite disillusioned with both political parties. In 1932, there was a Democratic national committee-woman who was also a member of the Party, and six NWP members who were elected delegates to the Republican convention, along with two committeewomen. But even with their own members present, no progress resulted. In 1936, the NWP was again dissatisfied with both parties, although giving the Democrats credit for opening a few new government jobs to women. The Party simply urged women to canvass all office seekers "to see whether there are any candidates under the banner of either Party who are ready to give a fair deal to women."[13]

Politicians had been uncertain about the effects of the "woman's vote" in the years immediately following suffrage, and therefore were more inclined to lend support to bills sponsored by organized women's groups, but there was increased resistance to women's legislation by the mid-twenties. The Child Labor Amendment failed to be ratified by the important states of New York and Massachusetts, the Sheppard-Towner Act was extended for two years only to expire permanently in 1929, and the drive for jury service was unsuccessful after 1923 except in the District of Columbia and Rhode Island. The NWP did not actively work for the maternity act or the Child Labor Amendment as an organization, although individual Party members often supported these measures. Even jury service campaigns were frequently left to the initiative of the League of Women Voters, although Party feminists actively backed all such bills as part of their equality campaign.[14]

The NWP was also concerned with obtaining equal nationality rights for married women. A number of its own members, including Inez Milholland, Consuelo Vanderbilt, and Harriot Stanton Blatch, had previously lost their citizenship through marriage to aliens. The 1922 Cable Act had given some relief to women who married aliens, but without equalizing citizenship rights, and specific bills were proposed throughout the twenties to remove the remaining disabilities of married women. The new Cable Act of 1930 left only a few inequalities for women. An American woman marrying an alien ineligible for U.S. citizenship still lost her citizenship, and a woman marrying an alien eligible for American citizenship had to choose between her husband's or her own. There were different naturalization requirements for men and women, while children born abroad still took their father's citizenship. By the mid-thirties, the Party's approach to solving these remaining differences had shifted to the Equal Nationality Treaty, rather than further amendments to the Cable Act. The NWP also worked for Congressional equality legislation for the District of Columbia, Hawaii, Alaska, Puerto Rico, and the Philippines. A woman's suffrage bill for Puerto Rico was passed in the twenties, the power of married women to make contracts in the District of Columbia was obtained in 1926, and jury service was granted to D.C. women in 1927. Equal inheritance bills, equalization of dower and curtesy rights, and equal pay bills for the District of Columbia were defeated. Summing up Congressional legislation in 1937, lawyer Emma Wold noted that women had the vote in all places under U.S. jurisdiction except the Philippines, but were still excluded from jury service in twenty-seven states, Hawaii, and Puerto Rico.[15]

The NWP expended a great deal of effort toward the passage of state equality legislation in the twenties, although most gains were made in the period between 1921 and 1923. Much of this legislation dealt with the parents' relationship to their children, property rights, the right to hold office, and jury duty; other women's groups also frequently sponsored or supported these equality bills. In 1925, Emma Wold had pointed out the major areas in which state laws discriminated against women. Equal rights for parents included custody, direction of education, and inheritance, as well as the burden of illegitimate children. Married women's disabilities included the use and control of property, the making of contracts, the claim in community property, the choice of legal residence, the grounds for divorce, and the right to retain maiden names. All women were affected by state laws concerning inheritance and the administration of estates, age of majority, higher entrance requirements to state colleges and universities, the right to serve as public officials, jury service, protective labor legislation, and the double standard of morality which made prostitutes but not their customers liable to prosecution.[16]

State legislative gains were slight in 1925. The NWP drafted and successfully sponsored specific equal rights legislation in California, Delaware, New Jersey, New York, Pennsylvania, and South Carolina; the Party supported, although it did not initiate, equality bills in Iowa, West Virginia, and Texas. But the defeats outweighed the victories that year. Jury service bills were lost in thirteen states, along with many other equality bills. There were also instances where women lost previous rights through legislation, such as the Connecticut law requiring married women to adopt their husbands' legal residence and the Maine law requiring women to use their husbands' name in registering for elections. In Massachusetts a resolution restricting the employment of married women was narrowly defeated, and in Pennsylvania the legislature passed a bill, later vetoed by the governor, excluding women over sixty-five from juries. The Party had prepared 127 bills that year, of which 39 were introduced and only 9 enacted. "It is not that the work is prosaic;" Emma Wold concluded, "it is futile and ceaseless."[17]

In New York state, where the NWP branch was strong and active, discouragement with state work had also set in by the mid-twenties. In 1925 the Party introduced ten bills, but only one was passed. The jury service bill failed again, along with equalization of guardianship, domicile rights, and others. Jane Norman Smith summed up the growing disillusionment of women during the twenties, as the equality legislation got down to the more controversial bills such as the wife's right to her own property and choice of domicile, the responsibility of support for illegitimate children, the equal treatment of prostitutes and their customers, and the mandatory jury service bill sponsored by the League of Women Voters and the NWP. "Immediately," she observed, "there was an increasingly hostile attitude toward passing any more Equal Rights bills." Although Smith believed state work was educational, it was both arduous and insecure in the long run, and she concluded that "if Equal Rights for men and women are to be secured during our lifetime, they must eventually be obtained through the only logical and permanent method, the amendment of the National Constitution."[18]

Smith's evaluation of the increased resistance to equality bills was correct. In 1926, none of the nine bills introduced by the Party in New York state passed. The Maryland situation was very similar. The NWP branch there was also large and active, but the results of state work were increasingly disappointing. In 1930, Party activist Dora Ogle summed up the last decade's work. In 1922 there were thirty-three major discriminations against women in the Maryland law and the Party introduced a blanket bill, "but it was simply laughed out of court and only one discrimination removed." That discrimination was a major one, however, the right of women to hold public office. In 1924, the Party was able to obtain equal pay bills for teachers and policewomen, along with equal inheritance rights for grandmothers, but the blanket bill was again defeated. During the next three years the only gain was the right of married women to administer estates, while the blanket bill and jury service bill failed year after year. "In 1929 we were much wiser, the blanket bill was left at home, our efforts and strength were concentrated on the Jury Service and Equal Guardianship bills," reported Ogle. The guardianship bill passed, and jury service failed again. The record for the Maryland branch was nine discriminations removed over a period of ten years. Ogle, like other women previously committed to state work, was discouraged.[19]

Underlying most of the NWP's more specific feminist goals was a belief in the importance of economic freedom and opportunity for all women. This was evident in the NWP state work for blanket equality bills and its work against minimum wage laws, restrictive hours laws, and any other labor legislation which applied to women only. The problem of protective legislation for women came to be the crux of the opposition to the ERA and also the focus in the struggle for leadership of the international feminist movement. It was not that there was disagreement between the NWP and other women's organizations on the right of women to work for pay, nor on the importance of economic independence with respect to women's status, but rather that there was disagreement on the method to achieve these goals.

By the late nineteenth century, feminist attention had centered on the importance of the vote, but a continuous strand of feminist thought was the assumption that women must have economic opportunity in order to develop fully. One of Charlotte Perkins Gilman's major contributions to feminist ideology was her repetition in a series of widely read books and articles that "the inevitable *sine qua non* for the final and complete emancipation of woman was economic independence." The NWP completely accepted the idea that women should do useful work, and this generally implied work outside the home for pay. Work furthered one's self-respect and gave dignity to life; the right to work was both fundamental and noble. Not all women were well suited to child care, the Party argued, and "personal service rendered to some man is not always the noblest form of enterprise of which married women are capable." The right to earn an honest living was the rock upon which modern feminism was founded, editorialized *Equal Rights* in 1933, and this was consistent with earlier Party statements that one of the uses of the vote was to expand women's economic opportunities.[20]

This emphasis on economic independence was not limited to the American feminists of the early twentieth century. It was also common in British feminist thought, and led to the same kinds of divisions among English feminists over the question of how best to achieve economic opportunity for women. In both England and America the major conflict generally centered on whether protective legislation or legislative laissez-faire was better for women. The double burden of housework and an outside job was discussed, but little effort was made to solve the problem. In fact, little analysis of the deeper problems involved in combining work with marriage and children was done by the NWP, the women's organizations favoring protective legislation, or the general public during these two decades. This was as true in England as it was in the United States, with only a few exceptions.

Olga Knopf was one of the exceptions to this generalization. In *Women On Their Own*, she argued that boys were the "natural heirs" to work opportunity and thus they were trained to be able to compete successfully. Girls were brought up differently, did not consider working outside the home as their normal future, and thus when they had to take jobs they lacked skill, experience, and the proper attitude. Volunteer work was no substitute for a man's experience, insisted Knopf, because "work which is not paid is almost invariably regarded as not quite serious." Knopf believed that the right of women to work must be established independently of the economic need of some women to work. Women remained incomplete without at least the opportunity to choose freely that job or career for which their capabilities suited them.[21]

The English writer Ray Strachey was another exception to the majority of feminists who did not attempt to analyze the ramifications of the problem of women and work. In an essay written in 1936, Strachey argued that the early nineteenth century emphasis on the right to work had been an essential precondition to women's emancipation, but suggested that it had led to the development of an ideal in which work became almost an end in itself. For feminists, work became a means to satisfy personal needs, an outlet for talents, and a way to express individuality. Early feminists had simply assumed that once a woman had attained economic independence she could, if she desired, add a husband and children to her life. Strachey noted that although relatively few women ever achieved this ideal, the ideal itself remained very important. During World War I, work became almost heroic, and women were encouraged to enter the labor force. When they were able to hold on to some of their gains after the war, however, it was because they were cheap labor and not because of any public acceptance of the right of women to work. In general, then, the nineteenth century promise of economic independence for women had not been fulfilled.[22]

During the twenties and thirties this lack of public acceptance became obvious to most women, even nonfeminist women. In 1933, the U.S. Women's Bureau identified three clear trends during the past one hundred years of women's work history: an oversupply of women looking for work, much lower wages for women than for men, and the movement of increasing numbers of married women into the work force. Even in the decade between 1920 and 1930, a period of shrinking opportunity for women workers, their absolute gain in numbers was about two and a half million, while in 1930 married women workers made up 28.9 percent of all women workers. Women in the professions had increased 48 percent between 1920 and 1930, although much of this gain was wiped out in the thirties. In April 1930, there were a half million women unemployed, and by 1933, three million. Many of these were married women, women over thirty, or women who were formerly white collar workers. By 1940, one-fourth of all women over fourteen years of age were employed, and out of every one hundred women workers, the Women's Bureau found, thirty held white collar jobs, twenty-four were in domestic or public housekeeping positions, seventeen did manual labor, eight were in other service positions, four were agricultural workers, and one worked at a trade or craft.[23]

Although the trend was clearly one of women moving into the labor force, public opinion was slow to accept this reality, especially in the case of married women. There was a real gap between the actual economic necessity which forced most women into the labor force, and the public conception that women, especially married women, worked for "pin money" which would be used primarily for luxuries. Nor were women's much heralded freedom and equality reflected in their treatment by their employers, who continued to consider them transient workers who should really be at home. The ambivalence in the American mind about married women working has continued into contemporary times, as Ellen and Kenneth Keniston have noted. The Kenistons' thesis is that many women themselves are aware of a conflict between a career and a set of roles centered around marriage and home. Conditioned by sex role assumptions and a Victorian outlook which they have inherited from their own parents, both men and women are confused about careers for married women.[24]

Although much too dependent on an Eriksonian view of women and their own distaste for what they term an androgynous world, the Kenistons have isolated two important factors. One is that the values commonly associated with the Victorian era have had a persistent hold on the American imagination and as a result have continued to be influential well into the twentieth century. The other important aspect of their work is that they stress the dichotomy which has always existed for most women with respect to a career and a marriage with children. Although the authors conclude only that female children need more role models of women who have successfully combined both marriage and a career, they fail to note that working outside the home is not now, and never has been, the norm for middle class married women with preschool children.

Robert Smuts' study of women and work also examines the values and attitudes underlying the "right" of married women to work. As he so perceptively notes, women's employment "involves two subjects which lie near to the center of human emotions: work and the relationship between men and women." Women's employment is frequently seen as threatening to the family, to the self-esteem of men, and to women's moral standards, so that although people could accept an economic "need" for women to work, they did not think women had any "right" to work. Although feminists were small in numbers, they were often highly educated, articulate, and frequently economically independent through their careers. Therefore they posed a threat simply by raising questions about the lack of economic opportunities for women. Since feminists did not openly question the value of maternity, but merely refused to accept the idea that a woman's life should be devoted to it, they encouraged married women to think in terms of outside employment. At the same time, the pecuniary value attached to outside work tended to devalue housework.[25]

Smuts' study suggests that many women gradually came to believe that they had essentially the same needs as men, and thus saw in work a chance for economic independence, an alternative to an undesirable marriage, a means of gaining prestige and success, as well as a path toward personal fulfillment. Men generally resisted the movement of women into the labor force,[26] and Smuts' explanation of this resistance is much like that offered by feminists of the twenties and thirties.

> The opposition to women's employment was concerned with far more than their place in the world of work. It was an integral part of a comprehensive effort to bring women back into the shelter of the home, to reemphasize their functions in the family, to reconstruct the supposedly tottering family around them, to reassert the authority of a strict moral code, and to restore a clear boundary between masculine and feminine character and behavior.[27]

In the context of the "new" woman of the twenties and the depression-engendered strains on the masculine role of the thirties, this explanation aids in understanding the increasingly virulent movement to restrict women's economic opportunities during the era. In addition, the question of protective legislation was central to those economic opportunities during the twenties and most of the thirties.

J. Stanley Lemons has argued that the NWP shifted its position on protective legislation between 1921 and 1923,[28] but it would be more accurate to say that the NWP gradually developed a position on protective legislation during this time period. It is true that early drafts of the Equal Rights Amendment contained tentative safeguarding clauses dealing with women's labor legislation, but the Party became convinced by 1922 that the primary effects of protective legislation were restrictive. One factor which helped equalitarian feminists arrive at this point of view was the postwar economic dislocation which fell so heavily upon certain groups of women workers, such as street car and railroad employees. Another factor was the experience of married women workers during the twenties, particularly married women employed by the government. Such growing groups as the Business and Professional Women and the government workers' associations also drew public attention to the great disparities between men and women in pay and opportunities for advancement.

In 1920 the old Party organ, *The Suffragist*, printed a balanced review of both sides of the protective legislation question, along with an article noting that certain groups of wage earning women were insisting that an equal chance to earn a living was essential to women's welfare. The NWP pointed out that although the Women's Trade Union League presented itself as a representative of wage earners, it was concentrating on protective legislation rather than the organization of these working women. By 1921, the Party had begun receiving direct requests to help fight protective legislation because it was costing some women their jobs. Mary Murray, Brooklyn rapid transit worker and later chairman of the industrial council, contacted Jane Norman Smith, the New York state branch president, about the position of the Party on protective laws. Shortly thereafter, Alice Paul, who had expressed no opinion on the Wisconsin clause safeguarding protective legislation, asked NWP members and officers what they thought. "Unlike many leaders," Jane Norman Smith later commented, "Alice Paul never made a decision on that important an issue and then expected those under her to comply with it." Smith had been convinced by wage earners that special legislation was restrictive and she voted to oppose it. With this decision, feminists such as Mary Beard, Lavinia Dock, and Hazel MacKaye withdrew from active support of the Party, although Dock and MacKaye soon changed their minds.[29]

In 1923, the industrial council in New York wanted to enter the local elections in support of a candidate for industrial equality, but Alice Paul thought this was unwise. The head of the council at that time was Frances Roberts, a former waitress who had worked her way up to restaurant manager. Roberts maintained that many of the women had joined the Party's council in order to do active work for economic equality and that she "could not hold the women together and would resign as chairman unless we worked actively for industrial equality." Although the working women supported the ERA as a long term goal, they emphasized that protective legislation was an immediate threat to them, and were especially worried about a women's eight-hour day bill before the New York legislature. In Jane Norman Smith's memorandum of this conference, she noted that the industrial council women, along with the New York Equal Opportunity League, tended to distrust the NWP. Smith asked Alice Paul to reassure Roberts about the importance of the industrial council and offered to pay Roberts' fare to Washington.[30] The problem was smoothed over and from that time on, NWP feminists were committeed to economic equality and the Party tended to attract other working women who shared the same concern with protective legislation.

Women government workers generally became more assertive during this period, and the NWP government workers' council demanded the opening of all civil service exams to women, a single appointment list for men and women, the removal of discrimination against women in appointment, assignment, title, promotion, and salary, along with some representation for women on classification boards. Married women were the first to be discriminated against in times of recession, and in 1921, a forerunner of the later government economy bill to dismiss married persons from the government service if their spouses were also employed by the government was introduced. The sponsor, Senator Porter McCumber, meant that married women should be dismissed and he admitted this was his intention. Women made up about 16 percent of all federal employees in 1923, although their proportion decreased slightly during the decade. By the mid-thirties they had regained their previous position, and by 1939 were nearly 19 percent of all federal employees.[31]

During these two decades, however, women were concentrated in the Post Office, Treasury Department, Veterans' Bureau, War Department, and the Works Progress Administration. Speaking of the concentration of married women workers in jobs with low pay and low prestige, outgoing council chairman Laura Berrien said in 1924: "But it is our own fault. We do not protest enough." After the 1924 elections, the effects of the Coolidge economy campaign began to be felt by married women who were civil service employees. The Personnel Classification Board considered a suggestion that when both husband and wife worked for the federal government, they should be penalized by "discredits" on their efficiency ratings. This suggestion brought objections from the National Federation of Federal Employees as well as from Jessie Dell. Dell had been able to convince the Commission to remove the rule which allowed employing agencies to stipulate which sex they preferred for the job, but this was countermanded during Roosevelt's presidency on the recommendation of Mary Anderson, who maintained it did not help women because they then had to compete with veterans who had qualified with lower scores.[32]

During the thirties, there were more direct attempts to eliminate married women holding jobs under civil service. When the Detroit post office requested a list of married women workers whose husbands also worked at the post office, Mary Anderson, Selma Borchard of the American Federation of Labor (AF of L), the NWP, and many others protested. Yet the following year, the federal government passed an Economy Act which included as Section 213 of its provisions a married persons clause. The NWP immediately launched a fund raising drive to work for the repeal of the clause, because it believed that "while the language indicates no sex bias, in practice this provision of the Act is aimed directly at married women." The Party argued that Section 213 set a precedent that would be followed by state and local governments, and that it encouraged divorces and penalized those hoping to marry. The NWP's government workers' council sent letters to more than three hundred women's clubs asking for support for the repeal of Section 213, organized councils in other cities such as Philadelphia where there were a large number of federal government employees, and cooperated with all organizations, including the League of Women Voters, in working for repeal of the clause.[33]

The other large group of married women who faced discriminations consistently throughout this period were teachers. As early as 1920, the eastern conference of the American Federation of Teachers listed as three of its major goals the right of married women to teach, to receive equal pay, and to have equal opportunity for advancement. A 1923 Illinois survey showed that men were paid more, were in all the top administrative and policy making jobs, and frequently did not have as high qualifications as the teachers they supervised. Teachers in Syracuse and Buffalo appealed to the NWP for help against the dismissal of married women in 1924, and in 1925 the NWP introduced equal pay bills for teachers in Minnesota, South Carolina, New Jersey, and Ohio. In Syracuse in 1928 the school board evaded a court decision based on the state tenure law which would have required it to retain some of the married women teachers; the board passed a rule making married women ineligible to teach in Syracuse and then declared jobs held by married women vacant.[34]

The NWP advised all women to canvass school board candidates carefully in order to avoid ever voting for "any public official who would participate in making such a law or rule placing marriage in the same category as misconduct, dishonesty, or gross inefficiency." Early in the depression, demands for the dismissal of married women teachers came from even more states, in spite of legislation which should have prevented such discrimination. The depression had encouraged many mayors and governors to suspend civil service regulations or teacher tenure laws as an "emergency measure" and the resulting loss of jobs fell most heavily on married women. By 1938, a National Education Association study of 291 cities showed that in 76 percent of these cities no married women could be hired as teachers, and in 46 percent of the cities, resignation was mandatory if a woman teacher was married.[35] Married women's hard-won gains in the teaching profession had been lost.

The drive to eliminate married women from the work force was not limited to those jobs paid by tax money, although this was the major area of discrimination. In 1926, the Baltimore and Ohio Railroad agreed with its unions that no married women whose husbands had jobs would be employed by the railroad. The Party urged women, especially its members traveling to Baltimore, to boycott the railroad. "It would be better to come in an oxcart to the conference," editorialized their journal, "than to travel in a B & O coach that daily rides down the right of a married woman to earn an honest living." That same year the Union Pacific Railroad replaced all its married women employees, except stenographers and comptometer operators, with men. Women's economic independence and opportunities ended with marriage, the Party concluded, and then women were "denied full opportunity because many women 'marry and quit' to use the inseparable phrase the executives employ." Although the B & O repealed its ruling against the employment of married women in 1927, the issue did not die. In 1928, a bill was introduced into the New York legislature to place a 20 percent tax on married women's incomes if their husbands were also employed and earned over $2,000 a year. The assemblyman who introduced the bill was quoted as saying that the bill was not to raise new revenue, but rather because "the old-fashioned wife to whom marriage is the only career is being replaced by many of those employed married women who flout the sacredness of marriage and militate against the purposes of marriage—the propagation of children.[36] By the time of the actual depression, railroads such as the Lehigh and Chesapeake and Ohio were furloughing married women with no need to justify their actions.

Many of the attacks on married women's right to employment were firmly backed by public opinion. There was more ambivalance during the twenties than during the early thirties, when the economy seemed to be collapsing and people sought any remedy for unemployment. When the Lynds surveyed "Middletown" in 1925, they found nearly one-fourth of all women working, and although the idea of married women workers was not readily accepted, twenty-eight out of every hundred working women were married. The proportion of employed married women who were mothers was also increasing, and in 1926, Secretary of Labor James J. Davis announced that in a survey of four major cities, about half the working women were mothers. Although Women's Bureau studies consistently showed that married women worked because of economic necessity, the public idea persisted that married women worked for luxuries and did not need their salaries in the same way as men and single women. Throughout the twenties, NWP members insisted that there was a human and even constitutional right to work for a living which could not be denied to married women. Not very tactfully, they suggested that married women often worked because their husbands were unable to support them and their children adequately. But the Party's major emphasis was on the right of married women to choose paid employment regardless of economic need.[37]

When the Lynds returned to do the field work in 1935 for their study, *Middletown in Transition*, they found that during the past decade women had been competing more aggressively with men for jobs, but that married women had suffered heavily due to the depression. Yet the Lynds concluded that the effect of the depression had been to put more strain on the traditional male role, while the female role expanded. "Women's place has been less exclusively in the home," they reported. The NWP argued in the thirties that women should not have to barter away their human rights for marriage, and that to deprive married women of employment would nullify great investments in education and training as well as cause other workers to lose jobs. In addition, the Party saw the drive against married women as only a forerunner to the drive against all women workers, who would then be forced to depend on their nearest male relative for support. Single women were being turned against their married sisters, the NWP warned, and must be brought to realize that the threat to married women's employment was a threat to all women's right to work. As Alma Lutz explained, married women often felt superior to single women, "and single women are encouraged to glorify all out of proportion marriage and the financial support furnished by a husband."

Women could not afford to be divided on so important an issue as the right to earn a living, the Party insisted, yet in 1936 a Gallup poll showed that 82 percent of the public believed a married women should not work if her husband were able to support her.[38]

The NWP did not hesitate to assign blame for the discrimination against women workers. As the equalitarian feminists saw it, the enemies were professional "uplifters" and men, often unionized men, while the tool was protective legislation for women only. The American Federation of Labor had never cooperated fully with the Women's Trade Union League in its early efforts to organize working women, and during the twenties resisted pressure by the WTUL to issue special charters for women's locals in industries in which the international unions refused female membership. Although special charters had occasionally been granted for Negro workers, unions opposed women's locals on the basis that women were only temporary workers. The NWP believed that the reason men supported minimum wages and maximum hours legislation for women while opposing it for themselves was because they knew it would make women less competitive. By 1925, the Party was openly accusing the American Federation of Labor of making women into scabs, and at the New York state industrial hearings that year, Doris Stevens characterized organized labor's policy toward women as "a policy of antagonism, hostility and exclusion."[39]

NWP members believed that men had been usurping women's jobs since the beginning of the Industrial Revolution. Although overall union membership had declined between 1924 and 1930, about 60 percent of the American Federation of Labor's unions remained stable. When labor unions endorsed protective legislation for women only or discriminated against their female members, the Party accused them of wearing "a mask of altruism." Labor leaders' arguments, according to the Party, were based on the idea that men should have priority for available jobs because of their family obligations, but in reality male workers simply could not compete with women workers. When a bill was introduced into the New York legislature in 1929 to exempt waitresses from laws that prohibited night work for women, the New York Federation of Labor testified against it, claiming it would throw 5,000 waiters out of work and serve as an entering wedge for breaking down other women's labor laws. The NWP felt totally vindicated by this incident. "It is precisely what we have been saying all along," editorialized their journal, "that labor men wanted protective legislation for women only, so that they could steal women's jobs away under cover of chivalry." Perhaps the issue really lay between the "sex struggle" and the class struggle, *Nation* had suggested in 1928. "The rub comes when the two struggles overlap," concluded the editorial, "and labor concedes the sexual *status quo* by appealing to the chivalry of the employer and the community for special labor laws for women."[40]

The NWP had never expected very much of the American Federation of Labor, pointing out that organized labor had refused to support the abolition of slavery or women's suffrage until the very last minute. The American Federation of Labor had betrayed its women members, charged Genevieve Sheldon after the failure of the 1933 American Federation of Labor convention to endorse her resolution for equal employment rights for women. Women union members had hoped too long, she said, and "are constantly being forced, almost without exception, into a position which closely resembles a 'back seat.'" Her suggestion, although not a new one, was that women form segregated feminist locals to look after their own interests. When William Green supported a proposed federal amendment in 1936 that would allow states to fix minimum wages for women only, the Party accused him of selling union women down the river. The NWP had more hope for John Lewis and the CIO, primarily because in 1937 he came out strongly for a minimum wage based on the job rather than the sex of the worker, and committed the CIO to the organization of women workers.[41]

Much of the opposition to the ERA during these two decades was based on the opponents' sincere belief in the necessity of special legislation. But philanthropists were the most dangerous kind of people, wrote Mrs. Hooker in 1923, announcing that one of the NWP's most important functions would be "to bring before the American people the futility, the injustice and the inadequacy of 'welfare laws.'" Frequently supporters of protective legislation for women interfered on the basis of sentimental instinct rather than rational thought, argued Rheta Childe Dorr in her *Good Housekeeping* debate with Mary Anderson. "Often I wish it could be bottled like a beneficent but pernicious drug," she wrote, "labeled with skull and crossbones, and inscribed 'To be well mixed with intelligence before taking.'" Harriot Stanton Blatch believed it was unfair that industrial women were always portrayed as "spavined, broken-backed creatures, and the sons of Adam as tireless, self-reliant, unionized supermen." Doris Stevens added that the two basic assumptions underlying special protective legislation were the questionable morality and biological inferiority of working women, which "asks women to set their pace with the weakest member of their sex."[42]

The League of Women Voters, Consumers' League, and Women's Trade Union League argued that women had special physical limitations, were not unionized, and were able to get legal protection in a way that men could not. But the Party rejected legislation based on women as an invalid group, concluding that those opposed to industrial equality assumed that a normal woman should be supported by some man, work only within her own home, and leave the field of industry to men. To NWP feminists, protective legislation for women was a badge of inferiority, and they maintained that "the sign of the crutch is an old brand and always signifies a man's woman, not a woman's woman." The Party also opposed special labor legislation because it usually combined women and children into one class. Lavinia Dock, along with most members, believed that children ought to be protected from industrial exploitation and argued that linking women with children had hindered efforts to eliminate child labor. The Party believed that in the nineteenth century both women and children had been exploited and thus were protected by being considered wards of the state, but insisted that this was no longer a valid concept. The NWP's industrial council agreed, pointing out that laws which classed women and children together tended to depress women's wages, make women unable to compete with men, and prevent children from obtaining adequate protection.[43]

The NWP's major objection to protective legislation was that it restricted women's opportunities. Party feminists did not oppose protective legislation as long as it applied to all workers, and was based on the job rather than sex. Otherwise women were likely to lose their jobs or be crowded into the lowest paid work. Nor should women be penalized by restricting their industrial opportunities on the basis that working women were also burdened with housework, argued the NWP. Women's unpaid labor had never been regulated, and it was only when women entered into competition with men for paid employment that there was any concern for their "welfare," the Party believed.[44]

Protection had a high price, Party members insisted. "Labor laws for women only are vertical," wrote Lavinia Dock in 1926, "and like a wall, may be so built as to shut out as many as they shut in." Not only did such laws infringe upon the liberty of the individual, but they also had the effect of closing off certain opportunities for women. Whole occupations might be closed to women as a result of legislation which prevented them from doing something like grinding their own tools, noted Elizabeth Baker. The Party agreed that "discrimination in one field reflects itself in all others," comparing the opportunities of women with the low paid, limited occupations available to southern Negroes. The NWP repeated again and again that the keystone of equality was economic equality, and that so-called protective legislation actually put women in a position in which they could be exploited by their male competitors. As Mrs. Hooker summed up in 1931: "The entire program of the Equalitarians is based on the assumption that no individual, man or woman, can really be free while he, or she, eats out of another's hand."[45]

The NWP argued consistently that women could and should be unionized, for then they could determine what sort of improvements in wages, hours, and conditions would be in their best interests. Women were in the labor force to stay and technological improvements had changed the nature of much industrial work; the massive unemployment of the thirties gave even more force to the Party's arguments. During prosperity men would not work for such low wages as women did, but the depression had intensified the competition for those jobs which were available. Women could not have protection and equal pay and opportunities too, the Party emphasized in its rejection of the protectionist Women's Charter in 1936. In other words, NWP members never deviated from the position they had taken in the early twenties, when Doris Stevens had insisted that "protection is a delusion."[46]

The most common kinds of protective legislation for women were minimum wages, regulation of hours, and laws barring certain occupational categories to women. The state of Ohio still prohibited women from some sixteen occupations in 1930, and most of these prohibitions, such as those barring women from working as street car conductors or meter readers, dated from the post–World War I economic dislocations. In 1923, the Party had pointed out that a precedent of restricting certain occupations to men only was dangerous because if unemployment increased "women will find themselves more and more barred from those positions desired by men." The Party consistently opposed any legislation which seemed to reduce women's competitive chances for employment, including laws sponsored by the Consumers' League requiring employers to give women paid leave before and after childbirth. The NWP's reasoning was that this would make employers even more hesitant to hire any women, and especially married women.[47]

The drive for minimum wages for women encountered increasing opposition during these two decades, and the NWP frequently worked against such laws. The Party was pleased with the 1923 *Adkins* decision striking down minimum wage laws for women only; Party feminists believed this decision marked a move away from what they considered to be the pathological concept of women presented in the frequently imitated Brandeis brief for *Muller* v. *Oregon*. In 1925, Senator Hiram Johnson proposed a constitutional amendment to permit minimum wages for women and children, and the NWP spearheaded the coalition of opposition groups among business and professional women. Such an amendment would mean that "women belong to a special class of incompetents requiring such special care as minors and defectives need, and not covered by other provisions in the Constitution dealing with freedom of contract," the Party argued. Although historian William Chafe has concluded that the minimum wage laws of the thirties did substantially improve the position of low level women workers, the NWP insisted that these laws too often cost them their jobs. Equalitarian feminists used as their example the Harvard scrubwomen, replaced by men at 34¢ an hour when the Massachusetts minimum wage law set women's wages at 37¢ an hour. Minimum wage laws for women deprived them of their rights, according to the Party and the U.S. Supreme Court through most of this period. When the Court reversed its stand on minimum wage laws for women in the late thirties, the Party decried it as "unsound doctrine" formulated in the "hysteria of politically created emergencies."[48]

Laws which restricted or regulated women's hours also restricted their employment opportunities, according to the NWP. Especially controversial was legislation prohibiting women from night work. The 1928 Women's Bureau study of the effect of protective legislation admitted that some women, such as pharmacists, some retail clerks, printers, and waitresses, did lose their jobs as a result of these laws. In the early twenties New York passed a law prohibiting night work for women which affected textile and clothing workers, as well as employees of bottling companies. Night work was often more highly paid than the day shift, the NWP pointed out, even if women workers could be absorbed into the day shift. Party feminists also objected to what they thought was the moral implication of such laws: "Women must not be allowed to work after dark lest they succumb to the dangers of the midnight streets." If night work were unhealthy, the Party argued, it should be prohibited for both men and women. "If night streets are unsafe for women," Doris Stevens further advised, "don't take away women's jobs—make streets safe." In 1924, the Supreme Court upheld the New York law prohibiting night work for women, turning down the contention that this denied women equal protection under the Fourteenth Amendment. The law remained in effect, modified only by exemptive legislation for women printers on newspapers, although the Party unsuccessfully supported several bills which would also have exempted waitresses.[49]

Other special hour limitations, such as an eight hour day, a forty-eight hour week, or prohibitions against working split shifts also harmed women, the Party maintained. Overtime work was highly paid and a way to promotion, not to mention those seasonal industries in which it was a basic prerequisite to employment. When the Party was unable to prevent the introduction of a forty-eight hour bill for women in New York in the mid-twenties, it countered by sponsoring a forty-eight hour bill for all workers. Since some legislators who were willing to vote for the women's hour bill feared that the demand would be widened eventually to include all workers, both bills were defeated. Forty-eight hour bills for women were reintroduced in New York in 1927 and 1930, only to fail in the face of protests from the NWP, waitresses, women railroad and transit employees, printers, biscuit and candy factory workers.[50] In the thirties, most hour legislation was part of the New Deal, and often covered both men and women.

Although the number of women in the labor force increased during the decade 1930–1940, it was generally in low paid seasonal employment or domestic service. Women holding higher level white collar jobs especially lost ground during this decade, and there was a great deal of public resentment at women holding any jobs while men were unemployed. A Women's Bureau study of unemployment among women in 1934 noted that the public, although shocked to find that girls and women had taken to the road in large numbers, believed that "such things were exceptional, that, in general, women's responsibilities were not so heavy as men's, and that on the whole they were probably getting along not so badly." As the study showed, this was not the case. Women had suffered from periodic unemployment even during the twenties, and were concentrated in industries and occupations where fluctuations were extreme and frequent. In her autobiography Mary Anderson concluded that women workers suffered more than men in the depression because they were the last to be hired back, received the worst jobs, and were underpaid. Yet during the thirties, the Women's Bureau did not change its attitude toward protective legislation for women and children. Its 1928 report on the effects of such legislation, particularly minimum wage and hours laws, had concluded that the advantages far outweighed the disadvantages, and the Bureau continued to support such legislation.[51]

The NWP joined other women's groups in denying that one of the causes of the depression had been the widespread movement of women into the labor force during the early twentieth century. The idea that women had usurped men's jobs was common, or as college president Samuel Harden Church expressed it in his letter to the *New York Times* in 1933, "the tragedy of this is that the man has no work at all—the women have crowded him out of his birthright." He suggested that for every four jobs, three men and one woman be hired, "until a fair balance between the sexes shall have been established." The idea that women worked only for pin money also persisted into the depression. Working women were "good lookers and good dressers," a New York City furniture dealer wrote to Jane Norman Smith in 1938. But even though they spent all their income on their looks, "they plainly show the wear and tear of twenty years' employment in an office or a shop." His suggestion was that a woman should be content to be the "leading lady" of home and family, rather than steal men's jobs. Whenever large groups of women were laid off during the era, the NWP tried to protect their right to work. In 1931, Josephine Casey, organizer and former union official, worked throughout the south and east in an effort to head off the growing tendency to dismiss women workers. Leaving suddenly to go to Rhode Island, she wrote to an NWP officer: "I wanted to stay in New York a few days but this made me a little anxious to step on it. You know the funny feeling we all get that we are the whole works." And after some 1940 layoffs of women textile workers, Caroline Babcock told Alma Lutz that "someone should have gone there the minute those girls lost their jobs."[52] The NWP never varied from its insistence that all women had as much right to work as men.

In one way Party feminists saw the depression as an opportunity. "Now is an excellent time to cut through to the hard fact underlying all sentimental generalizations about the difficulties of night work and long hours," wrote Muna Lee, "and force a comparison of these with the difficulties of existing in hard times with no work at all." Equalitarian feminists were quite encouraged at the political conventions of 1936, when Elinore Herrick of the Consumers' League, Molly Dewson of the Democratic National Committee, and the League of Women Voters all joined in protesting Section 213 of the Economy Act, and did not present any new proposals for minimum wages for women and children.[53]

Another thing which united women's groups in protest during this decade was the discrimination against women frequently embodied in the NRA codes and the lack of work relief programs for unemployed women. Industries employing the largest number of women frequently wrote a lower minimum wage for women into their NRA codes. Fully one-fourth of the codes discriminated against women in this way, with the support of labor unions which also managed to get provisions for separate seniority lists for men and women into a number of codes. Higher minimum wages for women, such as were proposed for the retail trade code, also discriminated against women because they would be replaced by men. Equal pay for equal work was the goal of all organized women, and in 1934 they protested the inclusion of any phrases such as equal pay for "female employees performing substantially the same work as male employees" because this was invariably used to justify lower pay for women. Mary Anderson personally enlisted the aid of Eleanor Roosevelt, sending her a copy of the memorandum which ten women's organizations had submitted to Hugh Johnson in protest. The NWP was also active in publicizing the discriminations in the codes and in lobbying government officials, especially Donald Richberg and Frances Perkins, for equal pay.[54]

The early New Deal work relief programs had done nothing for the "forgotten woman," *Equal Rights* maintained, "except further to sacrifice her to the forgotten man." The New Deal that women wanted, wrote Helena Hill Weed, would include the removal of legislative discriminations such as Section 213 and unequal minimum wages, the appointment of more women to responsible positions under the NRA, projects and opportunities in the PWA and CWA for women, along with an increase in the number of women who could qualify for work relief. But women could not depend on Franklin D. Roosevelt, warned Harriot Stanton Blatch in 1935. Concluding that his love of popularity was his great weakness, she advised members not to waste any time on him because "he is not with us and never has been." Combined protests caused some reorganization in work relief programs; by the mid-thirties there were special women's projects in the WPA. But generally the only women who could qualify for work relief were "married women who are economic heads of families, widows without resources, single women with dependent relatives, and unattached women who have to make their own way."[55] All adult unemployed men qualified for work relief, unless their family income exceeded the limit.

The NWP was not supported by other women's organizations, however, in its protest against interstate labor compacts. The Party's objection was that these agreements invariably set minimum wages and hours restrictions for women and children only, and thus were a means of circumventing the court decisions of the early twenties. In 1934, seven eastern states agreed to make uniform legislation for women and children which regulated their hours, established a mandatory wage for certain industries, and prohibited night work in manufacturing, mercantile, and mechanical establishments. President Roosevelt had encouraged this kind of compact since the early thirties, the Party pointed out, and women must fight back. The compact would set a menacing precedent for the restriction of women, the minimum wage invariably became the maximum wage, and the effect of such agreements was that men and boys could undercut women and thus women would lose jobs. Furthermore, Helena Hill Weed told a group of Maryland business and professional women, "the Constitution will indeed cease to function as the protector of liberty if this menace becomes a law." When NWP member Helen Hunt West was invited to the Southern Labor Conference in 1936, she joined with Frances

Perkins in proposing legislation which would apply equally to men and women. Although Perkins was willing to support legislation for women only, if laws applying to both men and women were impossible to pass, West protested against this as discriminatory.[56]

The struggle of these two decades over state equality legislation and the ERA were inextricably bound up with women's economic opportunity and the dispute over the effects of protective legislation. But when Professor Arthur Meier Schlesinger testified in 1943 that he could see no further objections to the Equal Rights Amendment since protective legislation for both sexes had been upheld by the Supreme Court,[57] he was mistaken. In the forties, fifties, and sixties the focus of the opposition to the ERA shifted from the economic to the social ramifications, although arguments against the removal of special labor legislation for women continued to be used by labor unions. During the twenties and thirties these fundamental disagreements over protective legislation for women and the conflict between the League of Women Voters' and the NWP's opposing viewpoints were reflected in the international feminist movement. So too was the conflict over "blanket" means to accomplish even agreed upon goals such as equal citizenship rights for married women. The international feminist movement, like the American movement, splintered as a result of these strains.

NOTES

1. NCL Papers, Box C 14 W 1, LC; Florence Kelley, "Conference with Representatives of the Woman's Party," December 4, 1921; Maud Younger to Ethel Smith, December 19, 1921, NCL Papers, Box C 14 W 2, LC.

2. Elsie Hill and Florence Kelley, "Shall Women Be Equal Before the Law," *Nation* 114 (April 12, 1922), 419–20; Zona Gale, "What Women Won in Wisconsin," *Nation* 115 (August 23, 1922), 184–85.

3. Editorial, "The Function of the Law," *ER* 1 (September 8, 1923), 236; Editorial, "An Unavoidable Obligation," *ER* 12 (November 29, 1925), 332; Editorial, "Are Women Persons?" *ER* 18 (June 11, 1932), 146; "National Woman's Party Explains Its Proposal for an ERA," *Congressional Digest* 22 (April 1943), 102; Editorial, "Whose

Creation?" *ER* 13 (April 10, 1926), 68; Editorial, "The Practical Solution," *ER* 23 (July 15, 1937), 98.

4. Emily N. Blair, "Are Women Failures in Politics?" *Harper's* 151 (October 1925), 513–22; Ruby A. Black, "How Indifferent Are Women Voters?" *ER* 14 (October 8, 1927), 277–78; Editorial, "By Their Fruits," *ER* 14 (December 3, 1927), 261; Anna Kelton Wiley, "Ten Years After," *ER* 16 (September 20, 1930), 261.

5. Carol Rehfisch, "The Woman's Party Is Right," *ER* 1 (October 20, 1923), 285–86; Inez Haynes Irwin and Florence Kelley, "The ERA," *Good Housekeeping* 78 (March 1924), 161; Anna H. Whittic, "Defense of the Blanket Amendment," *Woman Citizen* 19 (June 28, 1924), 17; Editorial, "The Opening of Congress," *ER* 11 (November 29, 1924), 332; Editorial, "Many Birds with One Stone," *ER* 1 (August 25, 1923), 220; Telegram, Judge Ben D. Lindsey to Maud Younger, n. d., printed in *ER* 11 (March 8, 1924), 27; Editorial, "A Practical Argument," *ER* 12 (April 25, 1925), 84; Editorial, "Elizabeth Cady Stanton's Message," *ER* 20 (November 10, 1934), 332; "Senate Hearing," *ER* 15 (February 9, 1929), 5; Editorial, "Support the Equal Rights Planks," *ER* 18 (June 11, 1932), 146.

6. Editorial, "Interpretation of the ERA by the Courts," *ER* 11 (March 1, 1924), 20; Burnita Shelton Matthews, "Women Should Have Equal Rights with Men: A Reply," *ER* 13 (May 29, 1926), 125–27; Editorial "What Can the Amendment Do?" *ER* 12 (September 26, 1925), 260; Rebekah Greathouse, "The Necessity of an ERA," *ER* 20 (March 17, 1934), 52–53; Editorial, "We Cross the Rubicon," *ER* 20 (May 19, 1934), 122.

7. Irwin and Kelley, "The ERA," p. 18; Editorial, "Sops," *ER* 1 (October 27, 1923), 292; Whittic, "Defense of the Blanket Amendment," p. 29; Doris Stevens and Alice Hamilton, "The Blanket Amendment," *Forum* 72 (August 1924), 152.

8. Editorial, "Why the Amendment?" *ER* 1 (October 6, 1923), 268; "Concerning Equal Rights," *ER* 12 (June 20, 1925), 147; Editorial, "False Prophets," *ER* 14 (January 21, 1928), 394; Editorial, "Elizabeth Cady Stanton," *ER* 20 (November 10, 1934), 322.

9. Editorial, "Equal Rights and Conscription," *ER* 1 (January 12, 1924), 380; Editorial, "Equal Rights and Conscription," *ER* 12 (January 23, 1926), 396; Editorial, "Equal Rights and Military Service," *ER* 14 (October 29, 1927), 300.

10. Alva E. Belmont and Burnita Shelton Matthews, "Program of the NWP," *Congressional Digest* 9 (November 1930), 263; Editorial, "Equal Rights For Women?" *New Republic* 94 (February 16, 1938), 34; Alice L. Manning, "May Day Surprise," *Independent Woman* 20 (June 1941), 184; Alice L. Manning, "Legislatively Speaking," *Independent Woman* 9 (December 1941), 372.

11. Ruby A. Black, "The Congressional Hearings," *ER* 12 (February 14, 1925), 5–8; Ruby A. Black, "Vigorous Congressional Campaign Begins," *ER* 12 (December 19, 1925), 357; "Plans to Push Amendment," *ER* 16 (September 6, 1930), 243.

12. "The Legislative Journey of the Equal Rights Amendment," *Congressional Digest,* 22 (April 1943), 105–6.

13. Editorial, "The Republicans and Equal Rights," *ER* 11 (June 21, 1924), 148; Editorial, "The Campaign and the Amendment," *ER* 11 (October 11, 1924), 276; "Amendment Campaign Outlined," *ER* 14 bis (December 15, 1928), 355; "The Woman's Party at the Chicago Conventions," *ER* 18 (June 11, 1932), 147; Editorial, "All That We Need," *ER* 18 (June 18, 1932), 154; Editorial, "A Tombstone Is Appropriate," *ERIFW* 2 (June 27, 1936), 130.

14. Chafe, *The American Woman*, pp. 26–29; Lemons, *The Woman Citizen*, 72–73; "Women as Members of the Jury," *ER* 1 (November 3, 1923), 301; Judge Florence Allen, "Woman Jurors A Success," *ER* 13 (February 5, 1927), 411.

15. *Equal Rights Weekly Bulletin of the NWP*, September 13, 1922, no page number; Editorial, "The New Cable Bill," *ER* 16 (April 12, 1930), 74; Editorial, "In the Balance," *ER* 19 (June 17, 1933), 154; Maud Younger, "Equal Rights and the 73rd Congress," *ER* 19 (June 24, 1933), 163; Mrs. O. H. P. Belmont, "Work of the Woman's Party for the First Five Years," *ER* 13 (May 15, 1926), 109–10; Emma Wold, "Women in Congressional Bills," *ER* 14 (January 28, 1928), 404; Emma Wold, "Changing Legal Scene," *Independent Woman* 16 (April 1937), 124.

16. "Progress of the Women's Party Campaign," *ER* 1 (June 9, 1923), 131; "Summary of the NWP Legislative Campaign (1921–1923)," *ER* 1 (July 21, 1923), 183; "Equal Rights and State Legislation," *ER* 11 (December 20, 1924), 259–60; Emma Wold, "Legal Status of American Women," *ER* 12 (April 11, 1925), 69–71.

17. Emma Wold, "Equal Rights in the Legislatures of 1925," *ER* 12 (October 24, 1925), 295–96.

18. Elizabeth Gifford, "The End of the Road," *ER* 12 (April 18, 1925), 75; Jane Norman Smith, "The Campaign in New York State," *ER* 12 (November 28, 1925), 333–34.

19. Florence Elizabeth Kennard, "Nationality Dinner Held in Maryland," *ER* 16 (February 8, 1930), 7.

20. Carl Degler, "Charlotte Perkins Gilman on the Theory and Practice of Feminism," *American Quarterly* 8 (Spring 1956), 31; Editorial, "The Right to Work," *ER* 1 (July 21, 1923), 180; Editorial, "Women's Souls," *ER* 1 (October 27, 1923), 292; Editorial, "Upon This Rock," *ER* 19 (June 3, 1933), 138; Lavinia Dock, "The Industrial Conference of the Women's Bureau," *ER* 13 (February 13, 1926), 3; Editorial, "For Economic Freedom," *ER* 15 (July 20, 1929), 186.

21. Knopf, *Women On Their Own*, pp. 189, 191, 193–94.

22. Ray Strachey, ed., *Our Freedom and Its Results* (London: Hogarth, 1936), pp. 122–24, 127–39.

23. U.S. Department of Labor, Women's Bureau, *Women At Work: A Century of Industrial Change*, Bulletin no. 115 (Washington, D.C.: GPO, 1933), pp. 1, 5, 7–8, 48–49; U.S. Department of Labor, Women's Bureau, *Women's Occupations Through Seven Decades*, Bulletin no. 232 (Washington, D.C.: GPO, 1951), p. 86.

24. Chafe, *The American Woman*, pp. 64–65; Ellen and Kenneth Keniston, "An American Anachronism: The Image of Women and Work," *American Scholar* 33 (Summer 1964), pp. 355–75.

25. Robert Smuts, *Women and Work in America* (New York: Columbia University Press, 1959), pp. 111–29.

26. *Ibid.*, pp. 132, 135–36.

27. *Ibid.*, 134.

28. Lemons, *The Woman Citizen*, 189.

29. Marie L. Obenauer, "Legislation for the Woman Wage Earner," *The Suffragist* 7 (March 1920), pp. 11, 20; Marie L. Obenauer, "The Enfranchised Woman in Industry," *The Suffragist* 8 (April 1920), 45–46; "Equal Rights Campaign—NWP," no date; Mary Beard to Jane Norman Smith, no date, Jane Norman Smith Papers, Boxes 1, 2, fs. 47, 60, SL.

30. Alice Paul to Jane Norman Smith, October 23, 1923; Memo,

"Conference between Adelaide Stedman, Mrs. Frances Roberts and Mrs. Smith," October 28, 1923, Jane Norman Smith Papers, Boxes 5, 2, fs. 111, 60, SL.

31. Lemons, *The Woman Citizen*, 78–79; U.S. Department of Labor, Women's Bureau, *Women in the Federal Service, 1923–1947*, Bulletin no. 230 (Washington, D.C.: GPO, 1949), pp. 18, 22.

32. "Government Workers Demand Equal Representation," *ER* 1 (April 21, 1923), 79; "Government Workers' Council Holds Convention," *ER* 11 (May 3, 1924), 93; "Discrimination in Government Service," *ER* 12 (February 14, 1925), 3; Editorial, "The Right to a Job," *ER* 12 (August 8, 1925), 204; "Justice for Married Government Employees," *ER* 12 (October 3, 1925), 270; Lemons, *The Women Citizen* p. 83.

33. "Defend Economic Rights of Wives," *ER* 17 (October 10, 1931), 284–86; Editorial, "Genuine Economy," *ER* 18 (November 5, 1932), 314; Abbie Ellis Owen, "Proposed Plan May Limit Section 213," *ER* 19 (May 27, 1933), 135; "Government Workers Plan Aggressive Campaign," *ER* 19 (January 27, 1934), 403.

34. Cora McCarty, "Women Teachers Demand Three Things," *The Suffragist* 7 (December 1920), 311; Rose M. Kavana, "Women Teachers in the Public School System of Illinois," *ER* 1 (December 19, 1923), 366; "Married Women Teachers," *ER* 11 (September 20, 1924), 151; "The Minnesota Tenure Bill for Teachers," *ER* 12 (July 11, 1925), 171; "Married Women Teachers in Syracuse," *ER* 14 bis (July 21, 1928), 191–92.

35. Editorial, "Pushing Women Out," *ER* 16 (September 6, 1930), 242; "Still Attacking Married Women," *ER* 17 (February 28, 1931), 29–30; Ruby A. Black, "The Very Same Old Story," *ER* 17 (April 25, 1931), 91–92; "Can Working Women Marry?" *ER* 24 (September 1, 1938), 315.

36. Editorial, "The B & O Agreement," *ER* 12 (January 16, 1926), 388; Editorial, "A Word of Warning," *ER* 13 (April 17, 1926), 76; Editorial, "A Railroad Boycotts Women," *ER* 13 (August 21, 1926), 320; Editorial, "We Commend the B & O," *ER* 14 (August 27, 1927), 228; "A Very Vexed Question," *ER* 14 (October 29, 1927), 299; Editorial, "A New Way to Fight Women," *ER* 14 bis (February 18, 1928), 12.

37. Robert and Helen Lynd, *Middletown* (New York: Harcourt, Brace, 1929), pp. 25–27; "Married Women in Industry Increase," *ER* 12 (January 16, 1926), 391; Editorial, "Economics and Egotism" *ER* 15 (July 6, 1929), 170; Editorial, "The Bar Sinister," *ER* 12 (October 3, 1925), 268; Editorial, "On Being Supported," *ER* 13 (April 17, 1926), 76; "Feminist Notes: Prejudice Against Married Women Workers Unwarranted," *ER* 14 (December 31, 1927), 368.

38. Robert and Helen Lynd, *Middletown in Transition* (New York: Harcourt, Brace, 1937), pp. 55, 57, 59, 61, 178–79; Address by Helen Elizabeth Brown, "Married Woman and Paid Employment," *ER* 19 (March 18, 1933), 52; Editorial, "His Sisters and His Cousins and His Aunts," *ER* 19 (January 27, 1934), 402; Alma Lutz, "What Price Marriage," *ER* 20 (June 9, 1934), 149–50; Laura B. Anderson, "Proceedings of the Washington Conference," *ERIFW* 1 (February 1, 1936), 379–80; Alma Lutz, "A Feminist Thinks It Over," *ER* 24 (October 1, 1938), 334; Editorial, "Mr. Landon Was Elected," *ERIFW* 2 (November 28, 1936), 306.

39. O'Neill, *Everyone Was Brave*, pp. 101–2, 247–48; Editorial, "Special Privileges for Women," *ER* 1 (March 24, 1923), 48; Editorial, "One Asset Anyhow," *ER* 16 (November 29, 1930), 338; "Industrial Hearing at Albany," *ER* 12 (March 21, 1925), 45–46.

40. Joseph G. Rayback, *A History of American Labor* (New York: Free Press, 1966), pp. 312–13; Editorial, "With the Mask Off," *ER* 13 (January 22, 1927), 396; Editorial, "Letting the Cat Out of the Bag," *ER* 15 (March 16, 1929), 42; Editorial, "Chivalry and the Labor Laws," *Nation* 128 (December 12, 1928), 648.

41. Editorial, "Is Organized Labor Opposed?" *ER* 13 (March 20, 1926), 44; Helen Black, " 'Women at War' for their Rights in Industry," *ER* 12 (August 1, 1925), 195; Theresa Wolfson, "Equal Rights in the Union," *Survey* 17 (February 15, 1927), 629–30; Genevieve Sheldon, "American Federation of Labor Fails Women," *ER* 19 (October 28, 1933), 303–4; Muna Lee, "Let Women Make Their Own Choice," *ER* 17 (April 11, 1931), 76; Vee Terrys Perlman, "Who 'In God's Name' Will Protect the Working Girl?" *ERIFW* 2 (March 28, 1936), 27–28; Ruth Gill Williams, "The Green Murder Mystery," *ERIFW* 2 (June 27, 1936), 131; "John L. Lewis Would Not Base Wages on Sex," *ER* 23 (May 14, 1937), 67.

42. "Suppose It Were You," *ER* 1 (October 20, 1923), 286; Editorial, "Why the Argument?" *ER* 1 (October 6, 1923), 268; Mary Anderson and Rheta Childe Dorr, "Should There Be Labor Laws for Women?" *Good Housekeeping* 81 (September 1925), 52; Harriot Stanton Blatch, "Do Women Want Protection?" *Nation* 116 (January 31, 1931), 115; Doris Stevens and Alice Hamilton, "Blanket Amendment," *Forum* 72 (August 1924), 149.

43. Editorial, "No More, No Less," *ER* 12 (February 21, 1925), 12; "The Mastick-Shonk Bill Dies," *ER* 12 (April 4, 1925), 62; Editorial, "The Sign of the Crutch," *ERIFW* 1 (January 18, 1936), 362; "Lavinia Dock Appeals to Nurses," *ER* 1 (January 5, 1923), 373; Lavinia Dock, "The Industrial Conference of the Women's Bureau," *ER* 13 (February 13, 1926), 3; Consuelo Furman, "Is Special Legislation for Women Desirable?" *ER* 1 (May 26, 1923), 115; Lucy Branham, "Subtracting Women from Children in Labor Legislation," *ER* 1 (December 15, 1923), 347; Editorial, "Industrial Axioms," *ER* 12 (January 9, 1926), 380.

44. Editorial, "Theory Vs. Practice," *ER* 1 (May 12, 1923), 100; Blatch, "Do Women Want Protection," p. 115; Jane Norman Smith to the Editors of *Nation, Nation* 116 (April 4, 1923), 393; Sue White, "A Recent Study of Women In Industry," *ER* 1 (February 2, 1924), 403; "News from the Field," *ER* 11 (February 16, 1924), 6; "Indusdustrial Hearing at Albany," *ER* 12 (March 28, 1925), 53.

45. Dock, "The Industrial Conference of the Women's Bureau," p. 3; Elizabeth Abbot, "The Case Against," *ER* 11 (January 3, 1925), 271; Frances Perkins and Elizabeth Baker, "Do Women in Industry Need Special Protection?" *Survey* 55 (February 15, 1926), 582–83; Editorial, "What Price Protection?" *ER* 13 (September 11, 1926), 244; Mary A. Murray, "Working Women Demand Industrial Equality," *ER* 14 bis (June 2, 1928), 133; "Banquet Attracts Brilliant Assemblage," *ER* 19 (November 11, 1933), 319; Editorial, "An Obvious Deduction," *ER* 17 (April 4, 1931), 66.

46. Lavinia Egan, "Figures on Industrial Discrimination," *ER* 1 (July 21, 1923), 179; Whittic, "Defense of the Blanket Amendment," p. 29; Speech by Ada R. Wolff, "Women in Industry," *ER* 13 (November 20, 1926), 325; Alma Lutz, "Shall Women's Work Be Regulated by Law?" *Atlantic Monthly* 146 (September 1930), 321, 327;

Rebekah S. Greathouse, "The Necessity of an Equal Rights Amendment," *ER* 20 (March 17, 1934), 53; Elizabeth Baker et. al., "About the Women's Charter," *Independent Woman* 16 (March 1937), 74; Stevens and Hamilton, "Blanket Amendment," p. 151.

47. Editorial, "Industrial Equality," *ER* 1 (March 17, 1923), 40; Editorial, "Women Learn Meter Reading," *ER* 14 (October 15, 1927), 284; Lutz, "Shall Women's Work Be Regulated By Law?" p. 324; Editorial, "Practice Vs. Theory," *ER* 1 (September 15, 1923), 244; Editorial, "The Farce of Restrictive Legislation," *ER* 17 (April 25, 1931), 90.

48. Editorial, "Minimum Wage Laws for Women," *ER* 1 (March 31, 1923), 56; Editorial, "The Minimum Wage Decision," *ER* 1 (April 21, 1923), 76; "Protest Meeting Held," *ER* 12 (November 28, 1925), 335; "The Johnson Amendment Introduced," *ER* 12 (December 19, 1925), 358; Editorial, "The Johnson Amendment," *ER* 12 (December 19, 1925), 356; Chafe, *The American Woman*, p. 82; Editorial, "The Scrubwomen Were Not There," *ER* 16 (February 8, 1930), 2; "A Surrender!" *ER* 23 (April 1, 1937), 43.

49. "Suppose It Were You," *ER* 1 (October 20, 1923), 286; Editorial, "The Position of the Woman's Party on Laws Prohibiting Night Work for Women," *ER* 1 (February 24, 1923), 16; U.S. Department of Labor, Women's Bureau, *The Effects of Labor Legislation on the Employment Opportunities of Women*, Bulletin no. 65 (Washington, D.C.: GPO, 1928); Editorial, "One Step Forward," *ER* 14 (September 14, 1927), 252; Crystal Eastman, "Equality or Protection," *ER* 11 (March 15, 1924), 37; Stevens and Hamilton, "Blanket Amendment," p. 150; Editorial, "The Supreme Court and Night Work Laws," *ER* 11 (March 22, 1924), 44; Mary Murray, "The Hearing on the Kirkland-Jenks Bill," *ER* 16 (March 15, 1930), 43; Muna Lee, "Let Women Make Their Own Choice," *ER* 17 (April 11, 1931), 76; Editorial, "We Repudiate the Compliment," *ER* 16 (March 15, 1930), 42.

50. Editorial, "Longer Hours for Women?" *ER* 1 (April 14, 1923), 68; Zona Clements, "Protective Legislation Based on Sex," *ER* 1 (December 15, 1923), 350; "The Mastick-Shonk Bill Dies," *ER* 12 (April 4, 1925), 62; "The Joiner Bill Fails," *ER* 12 (May 2, 1925), 93; Jane Norman Smith, "Wage Earning Women Oppose 48 Hour Law," *ER* 13 (January 29, 1927), 405-06; "New York Defeats 'Welfare' Bills," *ER* 16 (April 19, 1930), 85-86.

51. Smuts, *Women and Work in America*, p. 145; Howard Dozier "Women and Unemployment," *Review of Reviews* 85 (March 1932), 55–56; "Unemployment Among Women in the Early Years of the Depression," *Monthly Labor Review* 38 (April 1934), 790–99; Anderson, *Woman At Work*, pp. 154–56; Elizabeth Gifford to Jane Norman Smith, November 30, 1928, Jane Norman Smith Papers, Box 3, f. 70, SL; Editorial, "Chivalry and the Labor Laws," *Nation* 127 (December 12, 1928), 648; U.S. Department of Labor, Women's Bureau, *Women at Work* (Washington, D.C.: GPO, 1933), pp. 25–30. Some recent historical treatments have suggested that women suffered less from unemployment than men because women were concentrated in "feminized" occupations. See Ruth Milkman, "Women's Work and the Economic Crisis: Some Lessons from the Great Depression," *The Review of Radical Political Economics* 8 (Spring 1976), 73–97; see also Rosalyn Baxandall, Linda Gordon, Susan Reverby, eds., *America's Working Women* (New York: Vintage Books, 1976). This interpretation does not seem to be supported by the contemporary evidence, especially when underemployment and occupational "crowding" are taken into account.

52. "Shall America Go Nazi?" *ER* 19 (August 26, 1933), 237; D. W. Walker to Jane Norman Smith, December 20, 1938, Jane Norman Smith Papers, Box 1, f. 30, SL; Josephine Casey to Muna Lee, November 27, 1931, Jane Norman Smith Papers, Box 3, f. 78, SL; Caroline Lexow Babcock to Alma Lutz, January 20, 1940, Alma Lutz Papers, Box 6, f. 83, SL.

53. Muna Lee, "The Woman's Party Stands Guard," *ER* 16 (October 4, 1930), 278; Ruby A. Black, "Women and the National Conventions," *ERIFW* 2 (July 18, 1936), 156–59.

54. Chafe, *The American Woman*, pp. 85–86; Ruby A. Black, "Inequalities Under National Recovery Administration," *ER* 19 (September 2, 1933), 244–45; Press release, February 17, 1934, WTUL Papers, Box 6, LC; Memo, Mary Anderson to Mrs. Franklin Delano Roosevelt, February 19, 1934, WTUL Papers, Box 6, LC; Maud Younger, "The NRA and Protective Laws for Women," *Literary Digest* 117 (June 2, 1934), 27; Angus McDonald, "Sex Differences of the NRA Codes," *ER* 20 (September 15, 1934), 163–64; Editorial, "Women and the NRA," *ER* 20 (September 15, 1934),

258; "Reorganized NRA Asked to End Discrimination, *ER* 20 (October 13, 1934), 292.

55. Editorial, "The Forgotten Woman," *ER* 19 (July 29, 1933), 202; Helena Hill Weed, "The New Deal That Women Want," *Current History* 41 (November 1934), 179–83; Editorial, "Welcome in War—Outcast in Peace," *ERIFW* 1 (January 12, 1935), 10; Harriot Stanton Blatch, "The Most Vital of Human Rights," *ERIFW* 1 (June 29, 1935), 133–34; Ellen S. Woodward, "Jobs for Jobless Women," *ERIFW* 1 (July 20, 1935), 155; Editorial, "All Women, Here's Work," *ERIFW* 1 (July 20, 1935), 154.

56. Editorial, "The Menace of Interstate Labor Compacts," *ER* 20 (March 10, 1934), 42; Jane Norman Smith, "The Background of the Interstate Minimum Wage Compact," *ER* 20 (September 8, 1934), 251–52; Alma Lutz, "Women and Wages," *Nation* 139 (October 17, 1934), 440–41; Helena Hill Weed, "The Menace of the Interstate Compacts," *ER* 20 (November 17, 1934), 333; Helen Hunt West, "The Southern Labor Conference," *ER* 22 (February 1, 1936), 3; Jane Norman Smith to Helen Hunt West, January 27, 1936, Helen Hunt West Papers, Box 1, f. 8. SL.

57. Carrie Chapman Catt et al., "Should Congress Approve the Proposed Equal Rights Amendment to the Constitution? PROS" *Congressional Digest* 22 (April 1943), 114.

5
UNTIL ALL WOMEN EVERYWHERE ARE FREE

Both American social and equalitarian feminists believed that women were natural internationalists. Feminists had worked for peace, suffrage, and humanitarian causes on an international scale in the World War I era, and tended to support the establishment of the League of Nations and the World Court after the war. The NWP's underlying ideological framework was one of sisterhood which emphasized both the special characteristics of women and the common problems shared by women all over the world; these views were not unlike those of the social feminists. All international women's organizations favored independent nationality rights for married women and protested against the spread of fascism and its effects on women's status. But the NWP's activist program, including its blanket Equal Nationality Treaty and its Equal Rights Treaty which would have committed nations to granting equality to women within all the areas under their jurisdiction, aroused strong objections from the social feminists.

NWP members considered themselves part of a great historical movement toward equality, seeing similarities and encouragement in the struggles of women in other lands. Their sense of solidarity and fellowship was always strongest with Englishwomen, probably because there were so many similarities in the suffrage campaign and postwar economic problems in both England and America. However, Party feminists firmly believed that all women would bring special contributions to civilization because of their closeness to human problems, their shared motherhood, and their pacifism. Furthermore, Mrs. Hooker maintained, women had remained unspoiled "by ambition, by egocentric desire, by commercialism; they are impersonal and altruistic."[1]

The Party also argued that women could not be confined within narrow nationalistic bounds any more than within artificial bounds of political parties. "Feminists intuitively understand that they are citizens of the world and that only with this background can they be true patriots in their own countries," editorialized *Equal Rights*. After attending a 1925 socialist conference in Marseilles, Crystal Eastman expressed the hope that women might succeed where even socialist men had failed; women might spread peace and goodwill through the medium of international feminism. NWP feminists tended to blame the sorry state of world affairs on men's mismanagement, especially during the period of the post–World War I revulsion against militarism. During past wars, the Party declared, woman had been powerless, "a pawn in the hands of men and whoever has won, she has lost." In the mid-thirties Madeline Doty described the world as "a man's world, where national and international conflicts are settled by the resort to violence, bloodshed, war and militarism," rather than by woman's "spiritual power."[2] But perhaps the best summary of the Party's faith was given by Alice Paul in the spring of 1941.

This world crisis came about without women having had anything to do with it. If the women of the world had not been excluded from world affairs, events might have been different. This is a man-made world.[3]

But Paul believed that no matter who won the war, the women's movement would continue to grow. "Women are the same the world over, no matter what country they live in," she explained. "They want a world-wide movement—like a church. Something universal."[4]

The Party insisted that there was an interrelationship in the status of all women of all classes and in all countries. "As long as any woman is discriminated against simply on the ground of her sex," observed Mrs. Hooker, "all women, to a greater or less degree, will pay the penalty for her." American equalitarian feminists supported Lady Rhondda's attempt to be seated in the House of Lords as a peeress in her own right because they believed that when a woman was barred from any opportunity it implied the inferiority of all women. It was logical for European feminists who had gained the franchise to turn to the struggle for equal rights, according to the NWP; in order to attain equality women must abolish forever "woman's sphere, woman's work, woman's wage."[5]

Since feminists must work in the international field to achieve true equality, the NWP decided that its own special function would be to revitalize the international women's rights movement. Internationalism gave feminists a true perspective on their own position, the Party maintained, and American feminists must not become complacent about their own limited gains. "It is painful to patriotic Americans to recognize how far their country lags behind Soviet Russia in its treatment of women," observed Mary Winsor, Lucy Branham, and Ella Murray after their 1927 visit to the U.S.S.R. The Party not only approved of the Soviet Union's feminist advances, but also praised the recently passed social legislation of the Scandinavian countries.[6]

Still another rationale for international action during this period was that international bodies increasingly affected women's position. The Party feared that if feminists were not vigilant, some of these international decisions might simply reinforce the same inequalities already established in national laws. Very few women were involved in such groups as the Pan American Congresses, the League of Nations, the London Economic Conference, or the International Labour Office; men, therefore, would be controlling women's destinies again. Because of this, the NWP insisted, "our way leads straight to the halls of international councils as it led in the days of the suffrage struggle directly to the halls of Congress." Treaties were the most effective method; they were easiest to obtain and wasted less human and financial resources. "The Equal Rights Treaty is the inevitable outcome of the Equal Rights Amendment," declared Mrs. Hooker, "for both are born of the same idea, namely that the whole sex must cast aside its bondage in order to secure equal opportunity for any woman anywhere."[7]

In the twenties, the Party had protested against the challenges to women's right to earn a living, apparent even in the democratic countries like Great Britain. By the early thirties, NWP members were especially concerned with what they described as Germany's "reversion to barbarism." "Now, if ever, women must stand together," editorialized their journal, "not only to help their German sisters to resist to the uttermost, but also to prevent similar anti-Feminist movements from being started in other countries." The American equalitarian feminists supported and publicized the International Alliance of Women's call to women to resist being regarded simply in terms of their child-bearing functions, and joined British feminist protests against the imprisonment and execution of European women pacifists. "This one thing we know," wrote Alma Lutz after the fall of Czechoslovakia in 1938, "when Nazi philosophy enters, Freedom for women walks out."[8]

The Party also cooperated with women still trying to gain suffrage. After compiling congressional legislation relevant to Puerto Rican suffrage in 1926, the NWP advised Puerto Rican suffragists in their test case based on the Nineteenth Amendment. The Party lobbied Puerto Rican legislators during the mid-twenties in Washington, supporting a suffrage amendment to the Organic Act. The Party also aided the Cuban suffrage organization; when the 1928 Pan American Congress was held in Havana, NWP feminists staged suffrage demonstrations. To the usual techniques of parades, street speakers, and banners, the Party added a Latin American touch by releasing two thousand pigeons carrying papers with quotations from the patriot and national hero José Martí. Even the British women were not fully enfranchised until 1928, and the NWP contributed fifty marchers to the final Hyde Park suffrage demonstration. In France, where women did not receive the vote until after World War II, the Party supported the increasing militancy of French suffragists like Marie Verone, who organized a demonstration which disrupted a session of the French Senate. In 1929, after a similar demonstration resulted in the arrests of about fifty suffragists and charges of police brutality, Madame Verone remarked that such persecution would never stop the progress of justice. "Let us follow the example of the Anglo-Saxons," she said, "let us win by power what we have not been able to get by reason."[9]

Although American feminists were agreed on the need for international activism, protective legislation had become the ideological rock upon which the American women's movement split during the twenties, and the same issue divided the international feminist movement during these two decades. Internationally, the NWP and its equal rights allies opposed further passage or ratification of International Labour Office (ILO) protective labor conventions for women employed at night or in such hazardous work as the mines and the lead paint industry, for they feared the precedent which would be set if women were excluded from any employment opportunities. The League of Women Voters and its social feminist supporters considered such international conventions a logical extension of American protective legislation for women, who were at a disadvantage because of their maternal functions and thus could not compete on the same basis as male workers. Moreover, American social feminists believed that any setbacks in the movement for international protective labor conventions would weaken similar hard-won legislation for women in the U.S.

The postsuffrage leadership struggle between the National Woman's Party and the American social feminists had important ramifications for feminists and for all working women. The decade of the 1920s was characterized by economic dislocations which greatly affected working women in the United States, Great Britain, and other industrialized European nations. By the early thirties, the worldwide depression and the rise of fascism made it increasingly clear that women, especially married women, employed in business and the professions were particularly vulnerable.[10] Confrontations over how best to secure equality for working women occurred in both Europe and Latin America from the mid-twenties through the late thirties. In Europe the conflict took the form of a split in the International Alliance of Women for Suffrage and Equal Citizenship; this divided and diffused European feminist activities. The International Alliance of Women might have provided leadership against economic discriminations, but the application of the NWP for admission to this organization and the League of Women Voters' adamant opposition to the Party's membership precipitated the schism. While equalitarian feminists then concentrated their efforts on supporting a revision of the night work convention for women, opposing further ratification of protective labor conventions, and lobbying for League of Nations approval of the Equal Rights Treaty, social feminists combined to block these efforts.

Early in 1926, Mary Anderson and the U.S. Women's Bureau had sponsored a Conference on Women in Industry, which the NWP had disrupted with its demands for a reconsideration of the impact of protective legislation on women. In a letter discussing what she considered a major setback for the NWP, Anderson wrote that "now most of them have left for Paris to do what they can in the meeting of the International Suffrage Alliance." Although J. Stanley Lemons in *The Woman Citizen* has also suggested that the NWP turned its attention to international treaties and conventions in the late twenties because the Party was blocked in its American efforts, the NWP views on the Equal Rights Amendment and labor equality were gradually gaining support among uncommitted women's organizations.[11] But just as the bitter conflict between the NWP and the social feminists led by the League of Women Voters was brought out into the open at the U.S. Conference for Women in Industry in 1926, so the international phase of the struggle between these two groups over protective legislation and leadership of the feminist movement erupted at the meeting of the International Alliance of Women later that year.

In 1925, Alice Paul and Mrs. O. H. P. Belmont had recruited European feminists as members of the international advisory council of the NWP and had applied for membership in the International Alliance of Women. The Alliance had referred the NWP application for admission to the League of Women Voters, which was the only American member of the Alliance at that time. Ordinarily this procedure was merely a courteous formality and it was the Alliance's committee on admission that decided whether the applicant organization met the requirements of the Alliance constitution. But the executive board of the LWV voted unanimously against the admission, filing a formal protest that argued that the NWP did not educate women as citizens, was not organized into branches throughout the country, and was a "party" that engaged in partisan politics. The board also stressed the differences between the League and the Party in both policies and tactics, although a similarity in techniques and ideology was not required by the Alliance constitution. As Mrs. Carrie Chapman Catt wrote to LWV president Belle Sherwin, "the constitution, we must admit, is very loosely drawn and will admit a chicken yard if it applies."[12]

Mrs. Catt correctly concluded that since the admissions committee would not know what to do they would postpone action and refer the question to the 1926 Paris convention, where the League and the NWP would probably be expected to argue their cases before the delegates. "I do not recommend this plan," wrote Catt, and she then worked actively behind the scenes to prevent such a confrontation. The Leslie Commission, organized to distribute the remainder of the one million dollars left to the suffrage cause, was dominated by Mrs. Catt. The commission sent a formal letter of protest to the board of the International Alliance and to its admissions committee, charging that the NWP record was "one of continual prevarication with regard to organization, numbers and propaganda." Furthermore, warned the commission, "its presence in the Alliance may well lead to the withdrawal or alienation of other organizations."[13] This thinly veiled threat implied that the bulk of the financial support for the Alliance would be removed if the LWV should withdraw.

The president of the International Alliance, Margery Corbett Ashby, was placed in a very difficult position. She explained that the English suffragists had experienced the same problem, but had given some representation within the Alliance to the Women's Freedom League because "though we objected very strongly to their methods we realized that they did, as a matter of fact, represent a body of women who were working for our common object." But Mrs. Catt replied that the American situation was very different because the NWP had made little or no organizational efforts. "It has played the cuckoo," Catt wrote, "and laid its eggs in nests that had cost much to build." Catt also warned Sherwin that the British women had always resented the American control of the Alliance. In fact, she maintained, things had run smoothly when she was president of the Alliance only because "I held every rein in my own hands and raised the money for its maintenance." Yet Catt admitted that "behind this problem there is present the contention over the general question of equal rights." If the admission question were decided in favor of the NWP she believed the League of Women Voters should drop out of the International

Alliance, because if the NWP were to be admitted as an equal with the League "it will surely bring contention back to this country and do the League much more mischief." Sherwin agreed, but expressed the hope that the Party's application would be turned down.[14]

The executive board of the Alliance was the first to give in, and in November 1925, Mrs. Ashby wrote to Mrs. Catt giving her unofficial notice that the board had recommended against the NWP to the committee on admission. The following month, Ashby formally notified Alice Paul and the NWP that their application had been rejected, pointing out the objections of the League. Mrs. Ashby noted that under the Alliance constitution the NWP could still take its membership application before the conference delegates, "but it may be that your executive will prefer to withdraw it in these circumstances." Perhaps Mrs. Ashby really expected the Party to withdraw gracefully but she was to be disappointed. *Equal Rights* published the correspondence between Ashby and the Party, pointing out that the Alliance had solicited financial support from the Party and had suggested that it apply for admission. The NWP would never have applied for membership, Alice Paul insisted, if it had known that admission depended upon the approval of the League of Women Voters, "as their hostility to the Woman's Party campaign for equality between men and women in labor legislation is well known."[15] Thus the NWP decided to present its case for admission before the convention.

Unable to attend the Paris congress because of her health, Mrs. Catt sent Sherwin letters of opposition to be read to the delegates if necessary. "Do not be afraid of this rumpus," she wrote, "Remember that we are just washing our dirty linen in the International tub." Jane Norman Smith, Doris Stevens, and Burnita Shelton Matthews spoke for the NWP while other Party members attended either as fraternal delegates authorized by ten governors or as part of the very active NWP press contingent. Well-known British feminists such as Chrystal MacMillan, Mrs. Pethick-Lawrence, and Lady Rhondda supported the NWP's case, but the congress upheld the board's decision by a vote of 123 to 48. Eleven members of the Alliance executive board resigned over the issue and Lady Rhondda's Six Point Group withdrew its membership application. "The methods used in respect to the request for affiliation of the NWP, and with a view to preventing the affiliation," she wrote, "have been such that it would not be possible for the Six Point Group to associate itself with them."[16]

Alice Paul announced that the NWP would continue working for equality, and the Alliance board asked the Party to sign a statement to clear up any "false impressions" the public might have about the issues involved. This was designed to save face for all concerned and suggested that the League of Women Voters and the NWP were "willing to work side by side, each according to its traditions and convictions, fully aware of the great aims that unite them." The NWP representatives, of course, refused to sign on the grounds that they had no authority to do so, that it did not coincide with their intentions, and that it in no way expressed the Party's views or wishes. The damage was done, yet the NWP had not come to Paris with the intention of splitting the international feminist movement. When it became evident that those women's groups which favored labor equality might withdraw from the Alliance if membership were withheld from the NWP, Stevens cabled Alice Paul for instructions. "I feel that unless we are ready to carry on international movement ourselves," Paul replied, "we ought to support those doing it and not be responsible for split in their ranks."[17]

The League of Women Voters was forced on the defensive by the adverse publicity this whole affair engendered. In an effort to explain to its members "Why the League Objected," Gertrude Brown pointed out that the NWP often hindered the passage of the League's carefully selected bills because of the wide gap in their views about protective legislation. Concerning labor equality, Brown maintained that "the great mass of women are opposed to this viewpoint" and reiterated that because of their maternal functions women should be protected. The NWP also tried to clarify to its membership the differences between the League and the Party. It was not just the issue of protective legislation which had kept the Party out of the Alliance, Jane Norman Smith declared, but also the NWP's uncompromising attitude on women's need for total equality which was frightening to many women. The International Alliance, too, bore the scars of the conflict between the two groups of feminists. In its call for an eleventh congress to be held in Berlin in 1929, the Alliance attempted to hold together its remaining members by an ideological statement encompassing both gradual citizenship education and future work for total equality, but the result was the defection of the immediatists.[18]

The underlying problem within the Alliance in 1926 was its members' differing views about labor equality for women; this was also a major contributing factor in the LWV's opposition to the Party's bid for membership. The League had managed to prevent the Alliance from issuing any policy statement on the question of protective legislation during the twenties by insisting that the problem needed further study. In January 1926, however, the Alliance committee on like conditions of work for men and women had issued a preliminary report advocating equal educational opportunities for women, equality in the civil service, and equal pay for equal work. With these aims the LWV was in full agreement, but the fourth resolution, dealing with the right of married women to work, contained the recommendation that future labor laws should tend toward equality between men and women. "The problem before us," the committee noted, "is whether restrictions embracing certain groups of workers only inside the same occupation will not restrain or ruin their chances of earning a living." In March the committee resolved that future protective legislation should not be framed in any way that might restrict women's job opportunities, and LWV officials prepared a substitute resolution which they hoped would replace the committee's at the congress. The LWV resolution argued that because of national differences, legislation must be drawn up specifically with regard to "the needs and wishes of working women of that country."[19]

The only real chance of diverting the congress from accepting the committee's report was based on the League's dominant position representing American women, which would be weakened if the NWP were allowed to present its arguments against special legislation. This confusing issue was not settled by the compromise resolution finally passed by the Paris congress, which recommended that "no obstacle should be placed in the way of married women who desire to enter or continue in paid work, and that the laws relative to women as mothers should not be framed as to handicap them in their economic position." A resolution condemning the ILO conventions on night work and hazardous employment for women was defeated. American journalists correctly identified the question of labor equality as the basis of the schisms that were occurring in European feminism, or as the *Survey* reported, "by that issue more than any other one's degree of feminism is measured."[20] Little effort was made, however, to put this European feminist concern with women's right to work into the context of economic dislocations so evident in countries like Great Britain or Germany.

The NWP also emphasized the connection between its rejection by the Alliance and the controversy over labor equality. *Equal Rights* argued that labor equality, much like equal suffrage, could serve "to focus and vitalize the feminist movement." In Jane Norman Smith's notes on the Paris congress, she evaluated the schism in terms of a regrouping of feminists. The basis for this realignment, according to another NWP member, was evident. "They are reformers," she wrote, "we are Feminists."[21]

Feminists who, like the Six Point Group, favored industrial equality for women met to organize the Open Door Council in 1927. Although two NWP officers were present as fraternal delegates, the early membership was overwhelmingly British. The feminists announced that they hoped an international organization could be formed to work for women's labor equality and "to attack the anti-Feminist Labour Bureau of the League of Nations." By the summer of 1929, this hope had been transformed into reality by the organization of the Open Door International in Berlin, which included men as well as women. The ODI manifesto, calling for equal economic freedom, opportunity and status for women workers, expressed a fundamental belief "that a woman as well as a man is an end in herself." The Open Door International also issued an eleven point "Woman Worker's Charter of Economic Rights" demanding that restrictive legislation be based on the job rather than on the sex of the worker and stressing the right of the married woman to engage in paid work of her choice, free from restrictions related to maternity, with complete control over her earnings. The ODI believed that supporters of protective legislation for women were living in the past. "We look to the future, realizing that this economic emancipation has hardly begun," declared their manifesto. "The struggle has become international."[22]

American feminists also had always encouraged the growth of feminism in Latin America. The fifth Pan American Congress, held in

Santiago in 1923, passed a resolution to include a discussion of the rights of women at future conferences, and in 1926, an interAmerican congress of women meeting in Panama City passed an equality resolution. As Mrs. Catt became more involved in her peace work during the mid-twenties, the League of Women Voters' overtures to Latin American women declined, and the stage was set for the NWP to assume a leadership position in the Latin American feminist movement. When the sixth Pan American Congress met at Havana in 1928, representatives of the Party were present and succeeded in getting six countries to sponsor the inclusion of the Equal Rights Treaty, modeled on the Equal Rights Amendment, on the agenda of the seventh conference scheduled for Montevideo in 1933. Even more significant was the Congress' creation of an InterAmerican Commission of Women to study women's status. The Congress appointed NWP activist Doris Stevens as the chair of the Commission.[23]

Party members, delighted with this assertive move into internationalism, compared the influence of the Pan American conferences in the Western hemisphere with the League of Nations' influence on European countries. Pan American states which approved the principle of equal rights would be much less likely to discriminate individually or through international conventions. Such Pan American action would lead the way for the rest of the world, but *Equal Rights* also warned that "if we fail now through carelessness or lack of determination, our grandchildren will then face the always difficult task of abolishing inequalities established now." Since the NWP consistently maintained that feminism should not be limited by national boundaries but rather should encompass the whole world, it immediately announced its intention to promulgate the Equal Rights Treaty at Geneva. The Party believed that the success at Havana had provided a "conclusive demonstration" of "the proper method of procedure hereafter." As an *Equal Rights* editorial pointed out: "The few short weeks of intensive effort at Havana, the comparatively small sum of money invested in it, have already brought rewards greater a thousand-fold than could have been realized through purely national activities."[24] Longtime NWP member Lavinia Dock termed the Party's achievements "glorious" and "almost incredible." "I consider that Party members are classed with all the truly great crusaders," she wrote to Mabel Vernon, "and I don't

understand why everyone doesn't see it.'' In Doris Stevens' analysis
of the Havana accomplishments, she emphasized that women were
finally to be treated as colleagues rather than auxiliaries at international
conferences. Denying that the treaty method was revolutionary, she
cited the ILO conventions which dealt with women's work.[25] In her
speech to the Havana congress she had insisted:

> For you see, no man, no group of men, no government, no
> nation, no group of nations—ever had the right to withhold
> from us the rights we ask today. We ask to have restored rights
> which have been usurped. These are our human rights.[26]

Following its rejection by the International Alliance of Women, the
Party had turned to direct lobbying at the Havana Pan American Conference, the Kellogg-Briand Conference, the Hague Codification Conference, and the League of Nations. The only one of these activities
which could be described as militant was Doris Stevens' attempt to
present the Equal Rights Treaty to the participants at the Kellogg-
Briand Conference in 1928; this action became the most controversial
of the NWP's international efforts. The NWP had requested a one
hour appointment; when the French cabinet rejected the request, the
Party opened a Paris press headquarters and began an active campaign
which led up to the members' appearance before the gates of the
Rambouillet home of President Doumergue while the delegates were
lunching. Carrying a banner which read "We Demand A Treaty
Giving Women Their Rights,'' the women announced they sought a
brief audience. At this point the police intervened, arresting about ten
demonstrators for refusing to obey police orders to clear the area and
for not having their identity cards with them. The feminists displayed
bruises on their arms and wrists to support their charges that the police
had used "excessive energy" in detaining them, but on the whole they
were happy with the publicity resulting from the incident. "It was a
splendid battle,'' said Doris Stevens, "and we are proud of it.''[27]

Alice Paul agreed with this evaluation, and declared to the press:
"We rejoice at the protest raised in Paris. We will do all in our power
to help in the new movement for world-wide equality through international action which these women have so bravely forwarded.'' Other

Party members hoped that the action might hasten suffrage for French women, contrasting the "dignified and idealistic example" of the Pan American diplomats with the French response to women's demands. Mrs. Hooker insisted that since the women's reasonable, quiet, and proper request for a hearing had been ignored, they had no choice but to persist in their support of such an important cause by using other means. Denying that she had planned to disrupt the Kellogg-Briand Conference, Stevens explained that women were amateurs in diplomatic affairs. "We see only the forthright, common-sense way to proceed," she concluded. "That, I think, is often an asset."[28]

She was a bit more frank when speaking to the admiring militants of the Six Point Group in London. "Miss Stevens began by saying that she found it rather refreshing to come among her Feminist colleagues again after a long sojourn among the tribal fathers," Winifred Holtby reported. Stevens emphasized the importance of direct action, warned her listeners about the dangers of boredom, and concluded that "any movement may sag which just goes on in the same humble way from day-to-day." Both Mrs. Belmont and Doris Stevens attended the mass suffrage meeting in Paris endorsing the Equal Rights Treaty, and Stevens made another strong defense of militant actions such as those at Rambouillet. "Of course we lacked tact," she admitted. "We are in revolt."[29]

The first question on which the InterAmerican Commission decided to research and to make recommendations was the problem of married women's nationality. This issue was on the agenda of both the Hague Codification Conference of 1930 and the League of Nations Assembly; the International Alliance of Women had also passed a resolution advocating complete independence of nationality. But this question too became a focus for controversy between the League of Women Voters and the NWP. The League had always supported the principle of independent nationality and had worked throughout the twenties and early thirties for congressional bills which gradually removed the discriminations against married women. But the LWV seemed to fear that the Party would take credit for any advances toward equal nationality rights, and this was obvious by the hostility of the two groups at the Hague Codification Conference. The International Alliance, the League of Women Voters, and the NWP lobbied the conference.

At the first hearings League officials Maud Wood Park and Mrs.
Pittman Potter spoke on behalf of all women, but as LWV attorney
Dorothy Strauss reported, "other women, less reasonable in method,
appeared on the scene as spokesmen for less representative groups of
women and these were permitted to join this second meeting."[30]

The LWV had always objected strongly to being put on a "parity"
with the NWP, and the treaty method of obtaining nationality rights
was just as objectionable to the League as the amendment method of
obtaining equality. When these were combined with the third NWP
proposal, the Equal Rights Treaty, the League felt surrounded by the
threat of the "blanket" legislation to which it had always been opposed
and which it feared would destroy special labor laws for women. The
Hague Conference recommendation was that a woman's nationality
should remain dependent on that of her husband, and the efforts of
organized women shifted to the League of Nations where they lobbied
against ratification of the nationality convention.

In response to the Equal Rights Treaty, British feminists had created
a new organization, Equal Rights International, and in 1930, formally
extended an invitation to the NWP to join. But there was still resistance
within the Party itself to extensive international commitments which
might take precedence over state and national work. When the question
of affiliation with the Open Door International had arisen, there had
been protests that efforts for international equality might spread the
Party's resources too thin, although most members agreed with Mrs.
Belmont's often quoted statement that "no woman can be free anywhere until all women are free." *Equal Rights* stressed the similarities
between the position of the Equal Rights Treaty before the League of
Nations in 1930 and that of the federal suffrage amendment before the
U.S. Congress in 1912. In both instances, the Party journal pointed
out, Alice Paul stood ready to assume the direction of an efficient and
unified campaign. Internationalist members of the NWP believed
that Equal Rights International could provide a catalyst for the approval of the Equal Rights Treaty, and that its Geneva headquarters
could be immensely stimulating to European feminism. The NWP
affiliated with both the Open Door International and Equal Rights
International, and in 1931 the Women's International League for Peace
and Freedom endorsed the equality treaty. A growing nucleus of

feminist support for the Party's position was being established in Europe.[31]

Most of the NWP's European activities during the remainder of the thirties were designed to advance its Equal Rights Treaty through the complicated machinery of the League of Nations. If it had been able to achieve this goal, the treaty would have become an international convention recommended to all member countries for ratification. When first faced with persistent feminist lobbying, the League of Nations' response had been to create a Women's Consultative Committee in 1931, charged with reporting on the status of women and making recommendations concerning equality. But this committee split over the question of protective legislation in 1932, and although as a whole it ceased to function, the sub-committee on propaganda continued its activities on behalf on total equality. Not surprisingly, this subcommittee included six NWP members as representatives of the various participating women's organizations.[32]

The NWP had been able to obtain the support of more than a dozen nations which requested that the Party's equality treaties be brought before the First Commission of the League of Nations. Although the international feminist lobby was finding it increasingly difficult to influence the delegates, the treaties were placed on the agenda, and in 1935, the Juridical Commission spent five days debating the treaties. The Montevideo Equal Nationality Treaty was opened for adherence by all governments, but the League of Nations recommended that individual governments, women's organizations, and the International Labour Office (ILO) study the issues raised by the Equal Rights Treaty. In 1937, revision of the League covenant was on the Assembly's agenda, and the equalitarian feminists led by the NWP suggested four amendments. Social feminists could support the demands for woman suffrage, independent citizenship for married women, and the appointment of women as full voting delegates to all League bodies, but not the fourth suggested revision, the Equal Rights Treaty. Although NWP leaders believed that the suffrage and appointment amendments had the best chances for passage, no decision was reached on any of these equality amendments; in 1938, the League of Nations appointed yet another Committee of Experts to study women's status. Of the four women on this committee, only one, Kerstin Hesselgren of

Sweden, was even slightly sympathetic to total equality, and the U.S. representative was Dorothy Kenyon, a well-known lawyer closely connected with the League of Women Voters.[33]

According to Alice Paul, the equalitarian feminists' strategy was first to get the Equal Rights Treaty on the agenda of the League of Nations assembly, then to build up more support for the treaty by endorsements from international women's organizations, and finally to develop national support for ratification within individual countries. When the NWP did manage to get the Equal Rights Treaty on the agenda for the 1935 meeting, the League of Women Voters drew up a formal protest to be circulated among the League of Nations delegates, describing the treaty as unnecessary, impractical, and harmful, and suggesting that the status of women was a question which still needed intensive study.[34]

Only international organizations could circulate opinions in the League of Nations, but the International Alliance of Women would not annex the LWV statement. The League of Women Voters ultimately turned to the World YWCA to present the protest; the LWV strategy was carefully developed and made known to its officers in the form of a confidential paper. Its main effort would be to get the League of Nations to postpone the issue until further study was done. Other social feminist organizations would be approached for support on the basis that they could avoid expressing an opinion on protective conventions, "which statement they have been trying to avoid for years."[35] The strategy was successful and the League of Nations resolution recommended further study. The political status of women was assigned to individual governments for consideration while the question of protective legislation and its impact on women was assigned to the ILO for research.

It was Mary Anderson, the head of the U.S. Women's Bureau, who spearheaded the efforts of the social feminists to block the progress of the Equal Rights Treaty through the League of Nations. Although carefully instructed, American social feminists in international organizations had found themselves increasingly a distinct minority when advocating protective legislation in the 1930s. "There was practically no support to the [LWV] point of view outside the U.S. delegation," observed its representative to the 1935 Alliance of Women congress.

Mary Anderson encouraged social feminists to write the ILO stating their objections to the Treaty and their support for protective legislation. Anderson also corresponded with Grace Abbott, American delegate to the ILO after the U.S. joined in 1934.[36]

In a private report to American social feminists in June, 1935, Abbott observed that because of Hitler and Mussolini, European women were very much afraid of the closing of economic opportunities for women at all levels. "While we have felt some of the fear of these in the U.S.," Abbott wrote, "I was surprised to find how serious European women feel the situation to be." After consulting with social feminists in Geneva, she concluded that the Equal Rights Treaty had little chance of passage. However, she warned, the Open Door International had been actively urging the solidarity of women, and "the effect of this situation on women, not all of them 'feminists,' has been. . . that some who favor industrial legislation have concluded that at this time they ought to stand for the 'Equal Rights' Treaty."[37]

Throughout 1935, the new LWV president Marguerite Wells kept Secretary of Labor Frances Perkins informed of the social feminists' concern about the Equal Rights Treaty. Perkins responded by instructing the U.S. delegates to the ILO to encourage a full study of protective legislation, to agree with the League of Women Voters' position, and to oppose the Treaty. Social feminists also kept pressure on Harold Butler and other ILO officials. "Miss Paul does not represent the working women of the U.S.," Mary Anderson wrote to Butler. "Her views are diametrically opposed to those of working women, who believe in special legislation for women and work for such legislation through their trade union organizations." The NWP insistently demanded that Perkins urge the ILO to deal with the question of women's right to work, and in a memo to the Secretary of Labor, Anderson argued that the Party just wanted publicity. "It is for the purpose of showing the European women's organizations that they are all-powerful," Anderson wrote, "and for that reason they should support them in putting through the Treaty."[38] Both more accurate and more discouraging was the response of an ILO official to the League of Women Voters' Geneva lobbyist early in 1936. Governments were "nervous about taking a definite line," he wrote.

The resolution of last year is, of course, only a compromise between reluctance to offend the women's organizations and inability to propose any rational form of action by the League; and it seems likely to give us an ill-digested encyclopaedic mass of information but very unlikely to provide us with anything approaching a policy. Being convinced as I am that the most that can emerge from the League's discussion is some form of pious resolution . . . my fear is that the whole affair will slowly progress towards a fiasco which can only do the League harm.[39]

Anderson's most ambitious project was the development of the Women's Charter, intended to serve as an alternative to both the Equal Rights Treaty and the Equal Rights Amendment. In the summer of 1936, a small group of representatives from social feminist organizations began meeting to formulate a charter safeguarding protective legislation for women. Also actively involved in the early planning stages were Mary Van Kleeck of the Russell Sage Foundation, Frieda Miller of the New York State Department of Labor, and historian Mary Beard. Anderson informed Mme. Thibert of the ILO Women's Work division as well as Frances Perkins about the plan. "This is a good move," replied Perkins, "and I would suggest that you continue with the work of this Committee."[40] Although two NWP members had been appointed to the ILO's Correspondence Committee on Women's Work, the Party was excluded from knowledge of and participation in these meetings.

The Women's Charter group experienced difficulties from the beginning. Anderson, Van Kleeck, and a few others insisted upon a strong statement supporting protective legislation, but as one business woman noted, "there are hundreds and thousands of the group I represent who are muddled about this whole thing." Each attempt to broaden the unofficial committee to include other women's organizations, although still excluding the NWP, simply exacerbated the problems. The October meeting foundered over Mary Beard's suggestion that women should be trained to work and should expect to work, which won strong approval from some committee members and equally strong disapproval from others. Mary Anderson expressed the traditional view when she argued that a woman "must remember that when she marries and keeps house she also has a lifetime job." One representative voiced a hope that the Charter "would not be a defense of position against the Woman's Party but would be something else which would include their general idea of wanting to get better status for women." When Van Kleeck argued that the Charter was not merely defensive, another representative of professional women replied that "it was so interpreted by my group." There were heated discussions about whether to include a specific guarantee of the right of married women to work. "We cannot get together with the Woman's Party point of view unless they accept our point of view," insisted Mary Anderson, ". . . unless we sacrifice the working woman."[41]

Although the group managed to establish tentative procedures for publicity, promotion, and endorsement of the Charter, the fundamental problems revealed by the attempt to formulate an alternative to the NWP's equality program were never resolved. Even the social feminists of the ILO Women's Work section had objections to the draft of the Charter. It suggested "a demand for full responsibility and for special privileges at one and the same time," commented Alice Cheyney of the ILO staff in a letter to Anderson. Writing to a friend at the World YWCA six weeks later, Cheyney stated that she had rewritten parts of the Charter but was still not completely satisfied. "It seems to me. . . ," she explained, "to bear too strongly for general appeal, the mark of its immediate origin in a desire to make a case for protective legislation."[42]

In her autobiography, Anderson described the committee as trying to produce a document which all women could endorse, and her hope that "perhaps we could, with this charter, bridge the gap between ourselves and the NWP." This statement is disingenuous at best. The Charter specifically provided for protective legislation for women; when Van Kleeck sent it to Felix Frankfurter for his legal opinion she presented it as an alternative to equal rights. A suggested public presentation of the Charter which stressed its protective aspects was vetoed by representatives of both the LWV and the Consumers' League as impolitic. News of the text was kept from the NWP until Anderson sent it simultaneously to newspapers and women's organizations in December, 1936. Yet the Charter was not a success, in spite of all the careful planning. "But nothing worked out the way we had wanted it to," Anderson wrote. "The movement was a complete flop."[43]

The Charter failed for a number of reasons. The NWP emphasized the secrecy of the planning committee and questioned whether the women involved in drafting the Charter did so with the approval of the organizations they were supposed to represent. Groups like the Business and Professional Women and the American Association of University Women were already badly split over the question of protective legislation. Mary Beard publicly repudiated the draft, while even the American Home Economics Association journal recognized that there were two schools of thought about labor equality. To complicate the situation further, the NWP circulated an amended version of the Charter which substituted the concept of labor laws based only on the job and not on the sex of the worker. As one of the social feminists involved in planning the original Charter replied, "it seems hardly necessary to say that I completely disagree with the changes made by you and your associates, and would under no circumstances support such a revision." Furthermore, large women's organizations like the League of Women Voters insisted that the Charter go through their usual long and involved study procedures, and then often endorsed only the principles, not the actual document.[44]

By 1937, however, the social feminists had effectively blocked the progress of the Equal Rights Treaty through the ILO. At the labor conference that year, Grace Abbott successfully sponsored a resolution requesting further study of women's economic position, supporting the principle of equal pay, and calling for "legislative safeguards against physically harmful conditions of employment and economic exploitation, including the safeguarding of motherhood." The International Alliance of Women protested vigorously, but to no avail, that this action "could not be held to represent the views of women in general," and criticized Abbott for failing to consult with any international women's organizations. In America, Mary Van Kleeck announced the formation of a Joint Committee on Women's Work to implement the ILO resolution; this committee would be open to all women's organizations in sympathy with the Women's Charter.[45] By the end of 1938, the movement for the Charter had died.

The establishment of the World Woman's Party in 1938 was an

event which had been foreshadowed three years earlier by an appeal from Madeline Doty. In a report emphasizing the success of the ILO's Women's Consultative Committee, Doty asked the NWP for funds to acquire a permanent headquarters and staff. In 1936, Alice Paul received official permission from the NWP convention to make the Party an international organization, and two years later the World Woman's Party was established with the NWP as its American section. According to Paul, the WWP would help defend the women of the world while protecting American women against unjust treaties, and it was incorporated as an educational group whose object was "equality without distinction of sex." The thirty-eight incorporators were all NWP members; they elected Alice Paul president and selected an international board of thirty directors.[46]

Even the *Woman's Home Companion*, never a supporter of the NWP or its policies, noted the opening of the World Woman's Party Geneva headquarters with a friendly comment about the "brave and persistent fight" which the NWP had been carrying on for so many years. But the editors were quick to deny that they approved of the ERA, for "in some few ways women can never be on a level with men; not better or worse, not above or below, not less or more, but just different because nature made them so." However, the timing of the new international Party which was to combine all the disparate groups of European and Asian feminists could not possibly have been worse. Soon caught in the rising tide of World War II, groups like the Business and Professional Women of Hungary, the Woman Lawyers' Association of Poland, and other European feminist groups affiliated with the World Woman's Party just before being wiped out of existence. The international Party looked to the future, however, declaring that at the postwar peace conference it would demand that the principle of equality be included in all new constitutions and charters. Describing themselves as "the great new army without arms," the World Woman's Party feminists insisted that "no new world can be built without our advice, our help." But their newly opened headquarters at the Villa Bartholoni was able to do little more than provide temporary shelter for feminist refugees fleeing the advance of fascism. In 1941, Equal Rights International merged with the World Woman's Party, but Alice Paul was forced to return to America that same year. "Women must never again be excluded from the affairs of the world," she insisted to reporters. "There can be no democracy without the participation of women."[47]

The decade also ended badly for the NWP's leadership position in Latin America. The struggle between the social feminists led by the League of Women Voters and the equalitarian feminists led by the NWP was resumed at the Montevideo Pan American Conference in 1933. Sophonisba Breckinridge, a social feminist and U.S. representative, wrote Belle Sherwin that the women's meeting was confused, disorderly, and poorly conducted. The InterAmerican Commission of Women, led by Stevens, had been able to present both the Equal Rights Treaty and the Equal Nationality Treaty to the conference. Breckinridge could only hope that the Commission would be disbanded and that then those Latin American women "who do not share the characteristics of the leading members of the Woman's Party" could be reorganized. When the U.S. abstained from voting on the Equal Nationality Treaty, the publicity was very unfavorable and organized women other than members of the League of Women Voters expressed disapproval of the American action. As Doris Stevens had cabled to the newspapers, "the attitude of the U.S. delegation was not only a matter of great regret and disappointment, but came as a profound shock and surprise."[48]

Belle Sherwin had informed Cordell Hull that although the League of Women Voters favored equal nationality, it opposed the treaty method for achieving this equality, and simultaneously the League had released its objections to the press. Writing later to a member about the unfavorable publicity which resulted, Sherwin admitted that the first League press release had been hastily prepared, somewhat too grudging about the principle of equal nationality, and too flatly opposed to the treaty method in general. She explained that "the League of Women Voters is always on the defensive in respect to the action of the NWP," but went on to justify "the old policy of nonaggressive publicity in relation to points at issue with the NWP." Yet the League did feel compelled later to issue conciliatory press releases, and Dorothy Strauss wrote the *New York Times* to correct any misunderstanding of the League's attitude on equal nationality rights. Denying that Eleanor Roosevelt had intervened on behalf of the League of Women Voters with the State Department, Strauss explained that the League believed the treaty would not accomplish the desired goals and noted that the LWV's longtime interest in efficiency in government had led it to oppose "blanket" methods which might hinder more effective legislation. She also insisted that the League was not opposed to meaningful international agreements on nationality. Yet the underlying reasons for the League's opposition were its rivalry with the NWP and its fear of some future threat to protective laws in the United States. When League officials later testified against the ratification of the Equal Nationality Treaty at the Foreign Relations Committee hearing, it was on the basis that it would open all sorts of other areas to blanket legislation.[49]

The League of Women Voters also finally succeeded in ridding the InterAmerican Commission of Doris Stevens and the NWP influence. Instrumental in this accomplishment was Mary Winslow of the Women's Trade Union League, who began working behind the scenes a full year before the eighth Pan American Conference at Lima. Her first efforts utilized Mollie Dewson's influence in the State Department to get a reliable social feminist appointed to the delegation; this woman would be able to present a resolution safeguarding protective legislation yet speaking out for women's rights. Winslow and other social feminists drafted a resolution and circulated it quietly to selected women's groups. Two women went to Lima as technical advisers to the American delegation and Mary Anderson personally paid the expenses of a third woman, a journalist who would do publicity work. President Roosevelt had approved the resolution as modified by the State Department and had instructed the American delegates to support it. The League of Women Voters had arranged a communications system so that if further support were necessary, endorsements from women's organizations could be obtained and sent to Lima within twenty-four hours of notification.[50]

Social feminists also laid plans to have Stevens replaced as chair of the InterAmerican Commission by a State Department appointee. Mollie Dewson suggested Mary Winslow, while Elisabeth Christman of the Women's Trade Union League and Mary Anderson of the Women's Bureau quietly collected endorsements. Although the NWP leaders countered with a publicity campaign and by lobbying Congress, there is no doubt that they were taken by surprise, both by the Lima resolution and the move to replace Stevens. The State Department had announced Mary Winslow's appointment on February 1, 1939, and two weeks later Marguerite Wells sent her some observations from one of the technical advisers at the Lima conference. The latter believed that Stevens had somehow gained the loyalty of the *New York Times* and therefore was able to secure good publicity. Yet she also thought Stevens was "on the way out, both as a personality and the leader of her particular cause, but she may make quite a struggle getting out." Indeed, Stevens had earlier offered her resignation but the Commission had refused to accept it, so her personal position was somewhat strengthened. However, since she had not been appointed by the U.S., but rather by the Pan American Conference, her legal position was shaky.[51] The advisor suggested that the League of Women Voters make a concerted effort at lobbying, and concluded encouragingly:

> Don't let the people in Washington get discouraged—we had Doris on the run once—we can get her there again. I don't see why the whole thing can't be handled by clever administrative rulings and appointments. You must get the Pan American Union to get over being intimidated by Doris. It's a bad habit people have. She is vulnerable in certain spots.[52]

The NWP counterattacked vigorously by lobbying U.S. Senators and Pan American delegates. Although Stevens had considerable support among the delegates and Senators, including some prominent Democrats, the InterAmerican Commission was reorganized completely in 1940, a Latin American woman appointed chair, and Winslow finally seated as U.S. representative. "We have deplored the agitation regarding feminist issues that have [sic] taken place in South America," Elisabeth Christman had announced to the press in the midst of the leadership struggle, "and feel they have been a great setback to the interests of women."[53] The NWP continued its battle with the social feminists over which group could best represent women's interests. "The situation is and has been for months," wrote Mary Murray of the NWP's industrial council,

> The Governing Board has before it the name of an appointee to a place not vacant, presented by a person having no juris-

diction in affairs of the Board, said person being the highest officer of one of the most powerful countries in the Pan American Union. Not a pleasant position for Board members from neighbor countries.[54]

The NWP's international activism during the twenties led it to assume a dominant position in the Latin American feminist movement and to precipitate, although not cause, a schism in the international women's movement. During the thirties it presented the Equal Rights Treaty and Equal Nationality Treaty for endorsements by women's organizations and passage by international conferences, but it was blocked by social feminists who favored the protective labor conventions of the ILO. By the end of the decade, Alice Paul's attempt to unite European feminists had been overwhelmed by the rise of fascism, while the NWP's leadership in Latin American feminism had been challenged successfully by American social feminists. Both groups of feminists were uncompromising, because at the heart of the matter lay an ideological disagreement over the meaning of economic equality for women.

The final result of more than a decade of international struggle between American social and equalitarian feminists was the development of a total impasse. The ILO study, *The Law and Women's Work* (1939), discussed the problem of women's right to employment, noted that women had historically formed a reserve labor pool, and maintained that there were "certain problems that are always with us, such as the fact of maternity, which underlies them all." The conclusion of the 1939 ILO study differed very little from that of the 1932 ILO report on the same subject, neither condemning nor approving protective legislation for women.[55] And the outbreak of World War II made further debate on the question of women's right to work merely academic, at least for a few years.

NOTES

1. Lemons, *The Woman Citizen*, p. 196; Editorial, "An International Movement," *ER* 11 (November 22, 1924), 324; "A Living Center of Union," *ER* 12 (October 24, 1925), 291; Crystal Eastman, "The

British Labour Women's Conference," *ER* 12 (July 4, 1925), 165–66; Editorial, "The International Movement," *ER* 12 (April 4, 1925), 60; Editorial, "The Sisterhood of Man," *ER* 12 (May 16, 1925), 108.

2. Editorial, "The International Movement," *ER* 12 (May 9, 1925), 100; Crystal Eastman, "Socialist Women of Eighteen Countries Meet at Marseilles," *ER* 12 (September 26, 1925), 261–63; Dr. Caroline Spencer, "The International Parliament," *ER* 1 (January 5, 1923), 373; Editorial, "International Feminism," *ER* 14 bis (May 5, 1928), 100; "Doris Stevens Acclaimed Prize Columbia Alumna," *ER* 20 (February 24, 1934), 29.

3. "Alice Paul Returns," *ER* 27 (April 1941), 31.

4. *Ibid.*

5. Editorial, "The Significance of the Woman's Party," *ER* 14 bis (December 8, 1928), 346; Crystal Eastman, "London Letter," *ER* 12 (May 30, 1925), 125; Hazel Hunkins, "The Significance of the Peeresses Bill," *ER* 12 (August 22, 1925), 221–22; "After Equal Franchise—Equal Rights," *ER* 14 bis (November 10, 1928), 317; "British Women Phrase Demands," *ER* 15 (May 25, 1929), 124–25.

6. Editorial, "The Significance of the Woman's Party," *ER* 14 bis (December 8, 1928), 346; "Miss Gonzales Arrives; Mrs. Belmont Greets Commission," *ER* 14 bis (July 28, 1928), 197–98; Isabelle Kendig Gill, "Speech at the Business Conference, November 17," *ER* 1 (December 1, 1923), 334; Editorial, "An Enviable Record," *ER* 12 (May 2, 1925), 92; "Position of Women in the Soviet Union," *ER* 14 (November 5, 1927), 307; "American Investigation Committee on Conditions of Russian Women," *ER* 14 (January 21, 1928), 395–96; Editorial, "For Those Who Have Eyes," *ER* 14 (November 5, 1927), 308.

7. Editorial, "Our Rights in the Hands of International Bodies," *ER* 12 (August 15, 1925), 212; "Miss Gonzales Arrives; Mrs. Belmont Greets Commission," *ER* 14 bis (July 28, 1928), 198; Editorial, "Our Responsibility," *ER* 19 (August 19, 1933), 226; Editorial, "International Co-operation," *ER* 12 (July 18, 1925), 180; "Treaty Method Best for Wiping Out Inferiority Stigma; speech by Doris Stevens," *ER* 20 (June 16, 1934), 159–60; Editorial, "The Significance of the Woman's Party," *ER* 14 bis (December 8, 1928), 346.

8. Crystal Eastman, "English Feminists and Special Labor Laws for Women," *ER* 12 (April 18, 1925), 77; Helen Ward, "An English-

woman's Views on 'Protection,'" *ER* 12 (May 9, 1925), 102-3; Dorothy Evans, "Woman in the British Civil Service," *ER* 12 (May 16, 1925), 107; Editorial, "A Reversion to Barbarism," *ER* 19 (July 29, 1933), 202; "An Appeal to Women; Resolution adopted by IAWS and EC," *ER* 20 (July 14, 1934), 190; "Civilization Vs. Hitlerism," *ER* 20 (October 6, 1934), 284-85; Monica Whately, "Women Hostages," *ERIFW* 2 (April 11, 1936), 44-46; Alma Lutz, "A Feminist Thinks It Over," *ER* 24 (October 15, 1938), 346.

9. "Woman's Party Aids Porto Rican Women," *ER* 12 (May 16, 1925), 111; Zonia Baber, "Woman Suffrage in Porto Rico," *ER* 13 (July 3, 1926), 165-66; Katherine W. Fisher, "Votes for Porto Rican Women," *ER* 14 (June 11, 1927), 139, 144; "Events in Havana," *ER* 14 (January 28, 1928), 405; "Club Feminino Welcomes Emmissaries," *ER* 14 bis (February 11, 1928), 3; Mrs. L. S. Houston, "Intimate Glimpses of Havana," *ER* 14 bis (February 18, 1928), 13-14; Crystal Eastman, "British Women Fire the First Gun in Their Second Suffrage Battle," *ER* 13 (February 27, 1926), 22-23; "Woman's Party Banners Unfurled for Equal Political Rights in England," *ER* 13 (July 10, 1926), 171; Simone Tery, "American Apostles to France," *ER* 12 (June 20, 1925), 149; "French Suffragists Become Militant," *ER* 14 bis (May 5, 1928), 101-02; Katherine Fisher, "What Led to Militancy in France," *ER* 14 bis (September 15, 1928), 253-54; Katherine W. Fisher, "French Women Renew Campaign," *ER* 14 bis (January 5, 1929), 381-82.

10. Lois Scharf, "The Employment of Married Women During the Depression, 1929-1941," diss. (Case Western Reserve University, 1977); for European economic dislocations, see Renata Bridenthal, "Something Old, Something New: Women Between the Two World Wars," in *Becoming Visible: Women in European History* (Boston: Houghton Mifflin, 1977) edited by Renata Bridenthal and Claudia Koonz, pp. 424-44.

11. Mary Anderson to Mrs. Raymond Robins, May 17, 1926, Mary Anderson Papers, Box 3, SL; Lemons, *The Woman Citizen*, 196; Susan D. Becker, "An Intellectual History of the National Woman's Party, 1920-1941," diss. (Case Western Reserve University, 1975).

12. Belle Sherwin to Anna Wicksell, April 6, 1925; Elizabeth J. Hauser to Anna Wicksell, May 2, 1925; Anna Wicksell to Elizabeth J.

Hauser, May 25, 1925; Carrie Chapman Catt to Belle Sherwin, September 20, 1925; LWV Papers, Series II, Box 51, LC.

13. Carrie Chapman Catt to Belle Sherwin, September 20, 1925; Harriet B. Wells to the Committee on Admissions and Board of the IAWSA, September 22, 1925, LWV Papers, Series II, Box 51, LC.

14. Margery Corbett Ashby to Belle Sherwin, October 10, 1925; Carrie Chapman Catt to Margery Corbett Ashby, October 20, 1925, LWV Papers, Series II, Box 52 LC; Carrie Chapman Catt to Belle Sherwin, October 30, 1925; Belle Sherwin to Carrie Chapman Catt, November 25, 1925, LWV Papers, Series II, Box 51, LC.

15. Margery Corbett Ashby to Alice Paul, December 15, 1925, LWV Papers, Series II Box 51, LC; Crystal Eastman, "The Great Rejection, Part I," *ER* 13 (June 19, 1926), 149; "The International Suffrage Alliance," *ER* 13 (February 27, 1926), 24; "The International Suffrage Alliance," *ER* 13 (March 20, 1926), 48; Margery Corbett Ashby to Carrie Chapman Catt, (confidential letter), March 28, 1926, LWV Papers, Series II, Box 52, LC.

16. Carrie Chapman Catt to Belle Sherwin, May 12, 1926, LWV Papers, Series II, Box 52, LC; "Equal Rights Before the World Congress," *ER* 13 (June 5, 1926), 133–34; "Equal Rights Before the IWSA," *ER* 13 (June 12, 1926), 141.

17. "Equal Rights Before the IWSA," *ER* 13 (June 12, 1926), 141; Editorial, "A Gift of the Spirit," *ER* 13 (June 19, 1926), 148; "The Suffragist Fight Over Industrial Equality," *Literary Digest* 89 (June 12, 1926), 10; Crystal Eastman, "The Great Rejection, Part II," *ER* 13 (June 19, 1926), 149–50; Cable, Alice Paul to Doris Stevens, May 30, 1926; Cable, Doris Stevens to Alice Paul, June 1, 1926; Cable, Alice Paul to Doris Stevens, June 1, 1926; Jane Norman Smith Papers, Box 5, SL.

18. Gertrude Fendall Brown, "Editorially Speaking—Why the League Objected," *Woman Citizen* 11 (July 1926), 24; Jane Norman Smith, "The Different Purposes of the NWP and the League of Women Voters," *ER* 13 (September 18, 1926), 254–55; Editorial, "The Significance of the Woman's Party," *ER* 13 (September 18, 1926), 252; "Equal Rights the Ultimate Aim," *ER* 14 bis (December 22, 1928), 367.

19. IWSA, Committee on Like Conditions of Work for Men and

Women, "Appendix to the Preliminary Report, March 27, 1926," LWV Papers, Series II, Box 51, LC; "Resolution on Legislation for Women in Industry to be Proposed by the LWV," n.d., LWV Papers, Series II, Box 52, LC.

20. Edith Abbott to Belle Sherwin, April 13, 1926, LWV Papers, Series II, Box 101, LC; "Equal Rights Before the World Congress of Women," *ER* 13 (June 5, 1926), 133; "The Suffragists Fight Over Industrial Equality," *Literary Digest* 89 (June 12, 1926), 10–11; Cornelia S. Parker, "feminists and Feminists," *Survey* 56 (August 1926), 502–04.

21. Editorial, "Why the Emphasis?" *ER* 13 (June 12, 1926), 140; Crystal Eastman, "The Great Rejection, Part I," *ER* 13 (June 19, 1926), 150; "From Our Correspondents," *ER* 13 (June 19, 1926), 224; "Notes from 10th Congress, IWSA," 1926, Jane Norman Smith Papers, Box 1, SL.

22. Editorial, "The Six Points," *ER* 14 (June 25, 1927), 156; "The Open Door Council," *ER* 14 (June 4, 1927), 131; "Press Comment," *ER* 14 (July 2, 1927), 159; "Woman Worker's Charter of Economic Rights," *ER* 15 (July 20, 1929), 187.

23. U.S. Department of Labor, Women's Bureau, "Summary of Pan American Conferences Concerning Status of Women, August 1938," WTUL Papers, Box 8, LC; "Equal Rights in the Western Hemisphere," *ER* 14 (January 21, 1928), 395; "Pan American Committee of Seven Completed," *ER* 14 bis (November 10, 1928), 316.

24. Editorial, "Why We Are in Havana," *ER* 14 (January 28, 1928), 402; Editorial, "Showing the Way," *ER* 14 bis (February 25, 1928), 20.

25. Lavinia Dock to Mabel Vernon, May 7, 1928, in *ER* 14 bis (May 19, 1928), 120; Doris Stevens, "Feminist History Was Made at Havana," *ER* 14 bis (March 3, 1928), 29; "In Behalf of the Equal Rights Treaty; address by Doris Stevens," *ER* 14 bis (March 10, 1928), 37–39.

26. "In Behalf of the Equal Rights Treaty; address by Doris Stevens," *ER* 14 bis (March 10, 1928), 37–39.

27. "Equal Rights and the Kellogg Treaties," *ER* 14 bis (September 1, 1928), 235; "Demand for Treaty Causes Arrests," *ER* 14 bis (September 8, 1928), 245–46.

28. "Arrests Increase Support of Treaty," *ER* 14 bis (September 8, 1928), 246–47; Editorial, "Using All Means," *ER* 14 bis (September 15, 1928), 252; Helen Archdale, "International Developments in the Woman's Movement," *Current History* 29 (October 1928), 50–52; Helen Archdale, "A Tribute to American Feminism," *ER* 14 bis (October 13, 1928), 285; "Doris Stevens Addresses International Club," *ER* 14 bis (October 20, 1928), 293–94.

29. Winifred Holtby, "Doris Stevens in London," *ER* 14 bis (November 3, 1928), 310; "Paris Approves Equal Rights Treaty," *ER* 14 bis (December 1, 1928), 339–41.

30. "For Equality in Nationality," *ER* 15 (July 13, 1929), 180–81; Idella Gwatkin Swisher, "Program of the National League of Women Voters," *Congressional Digest* 9 (November 1930), 265–66, 288; IWSA, "Call for Demonstration at the Hague Codification Conference," March 14, 1930, LWV Papers, Series II, Box 101, LC; Dorothy Strauss, "Independent Nationality Through National Laws," *Congressional Digest* 9 (November 1930), 281–82.

31. Editorial, "Shall We Affiliate?" *ER* 15 (September 28, 1929), 266; "Plans for the Equal Rights Treaty," *ER* 16 (August 2, 1930), 203; Editorial, "The Long Arm of the Lever," *ER* 16 (September 27, 1930), 266; Editorial, "Equal Rights International," *ER* 16 (October 11, 1930), 282; Elizabeth Rodgers, "The Open Door International at Geneva," *ER* 16 (January 17, 1931), 397–98; "Open Door Council Meeting," *ER* 17 (May 16, 1931), 117–18.

32. Memorandum, Miss Quinlan to League of Women Voters, October 4, 1933, LWV Papers, Series II, Box 340, LC; Alice Paul, "Report to the Woman's Party Convention, Wilmington, Delaware, November 4 and 5, 1933, by the Committee on International Relations," *ER* 19 (November 25, 1933), 331–32.

33. Editorial, "For the Good of Humanity," *ER* 20 (October 13, 1934), 290; Madeline Z. Doty, "Equal Rights Placed on League Agenda," *ER* 20 (November 10, 1934), 326–27; "Debate at League of Nations," *ER* 21 (October 15, 1935), 1–3; Memorandum, Women's Trade Union League to the Secretary General of the League of Nations, August 23, 1937, WTUL Papers, Box 7, LC; Belle Sherwin to Marguerite M. Wells, August 20, 1935, LWV Papers, Series II, Box 342, LC; Lola Maverick Lloyd, "An International Magna Charta for

Women," *ER* 23 (June 1, 1937), 75; "Woman's Party Representatives in Geneva," *ER* 23 (September 15, 1937), 131; Lola Maverick Lloyd, "Equal Rights on the International Front," *ER* 24 (January 1, 1938), 190, 192; "League of Nations," *ER* 24 (March 1, 1938), 221.

34. Lola Maverick Lloyd, "Feminist Attack," *ER* 20 (November 17, 1934), 333; "Alice Paul Returns," *ER* 21 (July 15, 1935), 1; Alice Paul to Alma Lutz, July 20, 1936, Alma Lutz Papers, Box 6, SL; "Statement Drawn Up by the National LWV of the U.S.A." [1935]; Memorandum, Mrs. Johnstone to Miss Wells, February 25, 1936, LWV Papers, Series II, Box 340, LC.

35. Belle Sherwin to Marguerite M. Wells, August 20, 1935, LWV Papers, Series II, Box 342, LC; "Some Confidential Information of Which Miss Wells has come into possession from an unofficial source," n.d., [1935] LWV Papers, Series II, Box 340, LC.

36. Mollie Ray Carroll to Miss Marsh, February 10, 1935, LWV Papers, Series II, Box 370, LC; Josephine Schain to Mrs. Anne Hartwell Johnstone, June 12, 1935, LWV Papers, Series II, Box 340, LC; Lucy R. Mason to Harold Butler, May 18, 1935, Women's Bureau Papers, Box 843, NA.

37. Grace Abbott, "Women Delegates and the Subject of the Work of Women at the 19th Session of the ILO," typescript, June 1935, LWV Papers, Series II, Box 342, LC.

38. Marguerite Wells to Frances Perkins, October 9, 1935, LWV Papers, Series II, Box 340, LC; Marguerite Wells to Frances Perkins, October 14, 1935; Memo, Frances Perkins to Mr. Wyzanski, October 30, 1935, WRC, Frances Perkins Papers, f. 875, SL; Memo, LWV, January 31, 1936; Memo, Mrs. Johnstone to Marguerite Wells, February 11, 1936, LWV Papers, Series II, Box 340, LC; "Activities Related to International Alliance Since November Board Meeting," April 15, 1936, LWV Papers, Series II, Box 369, LC; Mary Anderson to Harold B. Butler, February 14, 1936, LWV Papers, Series II, Box 342; LC; Alice Paul to Frances Perkins, May 9, 1936; Abby Scott Baker to Frances Perkins, May 18, 1936; Memo, to the Secretary from Mary Anderson re: Miss Paul's Letter, May 21, 1936, Women's Bureau Papers, Box 848, NA.

39. H. McKinnon Wood to Mrs. Pitman Potter, May 26, 1936, LWV Papers, Series II, Box 369, LC.

40. Mary Beard to Mary Anderson, August 10, 1936; Mary Anderson to Mme. Marguerite Thibert, August 10, 1936; Memo to the Secretary from Mary Anderson, September 4, 1936; Memo from the Secretary to Mary Anderson, September 16, 1936, Women's Bureau Papers, Box 855, NA. The ILO Correspondence Committee on Women's Work included social feminists Mary Anderson, Elisabeth Christman, Mary Dingman, Elizabeth Morrisey, Mary Van Kleeck and Ethel Smith as well as NWP members Burnita Shelton Matthews and Lena Madesin Phillips.

41. Minutes, Conference, Women's Subcommittee on ILO, September 9, 1936; Minutes, Meeting of October 7, 1936, Rough Draft, Women's Bureau Papers, Box 855, NA.

42. Alice S. Cheyney to Mary Anderson, October 7, 1936; Alice S. Cheyney to Mrs. Beresford Fox, November 20, 1936, (copy), Women's Bureau Papers, Box 855, NA.

43. Anderson, *Woman At Work*, p. 211; Mary Van Kleeck to Felix Frankfurter, October 16, 1936; "Memorandum Regarding Interpretation of Women's Charter," from Mary Van Kleeck to Dorothy Kenyon and Lucy R. Mason, January 13, 1937; Mary Anderson to Lucy Mason, December 10, 1936, NCL Papers, Box C 16, LC; Note, December 23, 1936, WTUL Papers, Box 7, LC.

44. "A Dangerous Document," *ERIFW* 2 (December 26, 1936), 341; "Beware of the 'Women's Charter,'" *ER* 23 (January 15, 1937), 4; "Equal Rights Treaty vs. the Women's Charter," *ER* 23 (March 1, 1937), 27; Letters to members of BPW and AAUW, Alma Lutz Papers, Box 4, SL; "Proposal for a Women's Charter," *Independent Woman* 16 (January 1937), 10; Elizabeth Baker et al., "About the Women's Charter," *Independent Woman* 16 (March 1937), 72–74; *New York Times*, January 10, 1937, p. 6; Lucy R. Mason to Mary Anderson, May 20, 1937, NCL Papers, Box C 16, LC; "Women's Charter," *Journal of Home Economics* 29 (March 1937), 180–82; Lucy R. Mason to Edith Houghton Hooker, March 1, 1937, NCL Papers, Box C 16, LC.

45. *Minutes of the 81st Session of the Governing Body of the ILO, Prague 6–9 October 1937* (Geneva: ILO, 1937), p. 112; Ethel M. Johnson, "Women and the International Labor Organization, 1919–1945," mimeograph, Women's Bureau Papers, Box 1698, NA;

Katherine Bompas to Presidents of Alliance Auxilliaries, October 12, 1937, LWV Papers, Series II, Box 369, LC; Mimeograph, "Announcement of Organization of Joint Committee on Women's Work," March 10, 1938, Women's Bureau Papers, Box 855, NA.

46. Madeline Z. Doty, "Help Create A Feminist World Center," *ERIFW* 1 (June 22, 1935), 124, 126; "A Message From Alice Paul," *ER* 22 (November 15, 1936), 1–2; "World Woman's Party Launched," *ER* 24 (October 15, 1938), 343; "Official Action Creates World Woman's Party," *ER* 24 (December 1, 1938), 371.

47. Editorial, "Equal Rights," *Woman's Home Companion* 66 (April 1939), 2; Maximilian Kessler, "The WWP's War-Time Preparedness," *ER* 26 (February 1940), 7; Anna Hamburger-Ludwig, "The First Anniversary of the World Woman's Party," *ER* 26 (November 1940), 32; Amy C. Ransome, "The World Woman's Party," *ER* 26 (December 1940), 34; "Meeting of the Executive Council," *ER* 27 (January 1941), 27; "Alice Paul Returns," *ER* 27 (April 1941), 1.

48. Sophonisba Breckinridge to Belle Sherwin, December 8, 1933, LWV Papers, Series II, Box 340, LC; "First Equal Rights Convention to be Signed at Montevideo," *ER* 19 (December 23, 1933), 363.

49. Cable, Belle Sherwin to Cordell Hull, December 14, 1933; Belle Sherwin to Mrs. Henry Goddard Leach, December 20, 1933; League of Women Voters press release, December 20, 1933; Dororthy Strauss to the Editor of the *New York Times*, December 19, 1933, (copy), LWV Papers, Series II, Box 340; LC; League of Women Voters, "Statement to the Foreign Relations Committee Opposing Ratification of the Equal Nationality Treaty," n.d., LWV Papers, Series II, Box 295, LC.

50. Mary Winslow, "The Story of the Lima Conference, Confidential, Not For Release," April 1939, WTUL Papers, Box 8, LC.

51. *Ibid.*; Memorandum, Marguerite Wells to Mary Winslow, February 13, 1939, LWV Papers, Series II, Box 418, LC.

52. Memorandum, Wells to Winslow, 1939, LWV Papers, Series II, Box 418, LC.

53. *New York Times*, December 10, 1938, p. 8; December 19, 1938, p. 2; December 21, 1938, p. 12; January 8, 1939, II, p. 4; February 2, 1939, p. 21; February 3, 1939, p. 8; February 17, 1939, p. 3; March 3, 1939, p. 10; Press release, January 4, 1939, WTUL Papers, Box 8, LC.

54. Mary Murray, "Muchas Gracias, Senator Burke," *ER* 25 (September 1939), 111.

55. International Labour Office, Studies and Reports, Series I, *The Employment of Women and Children*, #4 *The Law and Women's Work* (Geneva: ILO, 1939), pp. ix, xi, 347, xi, 565. See also #2 *Women's Work Under Labour Law* (Geneva: ILO, 1932).

6

THEY ARE REFORMERS—WE ARE FEMINISTS

The NWP's activism brought it into conflict with almost all the other organized American women's groups during most of the twenties and thirties. Part of this conflict stemmed from the lingering antagonisms and personality clashes of the Party's militant role in the suffrage struggle, another part of the problem was the NWP members' tendency to present themselves as the only "pure" feminists of the postsuffrage period, but most importantly, the ERA along with the Equal Rights Treaty seriously threatened the social feminists' achievements in securing protective legislation for women.

The two major women's organizations that took the lead in opposing the NWP were the League of Women Voters and the U.S. Women's Bureau. Next in importance were the Women's Trade Union League and the Consumers' League, although both of these groups lost strength in the twenties and by the thirties were reduced to only skeleton organizations. On the other hand, the American Association of University Women and the Business and Professional Women were examples of neutral groups which retained their membership or even grew in strength during the era. The opposition within the AAUW was effectively neutralized by the late twenties while the organization studied the Equal Rights Amendment. The BPW became increasingly concerned about economic discriminations encountered by its members during the twenties, and in the thirties it became the first major women's organization to endorse the ERA.

Some other women's groups which were opposed to the Amendment but did not enter the struggle very actively were the National Council of Jewish Women, the National Council of Catholic Women, the General Federation of Women's Clubs, and the YWCA. Most of these organizations were part of the Women's Joint Congressional Committee during the early twenties; the Committee lobbied regularly against the Amendment after its introduction in 1923. But during the decade the Committee experienced the withdrawal of many of its supporting organizations such as the Daughters of the American Revolution, the General Federation of Women's Clubs, the Women's Christian Temperance Union, the Women's International League for Peace and Freedom, the National Association of Colored Women, and the National Council of Women, and these defections left it with much less influence on Congress.

Although no historian has dealt primarily with the NWP during these two decades, J. Stanley Lemons has studied its opponents, the social feminists, during the twenties. Social feminism reached its peak in the period between 1920 and 1925, but began to decline drastically after the defeat of the child labor amendment. Lemons believes social feminism was fragmented and weakened by a combination of attacks from conservatives, adverse judicial decisions, and the struggle with the equalitarian feminists of the NWP. Although he admits that Party members were well-educated, highly motivated, and talented, Lemons claims that their tactics included infiltration of professional women's organizations in order to divert the energy of these groups toward the ERA.[1]

Actually, in many cases the NWP members founded or were early members of these professional organizations because of their own personal qualifications and interests. Both Gail Laughlin and Lena Madesin Phillips were active in the early organization of business and professional women which led to the establishment of the BPW in 1919. Phillips also founded the International BPW in 1930, and was president of the National Council of Women from 1930 to 1935.

Burnita Shelton Matthews was elected president of the National Association of Women Lawyers in the same year in which she resigned from the Party's national council because of her disagreements with the Party old guard; Laura Berrien became president of the National Association of Women Lawyers in 1938, some time after they had come out in favor of the ERA. When Mrs. Harvey Wiley was elected president of the D.C. General Federation of Women's Clubs in 1932, she used the opportunity to resign as NWP chariman. Many NWP members had belonged to the Women's International League for Peace and Freedom in its prewar organizational days as the Women's Peace Party and had a genuine and sincere desire to work for world peace. It was also natural for many NWP members, as college graduates, to belong first to the Association of College Alumnae and later to its successor, the American Association of University Women. NWP members who had belonged at one time to the Consumers' League or the Women's Trade Union League, like Alice Paul, Maud Younger, Edith Houghton Hooker, Josephine Casey, and Florence Bayard Hilles, dropped out during or immediately after the suffrage campaign. Very few NWP members ever belonged to the League of Women Voters unless, like Caroline Lexow Babcock or Florence Kitchelt, they had worked within the League for years, become disillusioned with its methods and then joined the NWP.

William O'Neill has also dealt with the NWP in his history of feminism in the United States, *Everyone Was Brave*. Integral to his thesis is what he believes was the tremendous decline of feminism in the twenties, and he maintains that the equalitarian feminists were especially affected. Arguing that the NWP never really understood the "social feminist impulse," he points out that it underestimated the opposition to the ERA and overestimated its own potential strength. Describing the members of the NWP as haughty, uncooperative, truculent, tactless, and generally offensive, he concludes that they were basically agitators unable to make realistic political decisions. O'Neill characterizes the Party as caught in its own mystique because of the romanticism of its leaders, suggesting that such militant feminists could not avoid becoming man-haters or being drawn to other women in their movement. Although he is willing to concede that the NWP analyzed the woman problem more correctly than the social feminists, he insists that its militancy "insured the defeat of those hopes it meant to advance."[2]

By failing to note the Party's postsuffrage transition away from militant tactics and the very definite changes in the composition of its leadership and membership, O'Neill has been led to overstate his case. It is true that the NWP sometimes gloried in its solitary position, particularly in the early twenties. The equal rights movement, wrote Lavinia Egan, "is the only purely feminist movement in the world." NWP members also took for themselves the claim that they were the straight line descendants of the earlier women's rights advocates, insisting that their only novel idea was to write into the Constitution "a formal and decisive declaration of the Equality of woman with man." But they understood very soon after the introduction of their ERA that the major opposition centered on the effects of the Amendment on welfare legislation for women and children, particularly protective laws. By the late twenties, the Party concluded that many of its failures on the state level were due more to apathy than to direct opposition, but this only had the effect of encouraging them again to concentrate on the federal amendment.[3]

The NWP reaction to the opposition varied according to who opposed the Amendment, what tactics were used, and how discouraged the equalitarian feminists were at the time of the opposition. The Party had always favored public debate on feminist issues, convinced that reason, logic, and justice would win out in the end. The NWP believed that the arguments of the opposition often were as important as those of the proponents in convincing people to support a cause such as suffrage or the ERA. "All that a just case ever needs is to get the opposition out into the open;" editorialized *Equal Rights*, "then the jury of the people can decide." In 1924, when the struggle was just beginning in earnest, Lavinia Dock wrote that it was distressing to be "separated from old associates in the woman movement, and hard to differ from trade union friends, when one is still heart and soul in sympathy with labor." She argued that it was the mass of unorganized women in the home and their intermittent availability to the labor market that lowered the standards for women in industry. The solution, as Dock saw it, however, was not protective legislation but rather more trade union organization work among women.[4]

On the other hand, NWP members would not tolerate what they believed were the unfair tactics of the opposition. Both sides of the protective legislation question included women who had been active in the labor movement and were either working women or former working women. When the Consumers' League denied that NWP supporters were "genuine" working women, implying that the Party was the tool of exploiting employers, the NWP struck back editorially. *Equal Rights* denounced name-calling as the last resort of people beaten by fair arguments, and declared that "grave and inexcusable injustice has already been done a number of prominent labor women by this means." The editorial also noted that some members of Congress could not afford to be identified with employers and often had to sacrifice their real opinions if threatened with such embarrassing untruths.[5] But just as O'Neill claims, Party members were often tactless. In 1924, the militant NWP lawyer Gail Laughlin summed up the opposition to the ERA as follows:

> Some oppose our program because they still believe that women were created solely for the comfort and glory of men. Some oppose it because they think that "anything new is scandalous." Some oppose it because equality for women affects their selfish interests. Some oppose it because they would rather play up-lifter to the weak than give the weak a weapon which would make them strong; but, for the most part those opposed or indifferent are opposed or indifferent because they do not know the facts and have not been aroused to their responsibility to do justice.[6]

Briefly stated, this meant the opposition was either reactionary, selfish, patronizing, or stupid; Laughlin did not do justice to those who sincerely believed in the necessity of special labor legislation for women.

The NWP was more patronizing than harsh in its reaction to the opposition of groups such as the National Council of Catholic Women. In 1925, the Party noted that the Council had been asked by its executive board to oppose the ERA after having been told that women already had all the rights to which they were entitled. When the board's recommendation was accepted without protest, the Party pointed out that "subjected peoples acquire the psychology of subjection." Just as men long imprisoned might fear freedom, so some women might fear equality, and the timidity displayed by such women was just another argument for the ERA. Contrasting the American Catholic women with St. Joan's Social and Political Alliance of English Catholic women for equal rights, the NWP pleaded that if American Catholics could not help in the struggle for equality, at least they could refrain from obstructing it.[7]

By the late thirties, the opposition from some women's organizations had begun to dwindle and endorsements of the Equal Rights Amendment increased. But the League of Women Voters, the Women's Bureau, and the remnants of the Consumers' League and Women's Trade Union League remained adamantly opposed to the Amendment and the Party. NWP members were both confused and defensive. They admitted that women's opposition to feminist goals was always the most baffling and irritating, for it seemed like betrayal. Since the question of protective legislation had changed its complexion with the coming of New Deal labor legislation for both men and women, the Party could not understand further opposition to the ERA unless the real reason was that the opponents believed "honestly and sincerely, that women as a sex cannot go it alone." To equalitarian feminists, this was an intolerable philosophy which relegated women to a kind of subhuman position.[8]

The presence of the Roosevelts in the White House was also a source of continuing concern to equalitarian feminists, who described President Roosevelt as "a peninsula, almost completely surrounded by women who believe in protective labor legislation for women only." Party members also resented the fact that their motives were suspect by much of the media because of their social class, while the Roosevelts' were not. In 1938 a Party member replied to a query about what the well-dressed leaders of the NWP were going to do about fundamental economic problems by asking: "Why is it that so many writers like to jump all over the NWP and particularly like to refer to the 'well-dressed leaders'?" The NWP was not organized to solve fundamental economic problems, member Ruth Williams pointed out, and she concluded somewhat peevishly: "How is it that the NWP is suspected and ridiculed because of a few well-dressed members when the 'forgotten men and women' are supposed to be sincerely represented by such wealthy individuals as the President and Mrs. Roosevelt?"[9]

In her 1935 critique of feminism, journalist Genevieve Parkhurst expressed the confusion of outside sympathizers concerning the hostility among organized women's groups. Parkhurst believed the basic difficulty stemmed from the suffrage days and the disagreement over the tactics of the militants working for the federal amendment. This split on both principles and procedures, she maintained, had been carried over into the twenties and into the attempts to remove remaining laws which discriminated against women. It the meantime, more than eleven million working women were caught between the equalitarian feminists and the social feminists. Parkhurst believed that the economic situation of American women was especially serious, and blamed it on women's organizations. If they had just been able to come to some agreement, they could have protected women from the injustices of the depression. But instead, feminists had lost sight of women's basic needs, Parkhurst concluded, and "unable to agree on processes, they worked at fruitless and often destructive cross-purposes."[10]

In the thirties there was a slight increase in feeling among some members of both the NWP and the League of Women Voters (LWV) that cooperation might be possible, especially on the issue of married women's right to work. Organized women joined together in requesting the Women's Bureau to undertake a study of the effects of the married persons' clause of the Government Economy Act on women's job security. The preliminary study was completed in 1935 and a fuller study issued in 1936. Three-fourths of the "persons" who had lost their jobs under the application of the Economy Act were married women, and it had fallen with particular severity on lower grade employees in the Treasury and Commerce Departments and the Veterans' Administration.[11] The 1935 hearings on bills to repeal Section 213 were one of the few instances in which the NWP appeared on the same side as the League of Women Voters.

As late as 1940, Mrs. Harvey Wiley still had not given up hope of cooperation. Writing to Alma Lutz about conversations with a Boston officer of the LWV concerning married women's right to work, Wiley described the League member as very nice and not at all contentious. Both women had expressed the hope that the two groups could overcome their differences, and Mrs. Wiley suggested that Frances Perkins, whom she described as the "Number One married woman with a job, living husband, and all," might be willing to help. As Wiley concluded: "Maybe these dreadful attacks on women may serve to show the other side the light, that without implementation, their wishful hope that marital status should *not* be a bar to employment, cannot be granted without our amendment, or something like it."[12]

But the competition between the League and the NWP which began in the mutual dislike and distrust engendered by the suffrage campaign continued throughout the period almost unabated. The League of Women Voters, organized by Mrs. Catt as the states gradually granted suffrage, was uncertain in its purpose and direction during the first two years after the ratification of the Nineteenth Amendment. Its first president, Maud Wood Park, had noted that "the members were interested in peace almost to the exclusion of every other topic." Part of the League's confusion stemmed from an uncertainty as to whether women would be an independent force or would be integrated into the political system. The compromise the League reached was to support reform programs as well as to educate women so they could work more effectively within political parties. The League continued to be made up of middle and upper class women interested in a wide spectrum of issues, with a decision-making process based on the greatest possible study and consensus, and a reluctance to be identified as a feminist organization. But a major problem was the concept that within the League, women should be nonpartisan, but outside the League they should join political parties. Describing this as "an ambivalent, not to say schizophrenic attitude," Mildred Adams concluded that "the essence of the League, its pride and at times its stumbling block, lay in that word 'nonpartisan.' "[13]

At least part of the difficulty could be traced to the president emerita and her major influence on the League of Women Voters. Just as the NWP was closely identified in its objectives and tactics with the personality of Alice Paul, so the League took its image from Carrie Chapman Catt. Yet neither woman was active in the day-to-day decisions of her organization during the twenties and thirties. Mrs. Catt's international interests had led her to found the International Woman

Suffrage Alliance as early as 1902, and she continued to be active in promoting international feminism through the inclusion of Pan American women in the League of Women Voters' convention in 1922, her tour of South America in 1922 and 1923, and most of all, her organization of the Conference on the Cause and Cure of War in 1925. She actively supported the Kellogg-Briand peace pact, the World Court, and the cause of disarmament. In 1932 she retired as head of the Conference, but the next year led a petition campaign among prominent non-Jewish women to protest Nazi persecution of Jews. Her last activity was the plan for a 1940 centennial celebration of the origins of the women's movement at the World Anti-Slavery Convention of 1840.[14] Although Mrs. Catt did not really lead her organization during this period, like Alice Paul, she intervened in times of crisis, such as when the NWP applied for admission to the International Alliance of Women in 1926.

Mrs. Catt believed that after suffrage women possessed the tool which they needed to gain other reforms and that their task was to prove themselves worthy of the suffrage they had gained. She stressed citizenship education and welfare legislation as primary goals for women. Nations existed for their children, she argued, and women's task was to make a better world for the next generation. It was Mrs. Catt's hope that women and men could work together now that women had the vote; she saw no further need for purely feminist programs. Commenting on this ideal, Crystal Eastman wrote that "there is revealed a sort of high-minded altruistic confusion more inimical to the progress of feminism than the effects of the Catholic Church."[15]

Nation was not very impressed with the League of Women Voters in the twenties, either. Complaining that the League had avoided controversial questions such as birth control, opposed the NWP's policy of equality, and taken no stand on economic issues or the question of women in political office, *Nation* concluded that the League would never become "a fighting force." Anne Martin, who did not think too highly of her former associates in the NWP, nonetheless criticized Mrs. Catt harshly:

> There is no doubt that Mrs. Carrie Chapman Catt sounded the doom of feminism for many years to come when she urged the newly enfranchised American women humbly to "train

for citizenship," to join men's parties, "to work with the party of your choice,"—exactly where men political leaders wanted them, bound, gagged, divided and delivered to the Republican and Democratic parties. This cataclysmic blunder led to the colossal futility of the League of Women Voters' "Get Out the Vote" campaign in recent elections. Get out the vote? For what?[16]

The NWP did not come out much better in Martin's analysis, for she suspected the Party tended to put its own advancement first, and she criticized NWP members for being jealously exclusive about their feminism.[17]

Jane Norman Smith wrote to Martin about her charges that the Party had failed to cooperate with other women's groups, pointing out that in New York social feminist leaders had met at the instigation of the League of Women Voters in 1923 to draft and introduce legislation in such a way as to prevent the NWP from introducing its equality bills. The only instance of social feminist cooperation that Smith was able to recall was when the LWV invited the New York NWP to take a table at a large jury service bill luncheon and the NWP accepted. According to Mrs. Smith, the only "live" women's organization in the state was the NWP; other women's groups were overly cautious. "At their State conventions, the League of Women Voters admit that they cannot take action on any liberal subject without encountering intense opposition from their more conservative members," she wrote. "Many resigned over birth control!"[18]

The NWP had initiated an attempt to present a united front with its suffrage celebration ceremonies in 1921, in which all women's organizations were invited to participate. Writing to Maud Wood Park, Alice Paul emphasized that "in every way an effort will be made to give this ceremony a universal rather than a partisan character." The League's board of directors voted in writing, and decided to send a wreath to the ceremonies but not to attend. The League did agree to send a representative to the meeting for the exchange of legislative programs among women's organizations, but the old NAWSA members' distrust of the NWP was evident in the confidential comments of the League's board members. "Their requests seem simple enough," wrote one, "but if we are associated with them in any way it might result in harrassing entanglements later." Another member suspected that the NWP might try to duplicate the League's work, and replied that she wanted to keep away from the Party. "I am opposed to all connections or any connection with the Woman's Party and its convention," stated Mrs. James Paige flatly, and only Dr. Valeria Parker and Mary McDowell voted for participation. Although Mrs. Catt did not vote, she suggested that the League representative meet with the NWP, invite them to disband, and offer them the opportunity of gaining some positions and offices at the next League convention. The conference of women leaders met in December, 1921, but the failure to come to an agreement over the introduction of the ERA, the question of the Party's stand on protective legislation, or even the meaning of equality left the NWP isolated and in opposition to the majority of organized women again.[19]

The League of Women Voters began its opposition to the Equal Rights Amendment in the twenties, but it would be a mistake to believe that this opposition overshadowed all its other activities. League officers did fear, however, and with some reason, that many of their members did not clearly understand the reasons for the League's opposition to the Amendment and might be won over to the NWP. The League was caught between its established policy that it was bad strategy for women's groups to fight each other publicly, and the suspicion that if it did not counteract NWP publicity it would lose control of its own membership. In the early twenties, a New York League officer wrote to Maud Wood Park that the state League was trying hard to educate its members in the importance of protective legislation and to show them how the Amendment would destroy such legislation. Yet even this officer believed that personal antagonisms were the major cause of the struggle between the two organizations. "I have felt that in a number of instances the old suffragists who had been hampered, irritated and distressed for years and years over the members of the Woman's Party and their attitude," she wrote, "had been perhaps uncompromising in trying to get on with them." Jane Norman Smith of the New York NWP was appalled at the League tactics during the twenties and wrote Alice Paul "to tell her what a failure I was and that I was a mere babe in the woods compared to these women." Smith's complaint was that when the NWP did all the work and got the bills into the state legislature, the League would take credit for their passage. Contrary to the contemporary evaluation of Alice Paul by her enemies, she must be credited with her reply. According to Smith, Paul answered that "it makes no difference who gets credit for them, as long as they go through."[20]

The national League solicited opinions of eminent jurists against the ERA, while the local Leagues consistently opposed any blanket equality bills the NWP introduced in state legislatures. The distrust between members of the two organizations grew as it became increasingly difficult during the later twenties to get any "women's bills" through state legislatures. Jane Norman Smith had long suspected that Belle Moscowitz was obstructing NWP measures in New York state. "Undoubtedly the League of Women Voters and welfare workers are working quietly against us through her," she wrote. "I don't trust any of them." The League, on the other hand, collected stories which disparaged the working women whom the Party represented as being in agreement with industrial equality. The League also followed the NWP's example and took to the airwaves with its "Voters' Service" in the late twenties, causing one NWP member to complain that "it seems like the League of Women Voters has some awful personal drag with NBC."[21]

Both sides also rushed into print, with articles by individuals in popular magazines, printed debates, pamphlets, and other literature. Writing to the League of Women Voters president in 1924, Esther Dunshee urged that the League's activities against the ERA be more positive and aggressive. What really concerned her, she explained, was that some members thought that the League should support the ERA because the principle of equality "should be established at any cost as one of the basic principles of our government." After an NWP speaker addressed the Tacoma League of Women Voters in 1924, it endorsed the Amendment on the spot and sent a resolution to that effect to Congress. As the national League's executive secretary wrote to Julia Lathrop, "this raises a number of interesting questions as to the freedom of local leagues in matters of this kind."[22]

Esther Dunshee gave radio talks and wrote articles in the League's journal, the *Woman Citizen*, primarily to explain the opposition to the

ERA to the League's own members. In the twenties her main arguments were that the Amendment was vague and would be open to court interpretation, that it would wipe out twenty-five years of advances in protective legislation, and that it would not really accomplish its objective of equality. The well-known Dr. Alice Hamilton was also frequently pressed into service to present arguments against the Amendment. In a published debate with Doris Stevens in 1924, Dr. Hamilton stressed her objection to the admendment method because it would destroy protective legislation for women. She pointed out that women were usually in the labor force for a relatively short period, were difficult to organize into trade unions, and needed protective legislation to enable them to complete with men. "The belief in the 'equality of the sexes,' interpreted to mean their essential identity," she admitted, "is very attractive to many people." She confessed that this idea had once appealed to her, but insisted that her experience had shown her that while all workers in dangerous trades needed protection, the courts and legislatures would only agree to the special needs of women.[23]

The League also increasingly emphasized its objections to the legal aspects of the ERA. Executive secretary Gladys Harrison wrote to Belle Sherwin in the late twenties that there was a real analogy to be found with the Prohibition Amendment, "an example of bad lawmaking in the technical sense." It had been her experience in working against the Minnesota blanket equality bill that people were more impressed with the opinions of prominent jurists than with arguments based on protective legislation. Harrison wrote a widely distributed League pamphlet, "Against Equal Rights by Constitutional Amendment," in which she emphasized the legal objections to the Amendment. Literature produced by the League was submitted to a committee of experts for suggested revisions, and when Gladys Harrison sent the anti-ERA pamphlet to Sophonisba Breckinridge at the University of Chicago, she explained that the NWP's "plausible arguments make converts when they are not directly met." Harrison thought the League's pamphlet must be carefully reviewed "to be protected against any comeback" and concluded: "I should be very comforted to have your frankest comments."[24]

In the thirties the League continued to oppose the Amendment while attempting to pass specific state bills removing discriminations against women. The League opposed restrictions on business and professional women, the *Woman Citizen* insisted, but industrial women needed protection. A "panacea" like the ERA would not be beneficial to both groups. When the League's national chairman for the legal status of women tried to draw up a list of discriminations still in force, however, she encountered difficulties. "Our League has been without a chairman of this committee for some time," replied an officer of the Maryland League of Women Voters, "due chiefly to the fact that most of our women lawyers are active in the Woman's Party." In the thirties, the League's anti-Amendment arguments included the ideas that equality was relative, that the amendment was both unnecessary and uncertain, and that although ideally labor laws should apply to both men and women, half a loaf was better than none. After the passage of the Fair Labor Standards Act, the protective legislation argument was less prominent, but the opposition of the League became more intense as support for the Amendment increased both in Congress and among organized women. The League took the initiative in attempting to persuade the NWP to join them in a radio debate after the Republican platform of 1940 favored submitting the Amendment to the states, but NWP members were suspicious. They feared being too closely identified with the Republican party and did not want a confrontation with Eleanor Roosevelt and the Democratic women. As NWP activist Anita Pollitzer complained, "anyone might be enveloped in a web of insidious planning on their part."[25]

The differences with the League of Women Voters over the ERA did not end with the thirties, but continued into the 1940s. Even after the Amendment was reworded by the Senate Judiciary Committee, Carrie Chapman Catt still thought it was "a snare and a delusion." League president Marguerite Wells argued that the ERA would be another step toward the centralization of government control, and League lawyer Dorothy Strauss described it as "a glib formula [and] a panacea for existing discriminations, a get-rich-quick short cut to social justice." Other League stalwarts, such as Florence Kitchelt, were converted to the support of the Amendment. Writing to a friend still in the League, Kitchelt identified the source of the League's long opposition in the original suffrage split between the militants and the conservatives. "It was the militants who proposed the Equal Rights Amendment," she wrote, "and therefore we of the League, working day and night to get the League organized (1920-1923) would not touch it with a ten foot pole." She believed the League's position on protective legislation had been weakened because the American Federation of Labor obviously wished to reduce the number of women competing for jobs, and because during the New Deal protective legislation based on sex had become an anachronism. Kitchelt had asked the League officers to reopen study of the Amendment; when they refused, she joined the NWP. "But I do wish the tragedy of this old feud could be written off," she concluded, "by intelligent examination of the Amendment."[26]

The League of Women Voters played a leading role in opposing the NWP and the Equal Rights Amendment, but Mary Anderson of the U.S. Department of Labor's Women's Bureau was equally active in opposition. Anderson had been an industrial worker herself and was very active in the movement for protective legislation for women only. After World War I, the Women in Industry service had evolved into the Women's Bureau, headed by Anderson throughout these two decades; it primarily conducted research and issued studies dealing with women's employment. Anderson supported women's right to work and the concept of equal pay for equal work, but she was an implacable enemy of the NWP and the Equal Rights Amendment, as well as of any international treaties which would destroy special labor legislation for women. In her autobiography published in 1951, Anderson called the ERA "nothing more than a good slogan" and maintained that the advocates of protective legislation really tried to work with the NWP to find a compromise wording for the Amendment. Anderson claimed that the NWP at first denied the ERA would do away with protective legislation and later reversed its attitude, arguing that, since special labor legislation handicapped women, its elimination would be a good thing. She characterized NWP feminists as "past masters in the art of getting publicity," and admitted that in the twenties the Women's Bureau tried to combat Party activities directly. "But after a while we found it was not worth doing," Anderson concluded. "We could not meet their hysterical prejudices with any facts that would get their attention, so we gave it up."[27]

Actually, Mary Anderson was equally active during the thirties, working against the NWP both in the United States and abroad. There were several instances when Anderson and the NWP came into direct conflict, beginning in 1926 with the Conference on Women in Industry called by the Women's Bureau. The day before the conference the Party held a mass meeting on the restrictive effects of special legislation, leading a delegation of working women to see President Coolidge. During the conference itself, Party delegate Gail Laughlin moved to change the next morning's program to a discussion of equal rights in industry, and when the chairman refused to accept the motion, pandemonium ensued. Finally an additional evening session, with special rules for debate and procedure, resulted in the appointment of an advisory committee to investigate the effects of protective legislation. The committee included Alice Paul, Doris Stevens, and Maud Younger of the NWP, Sarah Conboy of the American Federation of Labor, Mabel Leslie of the Women's Trade Union League, and Maud Wood Park of the League of Women Voters; the investigation and report were to be directed by Mary Winslow, with the assistance of a technical committee including Mary Van Kleeck, Dr. Charles P. Neill, and Mrs. Lillian Gilbreth.[28]

According to the Party's version of their members' activities at the conference, they had succeeded in their aim of publicizing the need for industrial equality. Mary Anderson's view, expressed in a letter to Mrs. Raymond Robins, was that "I think now that we have the Woman's Party a little where we want them." Anderson believed that the NWP could not refuse to be on the committee without appearing to be afraid of the facts, and that if it joined the committee, the facts would undoubtedly prove the advantages of protective legislation. She also thought the equalitarian feminists' tactics at the conference had already alienated many other women who "had never seen them in action before and will go back home and tell what an insane crowd they are."[29]

By May the advisory committee had fallen apart. The Party had lobbied Congressmen, written to the chairmen of the appropriations committees in both the House and Senate, protested the refusal to hold open hearings, and had charged the Women's Bureau with partiality. Conboy, Leslie, and Park resigned and Mary Anderson dissolved the committee since it was no longer bipartisan. In Mabel Leslie's letter to the Women's Trade Union League she explained that she had intended to cooperate, but found it impossible to work with the NWP. Leslie pointed out that Conboy and Park agreed with her that the Women's Bureau policy of conducting confidential interviews was a necessity, because in open hearings workers would be afraid to testify that they wanted protection.[30]

Actually, the NWP was correct in averring that the Women's Bureau, Mary Winslow, and Mary Van Kleeck were all biased toward protective legislation for women. In 1921, Van Kleeck had anticipated the division between the interests of professional women and women working in mechanized industries. She saw this as the difference between a career and a job, an individualized situation and an interdependent situation, voluntary and involuntary working. But this was an oversimplified analysis which lumped waitresses, secretaries, and sales clerks in the category of professional women, and Van Kleeck had further insisted that "no one with any dependable information about present conditions could possibly believe that men could also be included within the protections of special labor laws."[31] Mary Winslow, of course, had long been active in the Women's Trade Union League working for protective legislation far more than for unionization of working members, as well as being a director of special studies for the Women's Bureau.

Mary Anderson did not trust the NWP and had a strong sense of class differences. In 1923, she wrote to Elisabeth Christman that "the Seneca Falls Conference was conducted practically under the noses of the Rochester Chamber of Commerce," and suggested that the NWP had become a tool of the National Association of Manufacturers. Referring to some articles in *New Majority* which took a neutral stance on special legislation, Anderson concluded that "it is a question of whether Mrs. O. H. P. Belmont with all her millions and Alice Paul with a great deal of her own money, as well as other members of the Woman's Party, all rich women, are going to dictate the policies of the labor paper." She wrote to NWP sympathizer M. Cary Thomas in 1924 to find out whether the rumors that she supported industrial equality were true, and arranged a conference with Rose Schneiderman, Ethel Smith, and others when Thomas replied that she did believe special legislation restricted women's opportunities. Writing about the NWP to Mrs. Raymond Robins prior to some legislative hearings, Anderson commented that "I think they are without doubt the biggest liars that ever lived," and she did her part in the public debate to convince uncommitted women. Anderson appeared in person at the New York state hearings on a forty-eight hour law for women to read from the Women's Bureau preliminary report on the effects of protective legislation; she also arranged for the report to be presented to the National Council of Women's convention in 1927.[32]

After the advisory committee for the Women's Bureau had been dissolved, Anderson wrote to Mrs. Robins that she did not believe that the NWP had "ever had such a blow—even their star performance—publicity—did not work very well." But Anderson admitted in her autobiography that the 1928 report did not effectively stop the Party's campaign against protective legislation, confessing that "we have felt very bitter about the way they have impeded passage of special legislation for women." The Women's Bureau study was not neutral, and although Anderson thought the NWP was hurt by the episode, Party members believed that they had won because the debate focused public attention on the problem.[33]

The depression made competition for jobs more intense, and in 1930, Mary Anderson had to plead that "as there is today no sex line in the matter of economic responsibilities there should be no sex discrimination in the award of jobs." But Anderson never changed her position on the Equal Rights Amendment, testifying at the 1943 hearings against the amendment on the basis that it was still impractical, dangerous, abstract, vague, and legally unsound.[34]

Mary Anderson opposed the NWP international activities, particularly any attempts to get the Equal Rights Treaty endorsed, because this would mean that international conventions protecting women workers would be nullified. In the twenties Jane Addams had called on Anderson to help counteract the Party's influence within the Women's International League for Peace and Freedom, while Margery Corbett Ashby kept Anderson informed on the progress of the Party's bid for admission to the International Alliance of Women. Anderson also corresponded with ILO officials about the declining influence and importance of the NWP. But when Anderson planned to appear in person as unofficial observer at the 1931 ILO conference in Geneva, the NWP made certain that the newspaper publicity was unfavorable, and the Secretary of Labor was forced to order Anderson not to attend. Although both the Women's Trade Union League (WTUL) and the League of Women Voters strongly supported Anderson's right to attend the conference as a private individual, the State Department was adamant. She stayed outside Geneva while Elisabeth Christman of the WTUL represented the interests of protective legislation advocates.[35] Two years later, Roosevelt appointed Anderson as the head of the official U.S. observers at the ILO, which helped to prevent any real revision of protective conventions during this period. In the late thirties, Anderson's major attempt to counteract the NWP's equality program was her sponsorship of the Women's Charter.

The membership of the Women's Trade Union League often overlapped with that of the League of Women Voters; many members also had a close association with the Women's Bureau. The WTUL had been organized in 1903 through the combined efforts of settlement house workers and labor officials with the purpose of organizing women into trade unions. It was not until about ten years later that the WTUL turned to the advocacy of protective legislation for women. By the mid-twenties, however, the WTUL's support from both individuals and trade unions had declined precipitously. By 1925, the WTUL had only about one thousand members and in the 1930s they were able to retain only a skeletal staff in Washington, had no full time field representatives, and operated on a minimal budget.[36] Margaret Dreier Robins and Julia Lathrop were representative of one type of the early members. Mrs. Robins was a middle-class progressive reformer whose major interest had been social work, and she was president of the WTUL until 1921. Julia Lathrop also came from a social work background, and through her work with immigrants and as a factory inspector in Illinois she became interested in protective legislation. During the twenties Lathrop was president of the Illinois League of Women Voters and a member of the national board of the WTUL.

Another kind of member was typified by Mary Anderson, Agnes Nestor, and Rose Schneiderman, all active during the twenties and thirties. Anderson had been a capmaker and among her closest friends were glovemakers Agnes Nestor and Elisabeth Christman, and United Textile Workers' official, Sarah Conboy. Anderson retained a deep respect for and longlasting friendship with Mrs. Robins, whom she described as "the finest person I ever knew," corresponding regularly to keep Robins informed through the period. In her autobiography, Agnes Nestor maintained that the WTUL leaders recognized the threat from the NWP in the early twenties and called a conference to discuss what action to take. They decided to continue to work for protective legislation and oppose the ERA, but Nestor admitted that the many setbacks of these two decades were discouraging. Referring to the final passage of the Illinois eight-hour day for women in 1937, she concluded that "the victory did not seem as thrilling as that of the passage of the women's Ten Hour Day Law more than twenty-five years before." Rose Schneiderman had risen from a cash girl in a department store and a machine operator in cap factories. After working as an organizer for the WTUL, she served as its president during the late twenties and throughout the thirties, and also was a member of the NRA advisory board during the mid-thirties. Her dislike of the NWP stemmed from suffrage days. Even when she wrote her autobiography in 1967 at the age of eighty-three, she still maintained that the NWP had been supported by the National Association of Manufacturers and expressed her pleasure that after more than forty years the ERA was not yet a reality. Eleanor Roosevelt was also a long time member of the WTUL and retained her sympathy with their work during these two decades. She wrote personal letters to a number of prominent women in the thirties appealing for contributions to the WTUL, and tended to distrust women who were members of both the NWP and the Democratic Party.[37]

Mrs. Roosevelt might not have liked NWP feminists, but they were ambivalent about her and admired most of what she did so long as it did not involve special labor legislation. Journalist Ruby Black summed up the Party's view in her article, "Is Mrs. Roosevelt A Feminist?" Black approved of the first lady's activities, especially her defense of married women's right to work, her own writing that gave her some independent income, her defense of equal pay and work projects for women in relief programs, her encouragement of women reporters through special press conferences, and her active campaign for her friend Caroline O'Day in New York. But Mrs. Roosevelt, of course, was openly opposed to the ERA. Ruby Black thought that Mrs. Roosevelt's attitude probably stemmed from the work among exploited industrial women she had done in her youth. Yet Eleanor Roosevelt had proven that a President's wife could have opinions, activities, work, and a life of her own, so Black concluded that "she talks like a social worker and acts like a Feminist."[38]

The Women's Trade Union League closely followed the lead of the League of Women Voters and the Women's Bureau in opposing the NWP's domestic and international equality programs. By 1922, WTUL members were convinced that they could not work with NWP members; Agnes Nestor encouraged Mrs. Hooker to resign from the Baltimore branch, while Maud Swartz led the WTUL into open opposition to the NWP's activities in New York state. The WTUL organized a formal protest to the President from unionized women at the 1926 Women's Bureau conference, and furnished letters of support to the League of Women Voters for use against the admission of the NWP to the International Alliance of Women. Since it had an active publicity bureau, the WTUL worked to offset the NWP's publicity by publishing and distributing literature against the ERA, and whenever possible, by circulating opinions in favor of protective legislation among members of the ILO and the League of Nations. In the mid-thirties it joined with other women's organizations, but separately from the NWP, in protesting discriminations against women in the NRA codes and the married persons clause of the Government Economy Act. Elisabeth Christman worked closely with Mary Anderson at all stages of the Women's Charter. The WTUL also supported the League of Women Voters in protesting any discussion of equality at Pan American conferences, and worked actively for the appointment of its member Mary Winslow to the InterAmerican Commission of Women.[39]

NWP members had always admitted that the WTUL was a wage earners' organization, although they thought that the social worker influence had misled the group into supporting protective legislation. But the Party's patience was fast running out in the late thirties when the WTUL continued to oppose the Equal Rights Amendment. In 1938, Mary Winslow urged branch members to write and interview

Congressional candidates, although she added in a postscript: "We think this should be done quietly and personally. Don't put it in your bulletin." When the WTUL began distributing new literature against the "threat" of the ERA, the Party accused it of obscuring the issue and of spreading misinformation through "substituting bugaboos for facts." NWP feminists could not understand why members of the WTUL, if they really believed in labor legislation for both men and women, did not work actively for it once protective laws for all workers were legitimatized by the New Deal. By the end of the decade the Party was convinced that the WTUL was opposing the ERA out of habit, except for some individuals like Mrs. Josepha Whitney who publicly announced their conversion to industrial equality. But at the 1943 Amendment hearings, the WTUL speaker still called the ERA "dangerous and vicious," and "a demogogic attempt to capitalize on that sentiment [for equality]."[40]

Like the Women's Trade Union League, the Consumer's League was closely identified with protective legislation for women, particularly the minimum wage. It, too, suffered a severe decline in both membership and finances during the twenties, but cooperated with other social feminist organizations in opposing the NWP's program. The three most outstanding members of the Consumer's League during the twenties and thirties were Florence Kelley, Mary Dewson, and Frances Perkins. Kelly died in 1932, Dewson became the head of the Democratic Party's Women's Committee with a great deal of influence during the thirties, and Perkins became Roosevelt's Secretary of Labor.

Florence Kelley had many personality traits in common with the members of the NWP, and, in fact, had abandoned her position as a vice-president of NAWSA to join the NWP. She left the Party in 1921, immediately going into active opposition to the equal rights program. Kelley was a natural leader who had both devoted followers and implacable enemies. Neither an effective administrator nor organizer, she brought to causes a moral fervor and crusading vigor which inspired others. But she was not without flaws. "Her great qualities cannot obliterate her faults," her friend and biographer Josephine Goldmark wrote, "her high temper, her impatience, and her tendency never to forget or forgive opposition." In 1921 Kelley wrote to Maud Younger that she could not stand by and see the NWP program wipe out her efforts of thirty-five years, and she began to speak and write actively against the ERA immediately after the failure of compromise efforts. In personal letters, she solicited legal opinions against the Amendment from Felix Frankfurter, Dean Acheson, and Ernst Freund, as well as lining up west coast judges who had previously sat on eight hour day or minimum wage cases.[41]

Writing to Newton D. Baker about her distrust of the NWP's intentions, Kelley characterized the demands for women's equality as "insanity." "The slogans of the insane are," she continued, "a fair field and no favor,—Equal Rights for women, nothing more—We ask no privileges now that we have the vote." Kelley also wrote a "blunt and bald" letter to Senator Curtis of Kansas before he was to introduce the Amendment. After some of her colleagues at the Consumers' League criticized the belligerent tone of her letter, she asked Frankfurter for his opinion. "The confusion created by this miserable amendment even before it has been introduced is so alarming," she wrote, "that I think it foolish to mince matters or delay getting into the fray." Actually Kelley never believed the ERA could be worded in such a way as to safeguard protective legislation, even if the Party were willing to compromise, and she had admitted this at the meeting with the NWP in 1921.[42]

Kelley's belief in protective legislation for women was rooted in the biological fact of potential motherhood; she believed women would always need different labor laws than men. She was especially wary of court interpretations of laws in ways never anticipated by the framers, and of the court's application of the Fourteenth Amendment in such a manner as to deny rights to certain citizens. She pressed the NWP to make public its stand on protective legislation for women, which it was reluctant to do before 1923. Early in 1922, Kelley wrote a widely reprinted pamphlet, "Twenty Questions about the Federal Amendment Proposed by the NWP," in which she dealt with four major areas including sex laws, marriage laws, legislation for wage earning women, and the police powers of the state. Critical of the Wisconsin blanket equality law even though it contained a protective legislation clause, she maintained that "years may pass before some case reveals the possibilities of this statute." Kelley insisted that equal rights should not mean identical rights, arguing that women must choose between the ERA and special labor legislation and concluding that the threat to protective legislation alone was reason enough to spur women's opposition to the Amendment, for "on this subject we are immovable."[43]

Kelley realized that part of the problem stemmed from the different experiences of wage earning industrial women and professional women, and wrote Ethel Smith of the WTUL in 1924, cautioning her to watch out for the doctors' and nurses' attitudes toward the ERA. "Their entire struggle from the beginning of their professional work has been to get equal standing with men," she explained, "and they cannot see why what is good for one goose is not equally good for another." When NWP members disrupted the 1926 women's industrial conference, Florence Kelley described them as coming in "like a pirate band attempting to sink a peaceful canal boat crew of Quakers." "You can see what Hell on Earth that honest Swede [Mary Anderson] is destined to experience in the next three years," she warned, "if indeed her Bureau is not wrecked by their perfidious underground methods!" Active until the end of her life, Kelley spent the first years of the depression trying to counteract the movement to dismiss married women employees.[44]

In many ways, Mary (Molly) Dewson was a more typical representative of social feminist reformers. From a social work background she emerged with a sense of mission and moral dedication to the amelioration of working conditions. Although the early Consumers' League worked with white lists and boycotts, like the WTUL it shifted toward protective legislation after 1910. By the 1920s Dewson had become active in Democratic politics, and during the New Deal she served on the advisory boards of both the NRA and the Social Security Administration. Yet women like Dewson enjoyed prominence in the New Deal not because they were women or feminists, but because they were primarily social reformers with personal ties to those in power. Dewson was very concerned about the declining financial and membership base of the Consumer's League during the era, and about finding a successor to Florence Kelley. She personally poached on the NWP's territory by persuading Mrs. Belmont's daughter-in-law to contribute $1,000 to the work of the Consumer's League in 1922. Dewson was anathema to the NWP, particularly when she was in a position to use her patronage in the New Deal. Jane Norman Smith had worked in opposition to her and the New York Consumers' League, and believed that Dewson had used lies and smear tactics against the Party. "Watch your step with Mary Dewson!" Smith wrote to a leader of the California Business and Professional Women. "Indeed, I usually try not to say unkind things about other women, but my contempt for Mary Dewson's methods of work is beyond words."[45] In the late thirties, of course, it was Dewson's influence which enabled Mary Winslow to undercut and finally replace Doris Stevens on the InterAmerican Commission of Women.

Neither Dewson nor Frances Perkins could replace the vigorous leadership the Consumer's League lost when Florence Kelley died. Perkins also had been a leader in the New York league and she joined the New York State Industrial Board in 1923, becoming its chief in 1926. But she, too, did her part in the war of words over the effects of protective legislation. According to Perkins, special legislation for women was practical and realistic in view of their observable exploitation by employers. Industrial work was different from a career, and women needed the special legislation in order to compete more equally with men. Perkins also stressed the difficulty of organizing women into trade unions and the hardships of the dual role of working wife and housewife. If the laws should unintentionally restrict certain women, such as women printers affected by the prohibition of night work, Perkins argued that they could apply for specific exemption. She rejected the NWP argument on behalf of the New York rapid transit workers, insisting that they lost their jobs as a result of the conversion to a peace time economy and the reemployment of former soldiers rather than because of the New York Women's Hours law.[46]

At the beginning of the depression Perkins had remarked that married women who worked for less than $3,500 a year were economic failures and this had infuriated Brooklyn Transit worker Mary Murray of the NWP. Everyone must realize it took time, experience, and training to be able to qualify for a high salaried job, Murray replied, and in the meantime most women worked because they had to earn money. Murray also questioned whether Perkins considered a man who earned less than $3,500 to be an economic failure, concluding with a personal

attack on Perkins for working although "she has an able-bodied husband and children." Yet Frances Perkins was one of the first public
women to reverse her stand and speak out against the discharge of
married women during the early years of the depression. She argued
that this did not solve the problem of unemployment and might well
create more problems in home-oriented service industries such as bakeries
and laundries. The NWP was delighted with Perkins for her conversion to the idea of women's right to work and her abandonment of
the "pin money" theory of working women's motivation. When
Perkins became Secretary of Labor over some objections from the
American Federation of Labor, *Equal Rights* practically overflowed
with good will. "We know of no predecessor in her office," editorialized the Party journal, "who has been so thoroughly imbued with
humanitarianism, who has tried so hard to get to the bottom of things,
who has been less actuated by political considerations, or who has been
more forthright in her approach to problems and people than Miss
Perkins." As Jane Norman Smith summed it up: "I've always liked
her and I think she is head and shoulders above most of the Consumers' League crowd."[47]

Toward the end of the era the Consumers' League efforts were confined to presenting written evidence that working women favored
minimum wage and hours laws, while the NWP accused it of emo-
tionalism and "good old-fashioned propaganda." The Consumers'
League did, however, participate in an unsuccessful attempt to form a
Committee of 500 in 1938 to defeat the ERA. This scheme, coor-
dinated by the League of Women Voters attorney Dorothy Strauss,
was aimed at getting ten influential women in each state to lead the work
against the Amendment. "It is appalling that the Woman's Party has
been able to marshall so much influence this year," exclaimed a
Consumers' League official. When Mary Winslow was appointed to
the InterAmerican Commission, the Consumers' League expressed its
approval to President Roosevelt, adding that its members were pleased
that NWP women who did not understand economic problems would
no longer be in a position to threaten women's welfare. But its troubles
with the NWP were not over, for when the 1940 Republican platform
approved submission of the ERA to the states, the Consumers' League
representative to the convention wrote that "Doris Stevens and her

gang had, as usual, worked completely undercover. We had been assured that there was no chance of its acceptance."[48]

The League of Women Voters, the Women's Trade Union League, and the Consumers' League also struggled against the NWP for influence within other American women's organizations. One of the first confrontations took place within the Women's International League for Peace and Freedom (WILPF), founded by Jane Addams during the World War I era. The purpose of the Women's International League was to remove the causes of war, although from the beginning the League had definite feminist overtones. Throughout the twenties, feminists introduced equality resolutions at WILPF conventions, but in 1926 a request to endorse the Equal Rights Amendment was tabled at the convention of the American section. That same year an English feminist introduced a resolution supporting total equality for women at the Dublin convention and it passed. In 1934 at the Zurich congress, Alice Paul obtained approval of the Equal Rights Treaty and the congress resolved to ask its national sections to work for it in their respective countries. By 1935, the Women's Trade Union League secretary wrote to a friend at the League of Nations that the Women's International League of Peace and Freedom, the Open Door International, and the International Alliance of Women now all stood behind the international equality aims of the NWP.[49]

When the Equal Rights Amendment was introduced in 1923, there was a united front of women's organizations opposed to it, but Party feminists were hopeful that with "education" these groups would reverse their stand. The General Federation of Women's Clubs, a huge conglomeration of disparate local groups, had resolved in 1924 to work toward equality by specific measures that would not harm special legislation for women. The debates in local federations continued during both decades, usually conducted by the NWP and League of Women Voters speakers. The League of Women Voters officers worried a great deal that the General Federation might endorse the ERA, but the Federation's decision-making process was so slow and cumbersome that there was little chance of reaching any national decision on such a controversial matter.[50]

Two of the strongest, most influential, and most active women's organizations of the era were the Business and Professional Women and the American Association of University Women. NWP members were active in both these groups and their point of view made considerable headway within these organizations, especially during the thirties. The AAUW opposition to the Equal Rights Amendment was neutralized to some degree when the resolution to continue opposition to the Amendment came up at their 1924 convention. The widely respected and admired M. Carey Thomas substituted a motion that the question be studied during the coming year and that in the meantime, the officers take no stand on the issue; Thomas' resolution passed by a vote of 229 to 177. The Consumers' League pamphlet was distributed to the members, along with literature supplied by the NWP. Thomas and Mary Van Kleeck debated the issue in 1925; the result was that the membership recommended further study of the Amendment. They were still studying it in the mid-thirties, although members were becoming more uneasy about discriminations against married women workers. When a man was appointed to replace president Mary Woolley at Mt. Holyoke, the AAUW decided this would be the issue on which to protest against economic and educational discriminations against women. Since studies of women in teaching and administrative posts had made their concentration at the bottom of the job and prestige scale very clear, the AAUW asked publicly: "Are women being educated to a dead end?"[51] But the AAUW still did not endorse the ERA.

In 1938, an official statement from the AAUW board was used against the Equal Rights Treaty at the Pan American Conference in Lima, and the NWP immediately protested this abuse of the impartial position the officers were supposed to be taking on the Party's equality proposals. The NWP also opposed the inclusion of AAUW statements in the hearings on the ERA, and AAUW conventions continued to schedule speakers on both sides of the Amendment issue. At the 1939 convention, the speaker opposing the ERA told the delegates in no uncertain terms that equal rights was "one of those weasel-like phrases like 'fraternity,' 'equality,' and 'democracy' into which we all fall so easily," and the convention finally voted against the Amendment officially. At the same time, however, delegates voted to work for the removal of discrimination in government employment on the basis of sex or marital status and failed to endorse any form of protective legislation for women.[52]

Two years before the AAUW had finally come to an official decision to oppose the ERA, the Business and Professional Women had arrived at the opposite decision. J. Stanley Lemons has suggested that the BPW supported social feminist objectives until about 1926, but that after that date the organization's program was narrowed to include only the immediate economic interests of its own members. Arguing that this was at the expense of the industrial women workers, he implies that the business and professional women workers were never really threatened by protective legislation. Yet legislation such as the 1927 California eight-hour day law covered all women except nurses, maids, and cannery workers, and the 1929 New York eight-hour bill included women in business offices. Lemons seems to think these were exceptional and neglects to deal with the outcry from waitresses, sales clerks, bank tellers, and other white collar workers who were affected by laws which not only limited their total work day but which sometimes prohibited split shifts. Lemons also fails to consider the breadth of membership of the early Business and Professional Women, which did include many clerks, typists, and waitresses who hoped to work their way up to managerial positions.[53]

During the early twenties, the official BPW journal, *Independent Woman*, searched for reasons other than discrimination to explain why women were not succeeding in business to the degree they had expected. Florence Sands suggested in 1924 that it might be primarily psychological, for perhaps women lacked confidence, initiative, vision, and even seriousness. But increasingly women became convinced that the artificial barrier of sex discrimination was hindering their advance. By the mid-thirties, articles dealing with the disillusionment of women workers dominated *Independent Woman*. Women had been unfairly penalized after World War I, argued Margaret Morann in her article, "Give Her The Fruit of Her Hands," and then had been dealt a nearly fatal blow by the depression. Women's opportunities had contracted more than men's; progress seemed impossible because of unfair discriminations. "It is a vicious system," she wrote, "that has dealt her equal responsibility without assuring her economic parity." Morann pointed out that the average business woman's salary was 30 to 50 percent lower than that of a man, and that a woman's economic insecurity increased as she grew older. As a young woman she had not dreamed of outstanding success, Morann explained, but neither had she ever expected to be a victim of such discrimination as she had encountered.[54]

In a 1935 article entitled "He Wants My Job!" Grace Fletcher discussed the back-to-the-home movement in Hitler's Germany and its American counterpart which called upon women to "make room on the payroll" for a man. "Married women are only the first victims," she warned. "The next step is obvious." In the late thirties, the Business and Professional Women sponsored a study of its members' dependents and wages. They found that only 3.4 percent had no economic "need" to work, and that the median income of women business and professional workers was still far below that of men.[55]

Local BPW clubs began endorsing the Equal Rights Amendment as early as the mid-twenties, when members began encountering sex discrimination in opportunities for employment and advancement. In 1926, the national federation decided to study the Amendment, but the 1927 convention avoided taking any definite stand for or against it. Local and state federation endorsements continued to increase, despite the efforts of the League of Women Voters to counteract the movement. The League repeatedly stated that it did not support protective legislation for business and professional women, and the Women's Trade Union League was also active in contacting members of the BPW and in furnishing them with literature against the Amendment. Lucy Mason of the National Consumers' League wrote to BPW president Geline Bowman in 1934 that in all her travels she had never discovered "a single case in which a woman lost her job because of the minimum wage laws," and Bowman replied that although many local clubs had endorsed the Amendment, the national federation would probably not be forced to decide on the issue yet.[56]

Speakers from the League of Women Voters and the NWP continued to oppose one another at the BPW conventions, but by the mid-thirties the League was reporting great sympathy with the Party's views against protective legislation. League officer Edith Valet Cook wrote in 1935 that she did not really fear passage of the ERA by Congress, but that she would hate to see such a large organization as the Business and Professional Women endorse it. She suggested the League intensify its efforts to prevent approval of the Amendment, adding that "so long as it is only the Woman's Party we can well afford to ignore it!" However, League president Marguerite Wells was more worried about the effect of a possible endorsement. Mary Anderson also noted that "the Woman's Party has been making real inroads" into the BPW; while she was traveling she spoke as often as possible against the Amendment. The 1935 BPW convention resolved to fight for the rights of women, including the right to paid employment, as did the meeting of the International Federation of Business and Professional Women later that year. International BPW president Lena Madesin Phillips had accused most women's groups of following a patchwork quilt kind of program composed of a multitude of reforms. "It is this diversity of interest, this complacency with the symbol, rather than with actuality, this conditioning to failure," she said, "which must be so heartily deplored today." The national BPW finally endorsed the Equal Rights Amendment in 1937, and Mary Anderson considered resigning. But Mary Van Kleeck and Dorothy Kenyon convinced her to retain her membership, and Anderson wrote to a friend that "they say that we might be able to stir up protest on the inside."[57]

Although the NWP feminists made a strong bid for leadership of both the American and international feminist movements and lost, it was not only for this reason that they failed to gain the support of large numbers of women for their equality program. Just as important as their failure to achieve a dominant position in feminist councils was their failure to analyze or even to attempt a systematic analysis of the ramifications of equal rights on the relationships among women, men, and children. This was especially true in the twenties when many women were concerned with the place of marriage and the family in the "new" woman's life, but also was important in the thirties when the NWP attracted but could not retain younger women concerned with economic discrimination in job opportunities. The core of the NWP membership, a transition generation between the Victorian era and the twentieth century, remained ambivalent about marriage and children. It is significant that the feminist revival of the 1960s emphasized the denial of "personhood" inherent in limiting woman's roles to those of wife and mother. At the same time, the National Organization for Women, in many ways the logical successor to the NWP, successfully spearheaded the drive to get the reworded Equal Rights Amendment finally passed by both Houses of Congress.

NOTES

1. Lemons, *The Woman Citizen* pp. 181, 224, 187, 192, 183.

2. O'Neill, *Everyone was Brave*, pp. 272–77, 281–83, 285, 290–92.

3. Lavinia Egan, "Keeping the Issue Straight," *ER* 1 (July 28, 1923), 188; Carol Rehfisch, "Historical Background of the ER Campaign," *ER* 1 (September 15, 1923), 245–46; Daisy Lee Worthington Worchester, "Welfare Legislation and the NWP," *ER* 11 (August 16, 1924), 213; Editorial, "Life Is Too Short," *ER* 14 bis (March 24, 1928), 52.

4. "The Woman's Party–Right or Wrong," *ER* 1 (October 20, 1923), 285; Elizabeth Evans and Carol A. Rehfisch, "Woman's Party, Right or Wrong?" *New Republic* 36 (September 26, 1923), 123–24; Lavinia Dock, "A Sub-Caste," *ER* 11 (May 31, 1924), 125–26.

5. "Unfair Tactics," *ER* 1 (January 19, 1924), 288.

6. "Speech by Gail Laughlin at NWP Headquarters: 'Why An Equal Rights Amendment?' " *ER* 11 (April 5, 1924), 61.

7. Editorial, "When Will Women Dare to Be Free?" *ER* 12 (December 5, 1925), 340; "Council of Catholic Women Opposes Equal Rights," *ER* 12 (December 5, 1925), 541; "The Opposition," *ER* 11 (April 5, 1924), 60.

8. Editorial, "An Intolerable Philosophy," *ERIFW* 2 (September 12, 1936), 218.

9. Editorial, "The Time Has Come For Action," *ERIFW* 2 (November 14, 1936), 290; "Ruth Williams Takes Issue with Columnist," *ER* 24 (November 15, 1938), 364.

10. Genevieve Parkhurst, "Is Feminism Dead?" *Harper's* 170 (May 1935), 736.

11. U.S. Department of Labor, Women's Bureau, "Preliminary Study of the Application of Section 213 of the Economic Act of June 30, 1932," LWV Papers, Series II, Box 340, LC.

12. Mrs. Harvey Wiley to Alma Lutz, November 21, 1940, Alma Lutz Papers, f. 100, SL.

13. Inez Haynes Irwin, *Angels and Amazons* (New York: Doubleday, 1933), p. 417; Chafe, *The American Woman*, pp. 34–35, 115; Mildred Adams, *The Right To Be People* (New York: J.B. Lippincott, 1967), 172.

14. Mary Grey Peck, *Carrie Chapman Catt: A Biography* (New York: H. W. Wilson, 1944).

15. Carrie Chapman Catt, "Too Many Rights," *Ladies Home Journal* 39 (November 1922), pp. 31, 168; "What Next?" *The Suffragist* 8 (November 1920), 278.

16. Editorial, "Women's Bloc?" *Nation* 119 (September 3, 1924), 230; Anne Martin, "Feminists and Future Political Action," *Nation* 120 (February 18, 1925), 185.

17. Martin, "Feminists and Future Political Action," p. 183.

18. Jane Norman Smith to Anne Martin, February 13, 1925, Jane Norman Smith Papers, Box 2, f. 62, SL.

19. Alice Paul to Maud Wood Park, January 3, 1921, LWV Papers, Series II, Box 6, LC; Executive Board Votes and Comments, LWV Papers, Series II, Box 57, LC; Ethel Smith, "Conference on the so-called Equal Rights Amendment Proposed by the NWP," December 4, 1921, WTUL Papers, Box 2, LC.

20. Mrs. Frank A. Vanderlip to Maud Wood Park, October 11, 1922, LWV Papers, Series II, Box 43, LC; "Equal Rights Campaign—NWP," Jane Norman Smith Papers, Box 1, f. 47, SL.

21. Jane Norman Smith to Fred Lee Woodson, March 13, 1924, Jane Norman Smith Papers, Box 2, f. 61, SL; Helen Hall to Ethel Smith, February 1, 1926, LWV Papers, Series II, Box 57, LC; Mrs. Petricha Manchester to Ethel Smith, February 15, 1926, Series II, Box 57, LC; Mary Moss Welborn to Jane Norman Smith, November 30, 1928, Jane Norman Smith Papers, Box 3, f. 70, SL.

22. Esther Dunshee to Belle Sherwin, July 7, 1924; Gladys Harrison to Julia Lathrop, July 19, 1924, LWV Papers, Series II, Box 43, LC.

23. "Miss Dunshee on Equal Rights," *Woman Citizen* 7 (March 8, 1924), 19–20; Hamilton and Stevens, "Blanket Amendment," pp. 152–60.

24. Memorandum, Gladys Harrison to Belle Sherwin, February 27, 1928, LWV Papers, Series II, Box 102, LC; Gladys Harrison to Sophonisba Breckinridge, October 23, 1928, LWV Papers, Series II, Box 185, LC.

25. Avis Ninabuck, "A Panacea is Questioned," *Woman Citizen* 14 (May 1929), 29; Lavinia Engle to Mrs. William J. Carson, September 29, 1931, LWV Papers, Series II, Box 163, LC; "Statement against the Equal Rights Amendment as presented by the Illinois League of

Women Voters by Mrs. Isabel Simons," February 26, 1935, LWV Papers, Series II, Box 340, LC; Jane S. Cramer and Genevieve Parkhurst, "Should Women Support the Equal Rights Amendment?" *Independent Woman* 14 (May 1935), 148, 171–72; Jane Smith and Dorothy Kenyon, "To End Discrimination Against Women," *Independent Woman* 16 (May 1937), 132; Mildred Palmer to Alma Lutz, October 19, 1940, Alma Lutz Papers, Box 6, f. 83, SL.

26. Carrie Chapman Catt, et al., "Should Congress Approve the Proposed Equal Rights Amendment to the Constitution? CON" *Congressional Digest* 22 (April 1943), 118–28; Florence Kitchelt to Mrs. David B. Fitzgerald, May 5, 1950, Florence Kitchelt Papers, Box 6, f. 168, SL.

27. Mary Anderson, *Woman At Work,* pp. 159–65.

28. *Ibid.,* pp. 168–69; Ruby A. Black, "Equal Rights at the Industrial Conference," *ER* 12 (January 30, 1926), 402.

29. Black, "Equal Rights at the Industrial Conference," p. 403; "Women's Bureau Report Not Impartial," *ER* 14 bis (December 8, 1928), 347; Mary Anderson to Mrs. Raymond Robins, February 4, 1926, Mary Anderson Papers, Box 3, f. 8, SL.

30. Mabel Leslie to Maud Swartz, May 4, 1926, WTUL Papers, Box 3, LC.

31. Mary Van Kleeck, "Women and Machines," *Atlantic Monthly* 117 (February 1921), 250–60.

32. Mary Anderson to Elisabeth Christman, December 1, 1923; Mary Anderson to M. Cary Thomas, February 4, 1924; M. Cary Thomas to Mary Anderson, February 5, 1924; Mary Anderson to Mrs. Raymond Robins, March 20, 1924, Mary Anderson Papers, Box 3, fs. 15, 16, 8; Mary Anderson and Rheta Childe Dorr, "Should There Be Labor Laws for Women?" *Good Housekeeping* 71 (September 1925); 53, 166, 173–74, 176; Jane Norman Smith, "Industrial Survey Commission Hears Testimony" *ER* 13 (February 5, 1927), 413, 415; Ella Sherwin, "What is a 'Clearing House?'" *ER* 14 (December 24, 1927), 361.

33. Mary Anderson to Mrs. Raymond Robins, May 17, 1926, Mary Anderson Papers, Box 3, f. 8, SL; Anderson, *Woman At Work,* p. 171; Chafe, *The American Woman,* pp. 120–21.

34. Editorial, "For the Benefit of the Women's Bureau," *ER* 16 (February 15, 1930), 10; "Against Sex Discrimination," *ER* 16 (Octo-

ber 11, 1930), 287–88; Catt et al., "Should Congress Approve the Equal Rights Amendment? CON," pp. 119–20.

35. Mary Anderson to Mrs. Raymond Robins, May 8, 1924; Margery Corbett Ashby to Mary Anderson, November 5, 1925; Mary Anderson to H. B. Butler, August 6, 1927; Mary Anderson to Dr. Marion Phillips, January 30, 1928, Mary Anderson Papers, Box 3, fs. 8, 17, 19, 20, SL; Anderson, *Woman At Work*, pp. 201–2; Rose Schneiderman to Elisabeth Christman, April 10, 1931, WTUL Papers, Box 5, LC; Press Release, May 15, 1931, LWV Papers, Series II, Box 101, LC; Rose Schneiderman to Secretary of State Stimson, May 29, 1931, WTUL Papers, Box 5, LC; Elisabeth Christman to Rose Schneiderman, June 5, 1931, WTUL Papers, Box 5, LC; Mary Anderson to Mrs. Raymond Robins, August 17, 1931, Mary Anderson Papers, Box 3, f. 9, SL.

36. Chafe, *The American Woman*, p. 69–76; Allen F. Davis, "The Women's Trade Union League: Origins and Organization," *Labor History* 5 (Winter 1964), 11; Lemons, *The Woman Citizen*, p. 122.

37. Jane Addams, *My Friend Julia Lathrop* (New York: Macmillan, 1935); Anderson, *Woman At Work*, pp. 35–37; Agnes Nestor, *Woman's Labor Leader* (Rockford, Ill., Bellvue Books, 1954), p. 277; Rose Schneiderman with Lucy Goldthwaite, *All For One* (New York: Paul S. Eriksson, 1967), pp. 123–26; Joan M. Erikson, "Nothing to Fear: Notes on the Life of Eleanor Roosevelt," in *The Woman In America* (Boston: Houghton Mifflin, 1965) edited by Robert Jay Lifton, pp. 268–83; Eleanor Roosevelt to Governor Ross, March 28, 1930, Sue White Papers, Box 3, f. 35, SL; Eleanor Roosevelt to Ruth Litt, January 18, 1933, Jane Norman Smith Papers, Box 4, f. 82, SL.

38. Ruby A. Black, "Is Mrs. Roosevelt A Feminist?" *ERIFW* 1 (July 27, 1935), 163.

39. Agnes Nestor to Elisabeth Christman, March 17, 1922, WTUL Papers, Box 2, LC; Unpublished autobiography, Jane Norman Smith Papers, n.d., Box 1, f. 47, SL; AFL Trade Union Women to the President of the U.S., January 21, 1926; Elisabeth Christman to Maud Swartz, April 16, 1926, WTUL Papers, Box 3, LC; Mary Winslow to Mary Anderson, June 21, 1926, Mary Anderson Papers, Box 3, f. 16, SL; Elisabeth Christman to the WTUL National Executive Board Members, June 19, 1929; Press release, May 1931; Elisabeth Christman to Mary Craig McCeachy, July 24, 1935; Press release, February

17, 1934; Elisabeth Christman to the WTUL National Executive Board Members, August 21, 1936; Mary Winslow, Minutes, June 1, 1936; Elisabeth Christman to Secretary of State Cordell Hull, October 6, 1935, WTUL Papers, Boxes 4, 5, 6, 7, LC.

40. Editorial, "Protected Against Their Will," *ER* 17 (May 2, 1931), 98; Mary Winslow to Local and State Leagues and National Committees, June 22, 1938, WTUL Papers, Box 8, LC; Editorial, "Tell Them the Truth," *ER* 25 (April 15, 1939), 58; Editorial, "Let's Think Correctly," *ER* 25 (September 1939), 106; Catt et al., "Should Congress Approve the Equal Rights Amendment? CON," pp. 122–23.

41. Josephine Goldmark, *Impatient Crusader: Florence Kelley's Life Story* (Urbana, Ill.,: University of Illinois Press, 1953), pp. vi, vii. 3, 58–59, 181–82; Letters to judges in NCL Papers, Box C 14 W 1, LC.

42. Florence Kelley to Newton D. Baker, June 3, 1921, NCL Papers, Box C 14 W 1, LC; Florence Kelley to Felix Frankfurter, October 24, 1921, NCL Papers, Box C 14 W 2, LC; Freda Kirchwey to Florence Kelley, January 11, 1922; Florence Kelley to Freda Kirchwey, January 16, 1922, NCL Papers, Box C 14 W 3, LC.

43. Elsie Hill and Florence Kelley, "Shall Women Be Equal Before the Law?" *Nation* 104 (April 12, 1922), 421; Florence Kelley, "Twenty Questions about the Federal Amendment Proposed by the National Woman's Party," n.p., 1922; Florence Kelley, "Blanket Equality Bill," *Woman's Home Companion* 49 (August 1922), 4, 89; Inez Haynes Irwin and Florence Kelley, "The Equal Rights Amendment," *Good Housekeeping* 78 (March 1924), 19, 163–65.

44. Florence Kelley to Ethel M. Smith, June 5, 1924; Florence Kelley to Mrs. Edson, January 28, 1926, NCL Papers, Box C 14 W 8, LC; Telegram, Florence Kelley to *Springfield Republican*, December 10, 1930, NCL Papers, Box B 4, LC.

45. James T. Patterson, "Mary Dewson and the American Minimum Wage Movement," *Labor History* 5 (Spring 1964), 135–52; Chafe, *The American Woman*, pp. 44–45; Correspondence with Grace Abbott, Mary Dewson Papers, Box 2, f. 18, SL; Florence Kelley to Mary Dewson, June 19, 1922, NCL Papers, Box C 14 W4, LC; Jane Norman Smith to Sue Brobst, November 21, 1932, Jane Norman Smith Papers, Box 3, f. 81, SL.

46. Frances Perkins and Elizabeth Baker, "Do Women in Industry

Need Special Protection?" *Survey* 55 (February 15, 1926), 529–30. See also George Martin, *Madam Secretary: Frances Perkins* (Boston: Houghton Mifflin, 1976).

47. Mary A. Murray, "Answering Miss Perkins," *ER* 16 (April 26, 1930), 95; Frances Perkins, "Wage Earning Wives," *ER* 16 (January 3, 1931), 383; Editorial, "Wise Men Change Their Minds," *ER* 16 (January 3, 1931), 378; Editorial, "Cheers For Miss Perkins," *ER* 19 (October 14, 1933), 290; Jane Norman Smith to Helen Hunt West, January 27, 1936, Helen Hunt West Papers, Box 1, f. 8, SL.

48. Mary Dewhurst Blankenhorn, "Do Working Women Want It?" *Survey* 57 (February 15, 1927), 630–31; "Consumer League Fails to Present Facts," *ER* 23 (May 1, 1937), 61; Mary Ellen Hughes to Mrs. John C. Hader, April 18, 1938; Mathilde C. Hader to Mary Ellen Hughes, February 4, 1938; Mary Ellen Hughes to Franklin D. Roosevelt, March 15, 1939, NCL Papers, Box C 16 IV W 14, LC; Mary Dublin to Margaret Wiesman, June 27, 1940, NCL Papers, Box C 15 IV W 14, LC.

49. Gertrude Bussey and Margaret Tims, *Women's International League for Peace and Freedom: A Record of Fifty Years Work* (London: George Allen and Unwin, 1965), pp. 47, 72; Sochen, *New Woman*, pp. 96–98; Editorial, "Equal Rights in a World Movement," *ER* 11 (May 17, 1924), 108; "WILPF Refuses to Act on Equal Rights," *ER* 13 (May 15, 1926), 112; "Women's International League for World Wide Equal Rights," *ER* 13 (July 24, 1926), 191; "WILPF Adopts New Statement of Aims," *ER* 20 (October 13, 1934), 294–95; Elisabeth Christman to Mary Craig McCeachy, July 24, 1935, WTUL Papers, Box 7, LC.

50. Anna Kelton Wiley, "Equal Rights Debate in the District of Columbia Federation of Women's Clubs," *ER* 20 (March 17, 1934), 51; Mrs. William F. Friedman, "The Viewpoint of the Opposition," *ER* 20 (March 17, 1934), p. 53.

51. Editorial, "University Women Withdraw Opposition," *ER* 11 (May 10, 1924), 99–100; Editorial, "A Specious Question," *ER* 12 (March 7, 1925), 28; Carolyn D. Smiley, "Are Women Being Educated to a Dead End?" *ER* 23 (March 15, 1937), 35.

52. "Is This the Real Attitude of the AAUW?" *ER* 25 (January 1, 1939), 4; Editorial, "History's Measure," *ER* 25 (May 1, 1939), 66;

Speech by Charlotte Hankin at the AAUW Biennial Convention, June 1939, AAUW Papers, Box 3, f. 55, SL; "Equal Rights Amendment Support Strengthened," *ER* 25 (August 1939), 99.

53. Lemons, *The Woman Citizen*, pp. 32, 43, 45, 199–200.

54. Florence Sands, "Why Many Women Do Not Succeed in Business," *Independent Woman* 9 (October 1924), 12–13; Margaret Morann, "Give Her the Fruit of Her Hands," *Independent Woman* 12 (July 1934), 200, 221–22.

55. Grace N. Fletcher, "He Wants My Job!" *Independent Woman* 14 (May 1935), 154, 167; Josephine Nelson, "She Supports A Family," *Independent Woman* 17 (March 1938), 81–82.

56. Editorial, "Delay—But Not Defeat," *ER* 14 (July 1927), 196; Elisabeth Christman to National Executive Board Members, June 19, 1929, WTUL Papers, Box 4, LC; Lucy Randolph Mason to Geline Bowman, June 22, 1934; Geline Bowman to Lucy Randolph Mason, June 26, 1934, NCL Papers, Box B 10, LC.

57. Jane S. Cramer and Genevieve Parkhurst, "Should Women Support the Equal Rights Amendment?" *Independent Woman* 14 (May 1935), 149, 172–74; "To Restrict Women Is to Hamper the Race; Resolutions adopted at the Northwest Biennial, Seattle, 1935," *Independent Woman* 14 (August 1935), 249; Edith Valet Cook to Marguerite M. Wells, February 18, 1935; Marguerite M. Wells to Edith Valet Cook, February 26, 1935; Edith Valet Cook to Marguerite M. Wells, March 21, 1935; Marguerite M. Wells to Edith Valet Cook, March 29, 1935, LWV Papers, Series II, Box 342, LC; Helen Havener, "International Board Meets in Brussels," *Independent Woman* 14 (November 1935), 376, 388–89; "Speeches at the Conference—Lena Madesin Phillips, President of the International Federation of Business and Professional Women," *ER* 21 (December 15, 1935), 1; Mary Anderson to Marian Parkhurst, August 4, 1937; Mary Anderson Papers, Box 3, f. 28, SL.

7

UNFORTUNATELY WE FALL IN LOVE

NWP feminists failed to explore the social and institutional ramifications of equal rights in depth because they never understood that equality might require a new kind of relationship between men and women. Party members accepted what they thought were basic differences between man's and woman's natures, but not role differentiation based on sex. This led to a certain ambivalence concerning men and especially marriage and motherhood, because the roles ascribed to wives and mothers were homemaking and childrearing. Equalitarian feminists consistently argued that women did not have to choose between marriage and a family or a career, yet recognized that women who attempted to have both were carrying a "double burden." Although they unofficially supported the endowment of maternity, uniform and easy divorce laws, alimony reform, and stood for the recognition of a housewife's contribution to her marriage and family, their underlying belief was that all women, except perhaps mothers of very young children, should work outside the home.

Party feminists always denied that they were anti-man, but inevitably their belief that marriage and motherhood limited women's opportunities outside the home caused them to ascribe certain characteristics to men as the dominant sex. The Party's distrust of men was most evident in its attitude toward prostitution, which it saw as stemming from the demands of men and the economic needs of women. The NWP feminists were caught in an ideological bind since they did believe that women were in many ways different from and superior to men. These differences were that women were more inclined to be altruistic and concerned with the quality of life; women as givers of life would also be peaceful conservers of life. Yet the whole logic of this argument was based on the biological role of motherhood, which the Party also saw as restricting women's opportunities at the same time that it gave them special characteristics to contribute to the world.

The basic flaw in the NWP's analysis of the woman problem in the 1920s and 1930s was the Party's failure to recognize women's confusion over their own sense of identity. It was a period in which two major roles, often mutually exclusive, competed for women's loyalty. The NWP, by encouraging women to believe they need not choose between a career and a family, did nothing to alleviate the stress women experienced when they tried to combine the two. Nor did equalitarian feminists develop or suggest any constructive ways in which to lessen the "double burden" of two jobs; rather, they simply affirmed the moderate, optimistic suggestions of Charlotte Perkins Gilman for the professionalization of shopping, cooking, cleaning, and child care. The Party occasionally attacked education, religion, fashion, language, and the custom of adopting the husband's name as factors contributing to what it frequently termed "women's inferiority complex." Urging women to cooperate and support other women, particularly those in business and the professions, the NWP tended to present exceptional women achievers of the past and present as role models for emulation.

The NWP feminists generally did envy what they considered to be men's privileges, thus taking an intellectual position which led them to demand identical privileges and opportunities for women. But although they distrusted men and believed that many undesirable male characteristics had been developed as a result of the inequality between men and women, Party members never questioned such basic middle class institutions as marriage and the nuclear family, nor the cluster of values included in the Protestant work ethic. Because so many of these feminists were solidly upper middle class in income, background, and education, they were blind to any possible class differences among women that might influence feminist goals and priorities. They accepted most middle class values almost completely, questioning only militarism and war, extremes of materialism, suppression of birth control information, and legal and economic discriminations against women.

The NWP never came to terms with its members' underlying attitudes such as distrust of men, fear of loss of identity and opportunity in marriage, or ambivalence toward the motherhood and homemaking roles of women. In her 1923 *Ladies Home Journal* article, "Women As Dictators," Mrs. O. H. P. Belmont wrote that men had done a poor job of directing the affairs of the world and that women should take over. "Perhaps there is something very glorious about being a help-mate," she argued, "but if so it's time some man shared that glory." Although Mrs. Belmont believed too many women were afraid of losing the admiration or love of men, she saw promise in the changing attitude toward divorce. "We have said to men:" she concluded, "you can't take us and use us as you choose, throw us aside and expect us to submit without a protest." Another clear expression of distrust could be found in the article Charlotte Perkins Gilman contributed to *Equal Rights* in 1923. Gilman examined the idea of men's protective instinct toward women, arguing that helpless women were exciting to men, while women who could defend themselves were considered "revolting" and "unfeminine." The harem was the ultimate symbol of male protection of women, Gilman believed, and men's "natural" protective instinct was "mainly jealousy and self interest." It was on this basis that women were divided into "good" and "bad" according to the degree to which they were under the control of their private male protectors.[1]

NWP feminists insisted that women were denied equal opportunities for personal development, career success, and the use of power. Although men might not have done it with a conscious purpose, the Party believed they had tyrannized over women. Women were denied the use of their education when they married, and the Party agreed with Pearl Buck's analysis that "a man is educated and turned out to work. But a woman is educated—and turned out to grass." In 1927, the prize winning *Equal Rights* essayist was Gwendolyn Jones, a Wellesley graduate who was at that time a second year medical student. She argued that the only real difference between men and women was the childbearing function, but that many unhealthy customs and conventions had crystallized around this difference. Thus women depended on men for all the necessities of life, making men selfish and possessive. In return, women catered to men's slightest whims; as a result, men became even more insensitive and arrogant. Alma Lutz also believed that the theory of male superiority affected men's personalities adversely, making them materialistic rather than idealistic.[2]

One of the NWP's Declaration of Principles had challenged the idea that men were the sole support of their families. The Party believed that only the childless idle wives of men with large incomes could be considered "supported." Yet it also recognized that the average man "honestly believes he supports his wife and family, he takes great pride in so doing, and he considers himself humiliated if his wife has to go out and 'work.'" In the twenties, Doris Stevens and Arthur Garfield Hays debated the question of whether wives should be paid from their husbands' income for the work done in the home. As one reporter noted, the debate began with gentle good humor, but as the audience become involved the debate became a "genuine sex conflict." Clarence Darrow insisted that women had no sense of fair play in money matters, while Hays argued that husbands would give their wives anything within reason, but to pay them for housework would create disharmony in the home. The NWP, of course, had never specifically suggested anything other than that the wife's contributions to the home should be recognized. The problem was exacerbated by the depression. Ruth Gill Williams maintained that there was a definite movement on the part of men to eliminate women from all but the most undesirable menial jobs, in order "to place women *totally* at the mercy of men." And sociologist Mirra Komarovsky discovered in her depression study of unemployed men and their families that none of the men found the slightest compensation in freedom from their work routine, because for the majority of American men, their occuption provided their primary identity and only means of self-expression.[3]

Both men and male culture were hostile to women and their interests, most Party members believed. Equalitarian feminists saw wars as conflicts between male governments, which women were powerless to prevent as long as they were not considered the equals of men. Rebecca Hourwich and her friends became annoyed at some men who had tried to start a conversation with them on a bus tour, but enjoyed the men's discomfort when they informed them loudly of the legal discriminations against women. "The intimation of sex antagonism by a man, however politely couched," Hourwich concluded, "is always meant as an insult." Ruth Gill Williams also found men insentitive and unfair with respect to women, writing of her disbelief "when men I have known have looked straight at me and made remarks concerning the ability and intelligence of women that were unbelievably insulting." Lawyer and novelist Blanche Crozier's explanation of this phenomenon was somewhat more analytical. Men did not realize how insulting they were when they criticized women in general to another women, "the assumption apparently being that the one addressed will feel honored by an implication that she is an exception, that she will be flattered by being allowed to be on the men's side."[4]

Men would have to be subjected to considerable pressure before they would give up their dominant position and privileges, the NWP believed; when given the opportunity, even great and talented men could take advantage of women without fearing the disapproval of society. Writing about Milton, one NWP feminist pointed out that "while the world has expressed much maudlin sympathy for the 'Blind Poet,' the victims of his religious bigotry and domestic tyranny—his two wives and daughters—have received none." Men could not even admire the outstanding achievement of a woman like swimmer Gertrude Ederle because this achievement involved the so-called manly virtues of courage, strength, physical skill, and endurance. Instead, *Equal Rights* editorialized, to protect their sex pride men insisted that women's bodies were better protected by fat.[5]

Although NWP members never really questioned white middle class male values, both Olga Knopf and Pearl Buck, authors widely admired by equalitarian feminists, were skeptical about these values. In 1935, psychologist Knopf pointed out that "we are living not only in a man's culture but in a white man's culture," and went on to note the parallels between Negroes' status and women's status. She also concluded that in American society of the thirties, "the most unfortunate position was to be both a Negro and a woman." Although *Equal*

Rights reviewed Knopf's book very favorably, the Party never adopted this line of analysis. Pearl Buck used a similar analogy in *Of Men and Women*, arguing that the strong always oppressed the weak. She identified the strong in America as "the white, Gentile, adult male" while the weak were a disparate group including women, Negroes, Jews, and the very poor. Implicit in both Knopf's and Buck's work was a questioning of the white male middle class power structure. Doris Stevens, like most NWP feminists, however, did not question the power structure but rather concentrated on how to gain women's equality within the existing system. Her theory was that in times of stress such as wars, revolutions, and their immediate aftermaths, men were more vulnerable to women's demands for justice. Women should take advantage of these crises to make gains, because during relatively secure periods "a woman is a woman, but a man is a human being."[6]

In spite of their pervasive distrust of men, NWP members claimed that men's attitudes would evolve eventually into respect for women. Feminists were often more concerned with what journalist Ida Clyde Clarke termed "the millions of sleeping beauties of our own sex." Ruby Black, reviewing Anthony Ludovici's *Lysistrata* and Dora Black's *Hypatia* in 1925, called the two books "the last clinch in the struggle between the sexes." Dismissing Ludovici's misanthropy and antifeminism as a product of some injury he had suffered in the past, the reviewer emphasized how typical Dora Black was of younger feminists who saw their enemies as fear, ignorance, and reaction, rather than men. "So the younger feminists have almost forgotten that there has been sex antagonism, sex hostility, sex warfare," she wrote approvingly. Jane Norman Smith believed there must be "good will and mutual understanding between the sexes" in order for feminism to succeed in achieving its goals, insisting that "I am not in the least bit anti-man." Even Mrs. Hooker dismissed Olive Schreiner's late nineteenth century writings as "dated" because they expressed hostility toward men. Maintaining that such problems were no longer of central concern to women, Hooker denied that the fight for equality was "a struggle to throw off the tyranny of men." Alma Lutz, writing in the late thirties, still believed women could change men's "medieval attitude." Men were at least willing to give women a chance to prove themselves, she thought, concluding that "I do not think men are formidable enemies in breaking down traditions."[7]

Yet men did regard feminist goals as threatening during the twenties and thirties. June Sochen has indicated that the feminist movement in Greenwich Village was at first considered a kind of game, and she quotes Floyd Dell as saying: "We thought they could be content with the joy of the struggle. But they needed the joy of achievement." By the mid-twenties, much popular magazine literature was devoted to the decline of the American man. In her satire, "The Great National Calamity," Rebecca Hourwich suggested that women give up "finding things for them and picking up after them" because such habits made men dependent and childlike. The NWP's position was that women had progressed so rapidly that it simply appeared to some observers that men had retrogressed. "Really men are just as good and virile and intelligent as ever," wrote Mrs. Hooker in 1929. "It is merely more difficult for them to get along solely on their sex than it was before."[8]

During the depression, Komarovsky found men looking for scapegoats to explain their long-term unemployment. Few men blamed the American capitalist system; most men blamed groups like married women, Negroes, and foreigners for taking their jobs. In William Chafe's analysis of women's greatly expanded economic opportunities during the 1940s, he stresses that women's work then was not perceived as a feminist threat, "part of an overt revolt against traditional values, or as a self-conscious movement for equality." But during the thirties, such activity was seen as threatening. As Robert Smuts has pointed out, "to a great many men the feminist demand for equal rights was an attempt to usurp masculine functions and prerogatives which could succeed only by forcing the traditional feminine role on men." His assertion is supported by articles like Eugene Pharo's "Emancipating the American Male," which appeared in the *American Mercury* in 1938. Pharo began by demonstrating that the employment of women had expanded during the depression, while that of men had contracted. He argued that if women wanted masculine privileges and equality, they should support men who could then devote themselves to culture. In Pharo's bitter description of this total role reversal, men would stay home, cook, and keep up their personal appearances, while women would be chivalrous, generous, powerful protectors and providers for the family. Pearl Buck believed that it was just such a separation between home and the world of outside work that had created troubled relationships between men and women. Men's respect for women was based on fear, Buck argued, and this fear motivated men to eliminate women from all possible areas of competition.[9]

NWP feminists also attacked the double standard of morality which granted more freedom to men than to women, although they believed most men were sexually immoral. Women should not be censured for smoking in public when it was permissible for men, insisted *Equal Rights* after the cancellation of preacher Maude Royden's tour because of her transgression. Mrs. Hooker, of course, believed that smoking was a filthy, unhealthy habit injurious to both sexes, but emphasized that the double standard must be eliminated even in trivial matters before men and women would be truly equal. The Party also protested against the double standard in the more sensational case of the U.S. immigration authorities' refusal to admit Lady Cathcart into the country because of her moral turpitude, while the Earl of Craven, named as corespondent in the divorce suit brought against her, was admitted. These incidents tend to support the view that one major issue of the twenties centered on the question of which sex would create the single standard of morality for both men and women, while during the thirties economic disequilibrium caused a realignment and reinforcement of traditional values.[10]

Nothing was more indicative of the NWP feminists' underlying distrust of men's moral character than the Party's attitude toward prostitution. The connection between sex and economics in both marriage and prostitution had been outlined clearly by the nineteenth century feminists. Prostitution was both an economic and a moral issue, the equivalent of female slavery and as such abhorrent to social purity reformers and feminists. The movement to license or in any way legitimatize prostitution had encountered tremendous opposition in both the United States and Great Britain by the turn of the century, but sporadic outbursts of indignation and panic over white slavery and venereal disease lasted well into the 1920s. In the mid-twenties, the NWP joined the New York League of Women Voters in actively campaigning to amend state laws so as to penalize the customer as well as the prostitute, and to make the customer liable to the same compulsory venereal disease examination as the prostitute. Prostitutes had always been singled out as a special class, made into scapegoats for other people's sins, and either abused or sentimentalized, wrote Crystal

Eastman. "But one thing they have never had yet," she added, "and that is simple justice."[11]

Men's moral code was based on complete sexual license for themselves but on chastity for the women in their families, claimed Mrs. Hooker. The majority of Party members agreed that "it is a great day for feminism when women of all classes demand justice for the prostitute." Many organized women were appalled when the League of Nations study on the Traffic in Women and Children, authorized in 1921, was finally made public in 1927 and 1928. The conclusions were published first, showing that the white slave traffic was still very extensive. As the NWP was quick to point out, all this traffic was financed by males who were neither pimps nor procurers, but "just an ordinary, everyday kind of man, the sort one meets and knows and is related to; some woman's husband, brother, father or son."[12]

Mrs. Belmont's indignation reached a new high with the publication of the actual evidence on the white slave traffic. Noting that countries where women's position was lowest provided the most "sex slaves," she warned women to be suspicious of all male chivalry and to redouble their efforts for equal rights. When Doris Stevens encountered objections from the League of Nations to the treaty method of gaining equality, she asked sarcastically: "Must we become sex-slaves before we can be judged fit subjects for action by convention?" Most NWP feminists never abandoned the Victorian stereotype of men as sexual predators, who saw women and girls primarily in terms of conquests. Men tolerated immorality and commercialized vice; their sex laws were "the laws of the wolf pack." As a result, boys were surrounded by temptation "and adolescence blossoms not fairly in the sun, but in the marsh-light of openly sanctioned brothels." Women must have equal rights, insisted Mrs. Hooker, otherwise "what matters it if thousands of young girls are annually offered up to the moloch of men's lust if a human existence counts for nothing?"[13]

Men had proven themselves unable to develop wise and ethical sex standards; American sex laws were "an enduring monument of the selfishness and sexual incompetence of men." "Beset by desire they rationalize their conduct," explained *Equal Rights*, "and then translate this rationalization into law." Mrs. Hooker insisted that women must face up to the persistence of prostitution, but she rejected the contention that men "needed" such an outlet. If it were true that men had such sexual needs, she wrote, prostitution would be "recognized as a useful trade, virtuous in proportion to the sacrifice." But men and women were not really that different in their needs, she maintained, arguing that both prostitution and the double standard were the result of men's lack of sexual ethics.[14]

Although most Party members believed themselves both ethical and modern in their approach to prostitution, venereal disease, and sex education, they implicated but refused to openly identify men as sexual oppressors. Nor did they understand the causes or results of the changing sexual relationship between men and women. The NWP firmly believed that the economic independence that would come with the ERA would end both prostitution and the subordination of women's interests in marriage. Yet in both these decades other feminists had moved beyond this kind of rather simplistic economic determinism. In her book *Concerning Women*, published in 1926 and dedicated to NWP members Ellen and Rebecca Winsor, Suzanne LaFollette had argued that when men used wives and prostitutes for different purposes, the results included "very considerable dehumanization." All women were trained to get approval, could not honestly be themselves even to themselves, and were socialized to stay in their "place." "The sum of these superstitions and prepossessions," concluded LaFollette, "may be expressed in the generalization that woman is primarily a function." Prostitution, according to LaFollette, reflected only men's taste and immorality—it had no bearing at all on the morality of women. Women might become prostitutes because it was the only way they could earn a living, because they had been "ruined" by some man, or because they prostituted themselves legally in marriage, "as women have been forced to do from time immemorial."[15]

Winifred Holtby also considered the problem of the relationship between men and women in *Women in a Changing Civilisation*. In societies where women's interests were always secondary to those of men, she observed, prostitution was the crudest, but not the only, violation of women's personalities. Holtby believed that the male moral code which made chastity "a social obsession" had handicapped all women immeasurably. From this intellectual position, she argued logically that access to birth control knowledge and legalized abortion would allow women to be free, "and yet not buy this freedom with celibacy." Women could then control and plan their own lives; both their attitudes and their place in society would be changed. The real battles of feminism, she suggested, were fought privately by women who refused to tolerate a double standard for adultery and who were no longer willing to be passive sexual objects subject to their husbands' wills. The actual feminist struggle, then, "centered round the determination of women to be recognized as persons in themselves, not merely the repositories of man's honour or his 'sin.'"[16]

The NWP never went as far as either LaFollette or Holtby in analyzing male-female relationships. At various times in *Equal Rights*, Party activists expressed their ideas on marriage, divorce, alimony, the home-versus-career question, motherhood, and birth control. But these expressions could not be said to form a coherent ideology, and were always of secondary importance compared with the Party's analysis of feminism and its techniques, its recognition of the legal and economic discriminations against women, or its development of a rationale for the ERA. The NWP may have been unwilling or perhaps unable to develop a systematic analysis of male-female relationships, but there were some consistent themes throughout much of the members' writings. Some Party members were optimistic, especially during the twenties, that the "new" woman would be able to join with a man in a new kind of marriage. Ruth Hale, whose own marriage, divorce, and subsequent "collaboration" with Heywood Broun were anything but conventional, wrote that traditional marriage was "a mundane institution, none too brilliantly done." Marriage should be an experiment, constantly revised to meet the needs of the times, and Hale opposed the concept that marriage was divinely sanctioned since this idea might hinder the development of friendship between husbands and wives.[17]

In 1924, *Equal Rights* described "the hope of the future . . . in the husband and wife walking side by side, equals, partners, friends and lovers." In general, Party members approved of Judge Ben Lindsey's ideas on companionate marriage, which involved a kind of trial marriage in which both members of the couple would work and would refrain from having children. After this trial period, the couple could begin their family if they wished to make the marriage permanent, or obtain a sort of no-fault divorce if they wished to separate. "In other words, he wants honesty, decency, fairness and normal and beautiful sex expression," wrote Ruby Black, adding that such an arrangement would tend to eliminate the concept of women as property which formed the basis for male jealousy and possessiveness.[18]

The Party was not so favorable in its view of Floyd Dell's "An Outline of Marriage," published by the American Birth Control League in 1927. Although agreeing with the main arguments for birth control and a marriage based on love and companionship, the NWP questioned the author's hypothetical description of the ideal married woman. Before her marriage she had worked; however, "this modern wife in her testimony is made to say that hers was not a life work, as her husband's was, that she willingly stopped it to produce her children, but that she hopes to return to it when the children are older." Party members like Doris Stevens argued that marriage was simply a business partnership that should be based on a contract providing for mutual support. Anything less than cooperation and friendship, especially any kind of authority and subordination model, could only result in a "third rate love" or no love at all. The more radical Vera Brittain argued that the claims of a husband on a woman's time and energy should be no more than "those of an intimate friend." Brittain did not believe that married couples should always be in "perpetual association" although she did think that "intermittent reunion is desirable." In her view, marriage should symbolize "the union of two careers and two sets of ideals and aspirations," and women should try to adapt marriage to work, rather than adapting work to marriage.[19]

Even in the twenties, however, feminist optimism about the emergence of a new kind of marriage was the minority view. In assessing the repeated failures of a Connecticut women's jury service bill, the Party blamed not only the apathy of women but also the fact that "their husbands have a death-like grip on the doors which might permit a new idea to enter." A married woman was the special target of all kinds of restrictions that tended to make her into an unnatural kind of parasite, totally dependent on her husband. Yet she paid a high price for such protection, the Party insisted, including in some cases bodily punishment. *Equal Rights* reprinted a New York newspaper exposé of wife-beating, in which the author had noted that wife-beating was unimportant as news, depended directly on the concept of women's subjection, and concluded that "the sinister fact is that slaves are always beaten." Austrian feminist Helene Granitsch, a member of the NWP's international advisory council, shared this gloomy view. The restrictions on married women were not new, argued Mme. Granitsch, but in earlier times there was little concern for the female victims "who, for the larger part of their lives, lived a joyless existence—without the light of intellectual activity." Even educated or trained women were expected to give up their outside work when they married, submerging themselves in housework. "Oh, the emptiness of it!" lamented Mme. Granitsch. "How tedious, truly how old-fashioned!" A series of adverse state court decisions on married women's property rights led Mrs. Hooker to conclude that their status was the same as slaves. If such discriminations continued, she had warned earlier, college educated women might decide in favor of "unlegalized unions."[20]

Although the majority of NWP activist members were married, they were disappointed if their own members' marriages interfered with feminist work. When author Inez Haynes Irwin declined a Party office in 1927, Mary Gertrude Fendall remarked that "she needs a lot of education as a feminist!" In the usual NWP manner of directly comparing men and women, Fendall asked: "What would we think of a man who said he could not be on a committee because one of his arduous occupations was being his wife's husband?"[21] But generally NWP feminists were not at all surprised to see their worst fears about the restrictiveness of marriage born out. Elizabeth Selden Rogers, a charter member of the NWP, reviewed a novel very favorably for *Equal Rights* in 1929, concluding:

> There is not a happy marriage in the book in any of the generations. Marriage has wrecked them all—men and women— in one way or another. Yet it is not a sad story. It shows the horrible slave-like lives of the women, dependent for every cent on their husbands.[22]

She did not like the novel's ending, however, in which a very modern woman found the "right man" in an old-fashioned husband. In fact, Rogers predicted that this was the kind of marriage which would "go straight on the rocks." But by the mid-thirties, unmarried feminists like Alma Lutz were in a position of vigorously defending single career women who had supposedly "missed the greatest thing in life and are unhappy in spite of their worldly success." Lutz observed that critics too often overlooked unhappy and disillusioned wives and mothers, yet she never deviated from the official NWP line. "There need be no choice between economic independence and babies," she insisted. "Both are possible and desirable."[23]

The NWP frequently referred to married women as a class, and argued that although they performed important services in the home, these services had no money value and thus their worth was not recognized. Given the existence of discrimination, the Party reasoned that women's upward mobility depended on the men they married rather than on any achievement of their own.[24] Although Mrs. Hooker stressed that business, professional, and all working women suffered from the restrictions of marriage, she took her example from the milieu she knew best.

> The debutante, or the girl who wishes she were one, the finishing school, a few feeble efforts at philanthropy, marriage; slam! slam! the door of opportunity is permanently closed on a seventeen or eighteen year old victim.[25]

But the Party never followed this line of thinking through to its logical conclusion and advocated neither revolutionary changes in the institution of marriage nor its total abolition. The same Mrs. Hooker who could say "thank God for the spinsters," credit unmarried women with winning the vote, and maintain that marriage "has done more to close the door of opportunity to women than any other institution," could insist "and yet we believe in marriage firmly when it isn't a trap, but an outlet." Party feminists failed to analyze carefully the institution which they so instinctively feared, and made no constructive suggestions about how to transform marriage into an "outlet" for women.[26] Even their strong implication that married women should work outside the home was never implemented by any positive advice about how a career and marriage could be combined. Certainly there were feminists both within the NWP and outside it during the twenties and thirties who had given these problems serious consideration. But they were isolated from the NWP consensus on the priority of legal and economic goals.

Rebecca Hourwich was an organizer for the Party in the early twenties, a free-lance magazine writer and a young wife and mother. Although she struggled to remain a Party activist and was to some degree successful, she suffered a breakdown from exhaustion and was temporarily out of touch with Party affairs after her husband's job took them to a small town in Maine. Her major concerns were how to raise her daughter as an equal and independent person and how to prevent her own career from being submerged in her roles as wife and mother. In 1926, Hourwich reviewed *Portia Marries*, describing the novel as unrealistic. It portrayed both husband and wife as well established professionals with a good deal of money, who lived in an urban area where services were plentiful. Furthermore, the novel did not deal with the couple's son until he was eighteen years old, leaving his childhood upbringing in obscurity. In the real world, Hourwich insisted, couples married before they were successful in their careers, had low salaries, and struggled to maintain a traditional home and family at the same time. Services were often either too expensive or unavailable, and Hourwich concluded that "any marriage is a gamble."[27]

Josephine Herbst, a writer and former editor of *Smart Set*, was primarily concerned with what happened to women in the creative arts when they married. She observed that older feminists had emphasized the need of independent work for women, but younger women had reacted against this, and "loved and married recklessly, instinctively knowing that the business of creative life in the arts was inexorably allied with a sex life." It was later that the couple found themselves trapped in a relationship quite different from what they had expected, particularly wives who in spite of themselves fell into "that fatal adaptivity and amiability of women in their lives with men." A wife ended up hating both herself and her husband and it was then "that she can see some sense, even if not a great deal, in the didactic struggle of the older crowd who separated careers and marriage as if they were oil and water." Herbst's only conclusion was that if women artists were aware of the dangers, they might juggle the demands on their lives and work more adroitly.[28]

Not even Suzanne LaFollette devoted much of her analysis of

woman's condition to the institution of marriage. She did object to regarding marriage as a mere condition for men but a vocation for women, because this meant that women's other interests were regarded as something which must be adapted to the marriage. The economic aspects of marriage still bore too close a resemblance to both chattel slavery and industrial slavery, LaFollette believed, and suggested that the tenacity of the institution of marriage was partly due to habit and partly because it enabled the state to exploit people economically. In her view, illegitimacy, marriage, and prostitution formed "a triptych of which the central panel is institutionalized marriage and the other panels the two chief aspects of its failure." But LaFollette, too, shied away from directly advocating the abolition of marriage and concluded only that the question of women's freedom was inextricably bound up in the larger question of human freedom from economic exploitation.[29]

In the mid-thirties, unmarried career women were likely to be on the defensive, and often were more direct in their criticisms of traditional marriage. It was always the woman, wrote Blanche Crozier, "who pays the cost of our system of marriage; and what she pays is such a destruction of her own potentialities." Crozier stressed that both public opinion and custom expected a wife to be supportive of her husband's career, and that this retarded her own development whether or not she realized it. Only work could offer a partial escape to married women, and this must be something more than just a hobby. The question of how to develop a better relationship between men and women in marriage was one which Crozier, like most Party members in the thirties, did not even attempt to answer. Yet as Dora Black had pointed out nearly a decade earlier: "Life isn't all earning your living. Unfortunately we fall in love and Feminism must take that into consideration."[30]

Party members' opinions on divorce, the other side of the marriage question, were consistent with their demand for total equality. As Edna Rostow has noted, divorce serves as a traditional way of accommodating the conflicts within marriage which are inherent during any movement for the "emancipation" of women. Or as Ruth Hale explained in the early twenties, "divorce has made marriage flexible, debatable." Feminists were concerned about the rising divorce rates throughout this period because they saw the increase as symptomatic of the failure of marriage as an institution to adjust to the changing times. Yet most regarded divorce not as a moral question, but rather as a simple cancellation of the marriage contract, believing that "the problem of the modern Feminist is to secure legislation whereby this cancellation may be as equitable as possible." But there was no real agreement among members on the best method for making divorce equitable. Ruth Hale favored individual state legislative reform which would make possible "cheap, easy, collusive divorce," while Doris Stevens supported a federal amendment providing uniform grounds for divorce. All equalitarian feminists agreed, however, that the grounds for divorce should be identical for men and women, and that a woman should be able to regain her own identity and not be punished for the failed marriage "after she has corrected the error by divorce."[31]

There was even less consensus or consistency in the feminist view of alimony during the twenties and thirties. In was difficult for NWP members not to feel that alimony was a kind of payment for the many disabilities suffered by married women. They tended to argue in the twenties that eliminating alimony without at the same time granting equal rights would cause great hardship to many women. "There is no justice in demanding that women regard sex in marriage as a dignified means to earning a living," editorialized *Equal Rights*, "and then all of a sudden cut the props out from under." On the other hand, feminists were unwilling to see alimony used as an argument against equality in marriage. Men would demand compensation if they had to support women with whom they no longer lived, and this compensation would further restrict the rights of all women. Feminists outside the Party also seemed to have mixed feelings about alimony. Suzanne LaFollette, in spite of her devotion to economic equality, believed that women were often victimized within marriage and suggested only that some fair and just basis for alimony be established. And Dorothy Thomas, writing for *Independent Woman* in the mid-thirties, maintained that even though alimony was an anachronism there were some women who deserved it. "The woman who has devoted her life to her husband and children and then is discarded for a younger mate must be protected," she insisted, voicing the worst fears of many married women. Thomas herself saw alimony as degrading, but also recognized

that women must have equal opportunity in order to provide for themselves economically.[32]

Equalitarian feminist thinking during this period, whether it was
about marriage, divorce, the home, motherhood, or woman's identity,
always returned to the possibility of a career or outside job and economic independence. In a way, this became as much of a focal point as the
suffrage had been for the earlier feminists. But while all women pre-
sumably could vote without causing strain on the performance of their
roles as wives and mothers, an outside job could not be so easily integrated into women's lives. Although there was a growing public
acceptance of middle and to some extent upper class unmarried women
earning their own living, it was not generally acceptable for any but
lower class married women to work for pay outside the home. Public
hostility was strongest against middle class married women with
children, but was extended to married women of all classes, with or
without children, during the depression.

In 1914, the young Walter Lippman had glowingly forecast that
"one of the supreme values of feminism is that it will have to socialize
the home." Feminists, including the NWP, agreed that the home
should be socialized, but gave very little thought to how this could
be accomplished. Like the male-female relationship in marriage, the
"politics" of housework was not a primary concern to most feminists
during the twenties and thirties. There were exceptions, of course. In
1920, Rebecca Hourwich tried to draw attention to the importance of
homemakers and their "domestic unrest," arguing that only a reorganization of the home would make equality meaningful for all women. By
the mid-twenties, Hourwich was insisting that husbands and wives
must share housework because it was important for the socialization
of children. Although Party members never doubted that the home
was the basic unit of society, they argued that it had shrunk in scope
and was often too restrictive for modern women. Wifehood and housework must be divorced, argued Doris Stevens in the twenties, and if
housework could not be standardized and done by specialists, then
wives should be paid from their husbands' incomes. Unfortunately,
the Party recognized, public opinion was that "work is not work if it
is done within the four walls of the home." Thus the NWP joined
with the other women's organizations in support of the Women's

Bureau efforts to include homemaking as an occupational classification in the 1930 census.[33]

The so-called "nervous housewife" received considerable attention in the popular literature of the twenties, but by the thirties she was more likely to be considered neurotic. The Party maintained a home-makers' council throughout both decades, which consistently argued that the "breadmaker" was as important as the "breadwinner." But NWP feminists also believed that much of the housework done in urban areas was wasteful, repetitive work which could be handled much better by hired specialists. Women should not have the double burden of an outside job and housework, argued the NWP, urging that homemaking be studied and then better adapted to the needs of working women. Equalitarian feminists resented any attempt to classify housework as women's work, calling this view "the kitchen complex," and they were even more disturbed by those critics of equal rights who accused feminists of trying to break up the home by forcing women into outside jobs.[34]

On the subject of housework itself there was very little disagreement between NWP feminists and those outside the Party. In 1921, Freda Kirchwey accused women's magazines of having as their common purpose "to make a domestic career endurable to all married women." This kind of unskilled labor was a community waste when it involved educated and highly trained women, the Party insisted. For creative women, housework could be destructive of their talents, as poet Anna Wickham explained in 1925. "Sometimes I think the reason why women have not distinguished themselves more in creative art is not because they bear children," she told Crystal Eastman, "but because they keep house." Or as Josephine Herbst concluded, "the machinery of female duties grinds the artist out of a woman unless she is thorough-ly aware of what is happening to her." The economic dependence of a housewife was also reflected in her relationship with her husband, Gwendolyn Jones explained, because "she is there to please him, to give him menial service, or sex service, or to act as a blatant consumer-by-proxy of his wealth." By the 1930s, the Party was characterizing housework without pay as debasing for the wife, as a bad example for the children, and as providing a rationale for the low pay of women working outside the home.[35]

Opinion outside the Party, except in women's magazines, also was frequently negative toward housework. In their first study of "Middletown," the Lynds found this division of labor "far-reaching as affecting the attitude of the sexes toward each other," and Komarovsky's depression study showed extreme friction when wives asked their unemployed husbands to help with the housework. "Housework is so closely identified with the woman's rather than the man's role in the family," she concluded, "that performing it is a symbol of degradation." Winifred Holtby maintained that "the tradition of woman as home maker encumbers her intellectual and economic progress at every turn," and suggested abolishing family homes for a generation. Pearl Buck saw the home as a stronghold of security, privacy, and noncompetitive work for women, which destroyed women by denying "the one great blessing of a man's life—the necessity to go out into the world and earn their bread directly."[36]

Perhaps the most revealing statements about women in the home were made by Mrs. Harvey Wiley and Mrs. Emile Berliner, both heads of the NWP homemakers' council. In the mid-twenties, Mrs. Wiley pointed out that about 22 percent of the Party's membership were full time homemakers, while nationally homemakers formed "a vast army" of women. Women should earn their own living first, and after they became housewives they should study home economics, Mrs. Wiley advised.

> Then, with a firm hold on God, a lively interest in outside affairs, and a strong hope for future freedom and self-espression after the home nest is empty, the home-maker, it seems to me, can weather the gale on the stormy sea of matrimony and make a safe landing on the Islands of Contentment.[37]

In 1930, although homemaking had been recognized by the census as an occupation, Mrs. Emile Berliner was less sanguine. Housework placed great demands on women who had neither special aptitude nor the training for it. Homemaking was monotonous, she noted, although occasionally there were compensations. However, her overall evaluation of the role was negative, for she concluded that "the drudgery is there, and work in a factory could be no more uninteresting and uninspiring than some housework."[38]

NWP feminists feared and distrusted men, perceived marriage and homemaking as threats to outside job opportunities, and were even more ambivalent toward motherhood. In 1920, Eleanor Taylor had pointed out to Party members that most women were or would become mothers and that any feminist movement which ignored their problems invited failure. Taylor's view of mothers, however, was not encouraging.

> Chained within four walls by the demands of the kitchen and the nursery, dependent for support and for her children's life upon the capability and unselfishness of one man, the mother, lower economically than the wage slave, herself handicapped in the expression of her personality, passes on her handicap to society, her children, and to other women.[39]

Taylor concluded rather paradoxically that mothers were too self-effacing and did not recognize their own worth.

An *Equal Rights* editorial of the mid-twenties described motherhood as a golden chain that in the past had bound women to the home, although the NWP believed motherhood should be viewed as a service to the nation and a sacrifice on the part of women for the continuation of the race. The Party advocated some form of the endowment of motherhood plans so widely discussed during the twenties, involving national payments before and immediately after childbirth. But a consistent underlying theme was that of the mother as martyr. In a review of the accomplishments of Edna St. Vincent Millay, an NWP member suggested that there were few great women poets of the past because of the large families women had. "Children are tangible, insistent appalling actualities," the reviewer wrote, "and their reality has a way of hushing the intensity that lies behind all abandon."[40] A few years later, *Equal Rights* responded to a challenge to produce "great women" from the past by arguing that all women understood

> that the reason why the members of their own sex had not excelled in the arts and sciences was because of their motherhood. They had sacrificed their own gifts, their own potentialities to their children, and their children, of the masculine

gender at least, had risen not to bless them, but to taunt them.[41]

The NWP joined all major women's groups in endorsing the Sheppard-Towner Maternity Act during the early twenties, and consistently supported legislation to make obstetrical care and information available to all mothers. A few Party feminists also shared some of the concerns of the eugenics movement, arguing that the finest women must become mothers for the good of the race. From their viewpoint, of course, the best mothers would be those who had education or training and the self-respect which came from equal rights. Party members rejected laws which they believed penalized maternity, such as those forcing pregnant school teachers to resign immediately and take two year leaves after childbirth. Costs of maternity care should be paid by public expense, the Party believed, for legislation requiring employers to pay maternity benefits simply cost women their jobs.[42]

Like most women's organizations in the twenties, the NWP did not take a clear stand on birth control because its own members were not in agreement on the issue. Some, like the author of an unsigned 1923 *Equal Rights* article, advocated free knowledge of birth control information "as a means of weeding out the garden of humanity, of eliminating undesirable strains." Another anonymous contributor saw birth control knowledge as potentially broadening women's opportunities, yet noted that it was the more highly educated women who were taking advantage of the chance to have fewer children, while the less educated were "reproducing in geometrical progression." Margaret Sanger, who had characterized birth control as "the fundamental freedom," was entertained at national headquarters in 1923 with a reception in her honor; in 1925, an admiring interview with Sanger, which described the birth control campaign as a creative effort, was published in *Equal Rights*. Mme. Granitsch was more forthright about birth control knowledge in her 1926 article, "The Revolution of Married Women." "Now woman shall be her own master," she wrote, "she shall herself dispose of her own body."[43]

But the NWP also included increasing numbers of nonprofessional working women, like Mary Murray of the industrial council, and the attitude of these women toward birth control was frequently one of opposition. In 1927, Murray was carrying on a public exchange of letters with a priest who favored protective legislation for women. In order to prove her credentials as a good Catholic, a working mother by necessity, and a patriot, Murray wrote:

> Perhaps it is the fault of the printer that the Reverend Father calls me a "miss." I want him to know that I am neither a young miss nor an old maid. I have gone through all the stages of a woman's life. I went willing down into the valley of death seven times to bring forth my loved children; I was left a widow with five little tots, the oldest seven years of age. I was forced to go to work to support them. I had two ready when Uncle Sam called, a soldier boy and a nurse, and now I am graduated into the class of grandmother.[44]

In 1933, Murray wrote angrily to *Equal Rights*, protesting an editorial praising Margaret Sanger's fight for birth control. Since Alma Lutz had written the editorial, she replied, making it clear that the editorial had represented only her personal opinion. The Party itself took no official stand on the birth control issue, Lutz explained, and apologized for having upset Murray and many of the industrial council members. Murray's reply was revealing: "You did not alarm me or my organization you just put us on the war path, they were not troubled—simply wild."[45] But Murray and the others were reassured and the NWP continued to avoid openly advocating birth control.

Party feminists were also in disagreement about whether mothers of preschool children should work outside the home. Mrs. Harvey Wiley thought women with young children should stay at home unless driven by extreme economic necessity. The Party's public image by the mid-twenties was often that of a small group of aggressive, unattractive, largely childless women; they especially suffered from such journalists as Hearst's Norman Hapgood, who described them as a "pugnacious but shallow little band of similarity maniacs." Increasingly put on the defensive by the spreading hypothesis that the children of working mothers would become neurotic, delinquent, and even criminal, the NWP confined itself to noting examples like Charles Lindbergh, whose mother taught high school. But it was difficult to argue against such a popular journalist as Dorothy Dix, who strongly supported married women's right to work outside the home, except for the woman with small children "because her job is taking care of them."[46]

Some equalitarian feminists during this period suggested day care facilities or a sharing of child care by husbands, but they were in the minority. In 1920, a *Suffragist* article suggested that since it would probably take at least a generation to shift some child care responsibilities to men, cooperative day nurseries should serve during the interim. The author concluded optimistically that the solution for working mothers "comes down to a matter of co-operation and organization." In the late twenties, Vera Brittain refined this argument in a way that suggested that women must free themselves mentally from the idea that child rearing should be their major task; fathers could share in child care and children could be left on their own more. In the early thirties Mrs. Hooker editorialized that maternity and paternity were of equal value, but stopped short of suggesting that fathers should help with child care. It might be argued that this failure of the NWP to reconcile the raising of children with women's careers at least partly explained such incidents as the one recounted by Olga Knopf in the thirties. A women's professional organization offered a prize to a woman both outstanding in her profession and married with children. "After much investigation they found their paragon," wrote Holtby. "A week later she suffered a nervous breakdown from overwork."[47]

The only member of the NWP publicly and consistently concerned with giving young children a feminist upbringing was Rebecca Hourwich. In a series of articles during the twenties she described her efforts with her young daughter Faith. When Faith rebelled against smocks and trousers and demanded dresses instead, Hourwich recognized the importance of peer group pressure and gave in to the child's wishes. Hourwich confessed that she had not wanted a son, but a daughter "who would grow up to be the perfect feminist and take her mother's place in the Woman's Party." But after a series of disappointments with her daughter, Hourwich admitted wryly that "my last hope for Faith was perhaps a nonactive membership in the League of Women Voters." By the time the child was six years old, her mother's hopes had revived. After spending a winter with her grandmother in a traditional setting, Faith reacted against "household strangulation" and became a tomboy. Even more encouraging, Hourwich was able to train her young daughter not to disturb her when she was working. Describing herself as the only "non-disturbable mother" in town, Hourwich concluded that "it has never even occurred to other mothers how often interruption brutally destroys any opportunity for clear thought or harmonious action."[48]

But the majority of Party feminists did not view childrearing as an important issue. Many of the activists, such as Mrs. Belmont, Mrs. Pell, Mrs. Wiley, Mrs. Hooker, Mary Murray, and Jane Norman Smith were older women whose children were already grown. Some, like Doris Stevens and Anita Pollitzer, were married but childless. A few, like Alice Paul and Alma Lutz, never married. Although *Equal Rights* reminded its readers in its 1924 Christmas editorial that no little girl yet had the gift of equal opportunity which was given to all little boys, and Alma Lutz reflected in the 1930s that feminists should not be careless about raising their children to be human beings in their own right, the Party journal almost never raised questions or made suggestions about child rearing. The only exception was in the thirties, when Mrs. Hooker and others argued that the depression should be a lesson to fathers to be certain that their daughters were trained to earn their own living. By the early forties, Mirra Komarovsky's study of women who were college seniors showed considerable role strain. The ideal of homemaker-mother could not be integrated with that of career woman and the results were uncertainty, insecurity, and cultural conflict among these young women. "What are assets for one become liabilities for the other," concluded Komarovsky, "and the full realization of one role threatens defeat in the other."[49]

But the NWP's main concerns about the motherhood role remained centered in its use by the proponents of protective legislation for women, or the biological implications relative to women's equality. Party feminists were even more sensitive to ideas or action which seemed to indicate contempt for women. The NWP viewed attempts to remove married women from jobs during the depression as "a supreme insult to all women," because it meant that women had no value except as mothers. The Party also believed that the suppression of women was fundamental to the fascist dictatorships, because they were dedicated only to war and needed women to produce the warriors. There were other ways in which the Party felt motherhood was unjustly denigrated. In 1926, Suzanne LaFollette had argued that the sentimental adulation surrounding motherhood was only present within the rules established by patriarchal society. In other words, LaFollette noted, unwed mothers were not tolerated because they defied the theory of male proprietorship and even implied sexual freedom for women. Prostitution like marriage, LaFollette reasoned, was based on economics and therefore was a noncompetitive institution. But illegitimacy was "a disturbing phenomenon, intimating as it does to virtuous women that the duplex morality to which their freedom is sacrificed is unnatural and unworkable." NWP members joined other feminists in championing the unwed mother and her child in much the same way as they championed justice for prostitutes. Reasoning that economics, rather than moral failure, had victimized both the prostitute and the unwed mother, Party feminists believed that illegitimacy laws were "legislation made by men in favor of men."[50]

The Party basically believed that although men, especially antifeminist men, professed to admire motherhood, they often held it in contempt. Pregnant women were considered "unsuitable" in offices and schools, and were generally barred by law or regulation from continuing to work. Women should be able to decide for themselves whether to continue working, insisted Mrs. Hooker, denying that anyone "should find anything unseemly in the presence of a woman among them who is fulfilling what many people seem to regard as the sole *raison d'etre* of any woman." Nor should women be regarded solely in the light of their children's achievements, argued the Party, for men were honored for their own accomplishments rather than for simply reflecting their children's glory.[51] In general, Party feminists agreed with Winifred Holtby's analysis:

> Maternity is considered so honourable that in its name divorce reform is delayed beyond all reason, women are underpaid, the education of many girls is crippled, women are denied the right of entry to many posts which they could occupy with profit, or are forced to resign from work which they can do and which needs doing.[52]

This ambiguity with respect to women's roles occasionally took the form of questioning the more symbolic aspects of women's identity. Party feminists were concerned, although infrequently, with questions of religion, education, clothes, and language as they related to women. Nineteenth century feminists had protested religious restrictions against women as ministers and one of the NWP's Declaration of Principles demanded that women no longer be barred from the ministry, priesthood, or any position of church authority. In 1923, Mrs. Hooker protested against the decision of Hebrew Union College to exclude women students, and when Methodists in the late twenties voted to bar women from mission work, the NWP pointed out that this interpretation of Christian brotherhood was "intolerant and intemperate, and altogether mediaeval." The Party believed that the attitude of organized religion toward women stemmed from the old idea of "woman's uncleanness" and the centuries long denial that women possessed souls. One NWP member even traced the root of the problem to the Reformation, arguing that "when Protestants began to make light of the Virgin Mary, the troubles of the modern woman began."[53] But the NWP's interest in religion was limited to the demand that the ministry be opened to women; it never engaged in the sort of analysis which Elizabeth Cady Stanton had attempted in the *Woman's Bible*. By the thirties, there was no further discussion of religious questions in the Party journal.

NWP feminists devoted only slightly more thought to education as it affected women. In the nineteenth century, women's educational standards had been an important feminist issue, and the long term trend had been toward similar curriculum requirements for both men's and women's colleges. But in the late twenties and thirties, there was considerable public disagreement about the value of a college education for the majority of women, who were destined to become homemakers and mothers. Some argued that women did not use their education or make it pay, and the NWP had to reject this argument. NWP feminists agreed on the necessity for women's colleges and supported similar educational standards for both men and women. As women's colleges struggled for endowments and financial contributions during this period, Vassar graduate Alma Lutz criticized women for not helping these colleges maintain their high standards of scholarship. Even more importantly, warned Lutz, "the dangerous reactionary tendency to feminize women's education must also be recognized and guarded against." In 1929, the Party supported the Smith College president's argument that women should be educated like men so they would share a common cultural basis. Courses preparing women for motherhood should not be offered, the Party maintained, in the absence of "fatherhood courses." But the real problem, as the NWP saw it, was that even well-educated college women who worked outside the home encountered job discrimination.[54]

While the equalitarian feminists were concerned primarily with support of women's colleges and equal educational and employment opportunities for women, Pearl Buck carried the analysis of women's education to its logical conclusion. The root of American women's discontent was that they were too highly educated for the place which society assigned them, Buck noted. Present methods of educating women were both cruel and wasteful; if women were to be happy in the home they should receive neither high school nor college educations. In addition to basic literacy courses, Buck suggested advanced courses "in cosmetics, bridge, sports, how to conduct a club meeting gracefully, how to be an attractive hostess, with or without servants, and how to deal with very young children in the home."[55] Her suggestion, of course, was only a device to persuade readers of her central thesis, that women should work outside the home on an equal basis with men.

Along with religion and education, some NWP feminists were concerned with women's visible identity. The identity of a woman was reflected by her clothing and her name, these feminists believed. Women should be free to dress as they pleased, the NWP argued during the popular uproar over "flapper fashions." Most Party members, however, did not follow current fashion trends. Some, especially those who were professional women, adopted a severely tailored style; some seemed to prefer more "feminine" dresses; others dressed like the respectable matrons they were. In a late twenties interview, a Wisconsin Party officer and attorney was asked why so many feminists seemed to adopt mannish dress. Dress was a matter of individual taste and preference, she replied, and the way women dressed "is just our interpretation of what makes each of us the mental picture of what we want to be." However, although most Party feminists wanted to be regarded as serious-minded professional women, the general public often believed they wanted to be men.[56] A woman's right to retain her own name was also an issue to some Party feminists. It was not uncommon for professional or well-known women of this era, like Margaret Mead, Amelia Earhart, Frances Perkins, or Caroline Ware, to keep their birth names. Even in "Middletown" in 1925, the Lynds reported, people occasionally discussed a woman's keeping her own name, but the community disapproved of the practice. It was NWP member Ruth Hale who founded the Lucy Stone League which took for its motto Stone's statement: "My name is the symbol of my identity and must not be lost." Mrs. Hooker described the giving up of one's name at marriage as an act which symbolized the old common law assumption that husband and wife were one, and that one was the husband. English feminists tended to agree. "A convention which continues to eclipse the distinguished woman," wrote Vera Brittain rather bitterly in the twenties, "is of course not ever challenged in those still all too frequent cases where a woman's only title to achievement is her acquisition of a husband." Dora Black described the taking of a husband's name as "one of the most devastating symbols of 'subjection' that remain," while Bertrand Russell admitted that "I should not like to have become Mr. Dora Black."[57]

The NWP objected more strongly to any government attempts to force women to use their husband's names. In the twenties the federal government attempted to require married women employees to use their husbands' names for payroll identification. The result was a suit utilizing a brief prepared by the legal research section of the NWP, which showed no statutory or common law support for the government's position. In the mid-twenties the federal government also began requiring married women to sign their husband's names in order to receive passports. The Party protested to President Coolidge, and NWP journalist Ruby Black successfully sued for a passport in her own name. The Party also protested, to no avail, the rulings of eastern railroads which required women to indicate their marital status by the title "Miss" or "Mrs." on commuter passes.[58] The practice of NWP feminists varied. Doris Stevens, Anita Pollitzer, Rebecca Hourwich, Ruth Hale, Crystal Eastman, and Josephine Casey never took their husbands' names or the title "Mrs." Older feminists such as Mrs.

O. H. P. Belmont, Mrs. Lawrence Lewis, and Mrs. John Winters
Brannan were known exclusively by their husbands' names. Others,
like Jane Norman Smith, Edith Houghton Hooker, Inez Haynes Irwin,
and Betty Gram Swing, used both their birth names and their husbands' names, usually with the title "Mrs." But it was never a real
issue, for the Party simply supported the woman's right to choose the
name by which she wished to be identified.

The equalitarian feminists then, in spite of considerable thought
about women's roles, never attempted to develop an ideology which
would help women integrate work outside the home with marriage and
children. Their interest in the social and psychological effects of inequality was always peripheral to their main concern—civil equality
which would bring in its wake the all-important economic equality
for women. Although they recognized the double burden which working women carried, NWP members' "solution" to this problem was
available only to middle and upper class women who could afford
to pay for household help. Believing that men and women were very
different from one another, yet demanding complete equality for
women, the equalitarian feminists of the NWP failed to convince most
women during the twenties and thirties of the need for the Equal
Rights Amendment.

NOTES

1. Mrs. O. H. P. Belmont, "Women As Dictators," *Ladies Home
Journal* 39 (September 1923), 7; Charlotte Perkins Gilman, "Her
Natural Protector," *ER* 1 (June 2, 1923), 125–26.

2. Editorial, "The Parting of the Ways," *ER* 11 (March 8, 1924),
28; Editorial, "A Peak In Darien," *ER* 11 (August 23, 1924), 220;
Editorial, "Insulting Monogamy," *ER* 11 (January 10, 1925), 380;
Pearl Buck, *Of Men and Women* (New York: John Day and Co., 1941),
83; Gwendolyn Jones, "The Prize Winning Essay: Equal Economic
Rights for Women," *ER* 14 (August 23, 1927), 85–86; Alma Lutz,
"That Much Maligned Feminism," *ERIFW* 1 (August 3, 1935), 171.

3. Editorial, "Who Supports the Family?" *ER* 13 (February 13,
1926), 4; Florence Loeb Kellogg, "Feminists and Family Income,"
ER 13 (February 27, 1926), 21–22; Ruth Gill Williams, "The Economic Pinch," *ER* 20 (March 23, 1934), 62; Mirra Komarovsky, *The Un-*

employed Man and His Family (New York: Dryden Press, 1940), 76.

4. Editorial, "Armistice Day," *ER* 14 bis (November 17, 1928), 322; Editorial, "A Study in Contrasts," *ERIFW* 2 (November 21, 1936), 298; Editorial, "The Vote Is Not Enough," *ERIFW* 2 (September 26, 1936), 234; Rebecca Hourwich, "She Must Be Crazy," *ER* 13 (February 13, 1926), 8; Rebecca Hourwich, "Sex Antagonism," *ER* 12 (August 29, 1925), 231; Ruth Gill Williams, "The Economic Pinch," *ER* 20 (March 24, 1934), 62; Blanche Crozier, "On the Woman's Side," *ER* 20 (April 21, 1934), 91.

5. Editorial, "The Importance of Sex Solidarity," *ER* 12 (February 28, 1925), 20; Kate C. Havens, "Milton's Views on Women," *ER* 12 (November 14, 1925), 318; Editorial, "The Fat Theory," *ER* 12 (October 10, 1925), 276.

6. Knopf, *Women On Their Own*, pp. 40–41; Buck, *Of Men and Women*, p. 114; Doris Stevens, "The International Road to Equality for Women," *ER* 20 (July 21, 1934), 195–97; Editorial "Where the Trouble Begins," *ER* 14 (February 19, 1927), 12.

7. Ida Clyde Clarke, "What Women Are Thinking," *ER* 11 (June 7, 1924), 134; Ruby A. Black, "What Is Feminism?" review of *Lysistrata: Woman's Future and the Future Woman* by Anthony Ludovici and *Hypatia: Women and Knowledge* by Dora Russell in *ER* 12 (October 10, 1925), 277; Jane Norman Smith to Ruth Pratt, May 1927, Jane Norman Smith Papers, Box 1, f. 16, SL; Editorial, "Progress," *ER* 14 (October 1, 1927), 268; Alma Lutz, "A Feminist Thinks It Over," *ER* 24 (September 1, 1938), 317.

8. Sochen, *The New Woman*, p. 130; Rebecca Hourwich, "The Great National Calamity," *ER* 12 (January 2, 1926), 371; Editorial, "Which Sex Has Changed?" *ER* 15 (August 31, 1929), 234; Peter Filene, *Him/Her Self: Sex Roles in Modern America* (New York: New American Library, 1974).

9. Komarovsky, *The Unemployed Man and His Family*, p. 119; Chafe, *The American Woman*, p. 193; Smuts, *Women and Work in America*, p. 133; Eugene Pharo, "Emancipating the American Male," *American Mercury* 44 (May 1938), 44–45; Pearl Buck, "Woman's Place," *ER* 26 (December 1940), 37–38.

10. Editorial, "Giving A Sex to Sin," *ER* 14 (February 4, 1928), 410; Ruby A. Black, "For A Single Moral Standard," *ER* 13 (February 20, 1926), 13; Editorial, "The Great Impediment," *ER* 13 (February

20, 1926), 12; Sidney Ditzion, *Marriage, Morals and Sex in America,* expanded ed., (New York: Octagon Books, 1969), pp. 378, 384.

11. Pivar, *Purity Crusade,* 17–18; "Equal Rights Campaign in New York," *ER* 11 (March 29, 1924), 54; Editorial, "An Ultra-Male Resolution," *ER* 12 (March 14, 1925), 36; Editorial, "The Proof of the Pudding," *ER* 12 (April 18, 1925), 76; Alison Neilans, "Equal Rights in Public Morality Laws: The Need for International Watchfulness," *ER* 12 (July 25, 1925), 187; Editorial, "Equal Rights in Chicago," *ER* 12 (August 29, 1925), 228; "A New Drive to Punish Women Only," *ER* 16 (June 28, 1930), 163; Editorial, "The Situation Is Too Disgusting," *ER* 16 (January 17, 1931), 394; Editorial, "Justice Is Expediency," *ER* 16 (January 31, 1931), 410; "When Is A Crime Not A Crime?" *ER* 1 (August 25, 1923), 219; Crystal Eastman, "Justice for the Prostitute—Lady Astor's Bill," *ER* 12 (September 19, 1925), 253.

12. Editorial, "Two Sides of the Shield," *ER* 12 (September 19, 1925), 252; Crystal Eastman, "The New British Commonwealth League," *ER* 12 (August 22, 1925), 219; Editorial, "Our Protectors," *ER* 14 (April 16, 1927), 76.

13. Mrs. O. H. P. Belmont, "A Parting Message," *ER* 14 (December 17, 1927), 353; "Traffic In Women," *ER* 14 (January 21, 1928), 393; Doris Stevens, "In Behalf of the Equal Rights Treaty," *ER* 14 bis (March 10, 1928), 38–39; Editorial, "The Single Standard," *ER* 1 (October 20, 1923), 284.

14. Editorial, "The Single Standard," p. 284; Editorial, "Many Birds With One Stone," *ER* 1 (August 15, 1923), 220; Editorial, "The Cry of the Unborn Race," *ER* 17 (June 20, 1931), 154; Editorial, "The Woman With Gifts To Bring," *ER* 1 (April 28, 1923), 85; Editorial, "Silence Gives Consent," *ER* 1 (June 23, 1923), 148.

15. LaFollette, *Concerning Women,* pp. 34, 39, 44, 55, 137, 140.

16. Holtby, *Women In A Changing Civilisation,* pp. 64–65, 68, 138–39, 61.

17. Ruth Hale, "Divorce," *ER* 1 (May 19, 1923), 107.

18. Reprint from the *Washington Herald,* April 6, 1924, in *ER* 11 (April 26, 1924), 88; Ruby A. Black, "Companionate Marriage," review of *Companionate Marriage* by Judge Ben B. Lindsey and Wainwright Evans in *ER* 14 (December 31, 1927), 369.

19. "An Outline of Marriage," *ER* 14 (October 22, 1927), 294–95; Doris Stevens, "Wages For Wives," *Nation* 122 (January 27, 1926), 82; Florence Garvin, "The Reason Why," *ER* 14 (September 3, 1927), 235; Doris Stevens, "A Chance to Share," *ER* 11 (February 7, 1925), 414–15; Vera Brittain, "The Passing of the Married Woman's Handicap," *ER* 14 (December 24, 1927), 364–65.

20. "Jury Service," *ER* 1 (February 24, 1923), 10; Editorial, "Interpreting Nature," *ER* 11 (May 31, 1924), 124; Editorial, "What Price Protection," *ER* 12 (May 30, 1925), 124; Helene Granitsch, "The Revolution of Married Women," *ER* 13 (June 12, 1926), 139; Editorial, "Wages for Wives," *ER* 13 (December 4, 1926), 340; Editorial, "The Disability of Married Women," *ER* 13 (August 14, 1926), 212.

21. Mary Gertrude Fendall to Jane Norman Smith, September 1, 1927, Jane Norman Smith Papers, Box 2, f. 67, SL.

22. Elizabeth Selden Rogers, "The Rebel Generation," review of *The Rebel Generation* by Jo Van Ammers-Kuller, in *ER* 14 bis (January 19, 1929), 398.

23. *Ibid.;* Alma Lutz, "That Much-Maligned Feminism," *ERIFW* 1 (August 3, 1935), 171.

24. Editorial, "The Great Illusion," *ER* 12 (October 17, 1925), 284; Editorial, "The Basis of Social Classes," *ER* 14 bis (March 31, 1928), 60.

25. Editorial, "The Basis of Social Classes," p. 60.

26. *Ibid.*

27. Rebecca Hourwich, "Portia Marries," review of *Portia Marries* by Jeanette Phillips Gibbs, in *ER* 13 (October 23, 1926), 295.

28. Josephine Herbst, "A Modern Juggler," *ER* 13 (July 17, 1926), 179.

29. LaFollette, *Concerning Women*, pp. 93, 195, 20, 22, 71, 73, 143.

30. Blanche Crozier, "The Woman Pays What?" *ERIFW* 1 (April 13, 1935), 44–45; Crystal Eastman, "Who Is Dora Black," *ER* 13 (June 5, 1926), 136.

31. Edna Rostow, "Conflict and Accommodation," in *The Woman In America*, edited by Robert Jay Lifton, p. 211; Ruth Hale, "Divorce," *ER* 1 (May 19, 1923), 107; Editorial, "Whither?" *ER* 1 (June 30, 1923), 156; Editorial, "A Grave Situation," *ER* 19 (October 21, 1933), 290; Doris Stevens and Ruth Hale, "The New Freedom In Divorce:

A Debate," *Forum* 76 (September 1926), 321; Rosika Schwimmer, "Until Death Do Us Part—But Not Divorce," *ER* 13 (December 11, 1926), 350.

32. Editorial, "Alimony and Equal Rights," *ER* 12 (October 3, 1925), 268; Editorial, "So That's That," *ER* 14 (November 26, 1927), 332; LaFollette, *Concerning Women*, p. 113; Dorothy Thomas, "Equality or Alimony? Women Must Choose," *Independent Woman* 14 (October 1935), 338–39.

33. Walter Lippman, *Drift and Mastery* (Englewood Cliffs, N.J.: Prentice Hall, 1961), p. 131; Rebecca Hourwich, "Feminism and the Home," *The Suffragist* 8 (April 1920), 40; Rebecca Hourwich, "Why Can't Daddy Help?" *ER* 12 (October 31, 1925), 299; Editorial, "The Sphere of Women," *ER* 1 (May 12, 1923), 100; Editorial, "The Home Maker and Congress," *ER* 11 (October 11, 1924), 276; Ruby A. Black, "Doris Stevens Speaks on Equality," *ER* 11 (January 31, 1925), 405–06; Doris Stevens, "Wages for Wives," *Nation* 122 (January 27, 1926), 81; Editorial, "Too Expensive," *ER* 13 (March 13, 1926), 36; Editorial, "Their Mutual Contributions," *ER* 12 (August 22, 1925), 220.

34. Excerpts from *The Nervous Housewife* by Abraham Myers in *The Suffragist* 9 (January–February 1921), 359, 365; Editorial, "On Being Supported," *ER* 14 (November 26, 1927), 332; Editorial, "Too Expensive," *ER* 13 (March 13, 1926), 36; Editorial, "Must the Job Be Double," *ER* 14 bis (December 1, 1928), 338; "Very Vexed Question," *ER* 14 (October 29, 1927), 299; "Feminist Notes: Prejudice Against Married Women Workers Unwarranted," *ER* 14 (December 31, 1927), 368; Mary Austin, "The Kitchen Complex," *The Suffragist* 8 (October 1920), 238–39; Editorial, "Wives and Husbands," *ER* 1 (March 17, 1923), 40; Editorial, "Women's Souls," *ER* 1 (October 27, 1923), 292; "We Do Not Oppose Equal Rights," *ER* 12 (February 28, 1925), 21; Elizabeth Gifford, "The End of the Road," *ER* 12 (April 18, 1925), 75; Editorial, "Remaking Public Opinion," *ER* 14 (December 24, 1927), 362; Editorial, "Home and Shop," *ER* 16 (August 16, 1930), 218.

35. Freda Kirchwey, "A Woman's Magazine and Why," *The Suffragist* 9 (January-February 1921), 356; Kathryn Manahan, "Equal Rights Question," *ER* 11 (June 21, 1924), 151; Crystal Eastman, "Anna Wickham: A Poet Without a Wife," *ER* 12 (July 18, 1925),

183; Josephine Herbst, "A Modern Juggler," *ER* 13 (July 17, 1926), 179; Gwendolyn Jones, "Prize Winning Essay," *ER* 14 (April 23, 1927), 86; Editorial, "Wives and Family Incomes," *ER* 20 (July 21, 1934), 194.

36. Lynds, *Middletown*, p. 117; Komarovsky, *The Unemployed Man and His Family*, pp. 43–44, 76, 80–81, 119; Holtby, *Women in A Changing Civilisation*, p. 146; Buck, *Of Men and Women*, p. 80.

37. Mrs. Harvey Wiley, "The Home-Maker," *ER* 11 (October 11, 1924), 279.

38. Mrs. Emile Berliner, "The Work of Homemakers," *ER* 16 (November 1, 1930), 310.

39. Eleanor Taylor, "Wages for Mothers," *The Suffragist* 13 (November 1920), 273–74, 290.

40. Editorial, "The Woman With Gifts to Bring," *ER* 1 (April 28, 1923), 85; Editorial, "A Good Example," *ER* 13 (April 3, 1926), 60; Genevieve Taggard, "Edna St. Vincent Millay," *ER* 12 (March 14, 1925), 35.

41. Editorial, "Producing the Evidence," *ER* 14 (May 7, 1927), 100.

42. Madeline Z. Doty, "The Maternity Bill," *The Suffragist* 9 (January–February 1921), 353–54; "For the Amendment," *ER* 1 (December 22, 1923), 359; Elizabeth Baker et al., "About the Women's Charter," *Independent Woman* 16 (March 1937), 74; C. W. Saluby, "The Vote and the Race," *The Suffragist* 8 (December 1920), 308, 319; Editorial, "Inferiority Complex," *ER* 1 (March 3, 1923), 24; Editorial, "Penalizing Motherhood," *ER* 12 (October 31, 1925), 300.

43. "The Sacred Torch," *ER* 1 (September 29, 1923), 259; "Will the U.S. Go Feeble Minded?" *ERIFW* 2 (May 1936), 68; Margaret Sanger, "Birth Control—the Fundamental Freedom," *The Suffagist* 8 (December 1920), 309; "National Headquarters Draws Prominent Visitors," *ER* 1 (May 26, 1923), 119; Hugh de Selincourt, "Margaret Sanger," *ER* 12 (July 4, 1925), 167–68; Helene Granitsch, "The Revolution of Married Women," *ER* 13 (June 12, 1926), 139.

44. "Mary Murray Replies Again," *ER* 14 (October 1, 1927), 267.

45. Mary Murray to Alma Lutz, December 19, 1933, Alma Lutz Papers, Box 5, f. 66, SL.

46. Mrs. Harvey Wiley, "The Work of the NWP," *ER* 1 (March 3,

1923), 20; "Comments of the Press," *ER* 1 (March 17, 1923), 38; Editorial, "This Freedom," *ER* 14 (June 18, 1927), 148; "Read Dorothy Dix," *ER* 14 bis (June 16, 1928), 150.

47. Margaret Lane, "Babies Plus Jobs," *The Suffragist* 8 (November 1920), 276; Vera Brittain, "The Passing of the Married Woman's Handicap," *ER* 14 (December 24, 1927), 364–65; Editorial, "Is She A Feminist?" *ER* 17 (September 12, 1931), 250; Knopf, *Women On Their Own*, p. 280–81.

48. Rebecca Hourwich, "Little Girls Shall Be Little Girls," *ER* 11 (July 19, 1924), 183; Rebecca Hourwich, "The Embryo Feminist," *ER* 12 (August 1, 1925), 199–200; Rebecca Hourwich, "Mother Must Not Be Disturbed," *ER* 12 (November 28, 1925), 334.

49. Editorial, "A Real Christmas Gift," *ER* 11 (December 20, 1924), 256; Alma Lutz, "A Feminist Thinks It Over," *ER* 24 (September 1938), 112; "Women and Wealth," *ER* 20 (November 24, 1934), 338; Mirra Komarovsky, "Cultural Contradictions and Sex Roles," *American Journal of Sociology* 52 (November 1946), 184.

50. Editorial, "Remove the Stigma," *ER* 20 (March 24, 1934), 58; Editorial, "The Handwriting on the Wall," *ER* 20 (September 15, 1934), 258; LaFollette, *Concerning Women*, p. 96–100; Burnita Shelton Matthews, "The Unmarried Mother and Her Child," *ER* 13 (August 14, 1926), 213–14.

51. Editorial, "The Contempt of Motherhood," *ER* 14 bis (February 25, 1928), 20; Editorial, "The 'Unsuitability' of Motherhood," *ER* 17 (February 7, 1931), 2; Editorial, "Whistler's Mother," *ER* 20 (April 21, 1934), 90.

52. Holtby, *Women In A Changing Civilisation*, p. 143.

53. Editorial, "Women and the Church," *ER* 1 (May 26, 1923), 116; "Women and the Methodist Ministry," *ER* 14 bis (July 14, 1928), 182; Editorial, "A Fearful Difficulty," *ER* 11 (January 3, 1925), 272; Editorial, "Equal Rights in the Church," *ER* 14 bis (March 24, 1928), 52; Ruth Pickering, "The Golden Age of Equality," *ER* 12 (February 21, 1925), 14.

54. Editorial, "School Days," *ER* 13 (September 25, 1926), 260; Editorial, "What Is Education?" *ER* 14 bis (May 26, 1928), 124; Winifred Smith, "Women's Colleges and the New Order," *The Suffragist* 18 (May 1920), 60–61; Alma Lutz, "Have Women the Welfare

of Their Colleges at Heart?" *ER* 14 bis (December 22, 1928), 365–66; Editorial, "Such Is Progress," *ER* 15 (February 9, 1929), 2; Radio Talk by Ida Kloze, "Women Are People," in *ER* 19 (March 11, 1933), 43–44.

55. Buck, *Of Men and Women*, p. 61.

56. Editorial, "Symptoms," *ER* 1 (July 7, 1923), 164; Editorial, "The Old, Old Story," *ER* 13 (December 18, 1926), 356; "Press Comment on Convention," *ER* 14 (July 30, 1927), 199–200.

57. Lynds, *Middletown*, p. 112; Ruth Pickering, "The Lucy Stone Pep," *ER* 12 (March 21, 1925), 43; Editorial, "What's In A Name?" *ER* 13 (June 5, 1926), 132; Vera Brittain, "Surnames of Married Women," *ER* 12 (November 14, 1925), 317; Crystal Eastman, "Who Is Dora Black?" *ER* 13 (June 5, 1926), 135.

58. "A Married Woman's Name; Government Insists on Husband's Name," *ER* 11 (August 30, 1924), 227; "Protest to Government on Married Woman's Name," *ER* 11 (September 20, 1924), 155; "President to Consider Surnames," *ER* 12 (May 9, 1925), 99; Anita Pollitzer, "Inferiority of Women Characterizes Modern Novels," *ER* 14 (January 7, 1928), 381; Charlotte H. Dixon, "It's A Poor Rule," *ER* 14 (December 31, 1927), 371; Editorial, "What's In A Name?" *ER* 16 (December 20, 1930), 362.

EPILOGUE

In 1949, 1953, and 1959, the U.S. Senate passed the Equal Rights Amendment, but with the "Hayden rider" which exempted all sex-specific legislation and thus made the Amendment meaningless. The House Judiciary Committee throughout the 1940s, 1950s, and the 1960s refused even to hold hearings on the ERA. The breakthrough finally occured in August, 1970, when Representative Martha Griffiths (D-Michigan) presented a discharge petition in the House of Representatives. The House then approved the ERA the same day by a vote of three hundred fifty to fifteen. Fifty thousand women marched for equality later that month in New York City, and anti-ERA groups immediately began organizing opposition to the Amendment. Once again the House approved the ERA in the fall of 1971, after rejecting a military exemption rider, and in March, 1972, the Senate passed the Equal Rights Amendment by a vote of eighty-four to eight. Although almost half the states immediately approved the Amendment, the ratification movement was brought nearly to a halt in the mid-1970s by an increasingly well-organized and well-financed coalition of opposition groups. Not even the three year extension of the 1979 ratification deadline has made final approval any more certain.

Political and legal equality for women had been the major goals of nineteenth century feminists, and in 1920, as a result of the federal amendment, women had finally received the vote. The National Woman's Party hoped to achieve complete civil equality for women through the Equal Rights Amendment, and the equalitarian feminists emerged from the suffrage struggle with certain advantages. They had a nucleus of experienced leaders, a small but dedicated group of members, a strong financial base, and the conviction that the vote had merely provided the means for further feminist advances. However, the NWP also suffered from certain disadvantages in 1920. The suffrage struggle had created antagonisms which would last well into the decade, antagonisms often worsened by the righteous attitude adopted by the equalitarian feminists in the postsuffrage era. Since NWP feminists believed that their militant actions had been responsible for winning the vote, they badly underestimated the more moderate, but very effective, work of NAWSA in convincing women of the need for suffrage. In addition, many NWP members had such strong feelings of personal loyalty toward Alice Paul that they resisted any alteration in the elite, hierarchical structure of the Party she had founded.

Although the equalitarian feminists believed in the absolute necessity of further advances for women, they were never able to agree completely about which advances should have priority. They claimed that the purpose of their Party was to work toward freeing women from all forms of subjection. In fact, the majority of Party members concentrated on legal equality, assuming that this would also entail economic equality. Social and psychological equality, they thought, would follow naturally. In other words, they did believe that equality could be legislated. Although they supported a wide range of options for women and women's right to choose among them, equality to most NWP feminists meant sameness with men. Thus, in attempting to destroy the double standard, they came close to accepting male defined standards. It was this lure of what seemed to be men's privileges which Mary Beard was criticizing when she accused the NWP of making equality with men the be-all and end-all of its efforts.

Actually, equality with men is essential to feminism, but it does not necessarily mean adopting male defined values without reflection or reevaluation. At its best, feminism is a humanistic outlook which involves rights and responsibilities, free from sex stereotyping, for both men and women. However, in the short term, obtaining women's rights must come first for feminists. The women of the NWP understood the importance of economic equality, but they very much underestimated the social and psychological aspects of equality. Most women in the interwar period realized that they were confronted with multiple roles, but were still primarily expected to fulfill those of wife and mother. The NWP argument that men and women were very different but should be treated exactly the same came perilously close to an acceptance of the nineteenth century cult of true womanhood combined with a demand for equality—a kind of separate but equal argument. The problem was that the logic of that argument could lead out into the world because the world needed women's special contributions, as nineteenth century feminist reformers and the NWP feminists thought. But that same argument could lead back into the home because the world could destroy women's special characteristics and women were needed in the home to provide a refuge for men and children.

The equalitarian feminists of the NWP distrusted men, feared marriage and motherhood, and assumed that all women, with the possible exception of mothers with very young children, should work outside the home. Yet their faith that the ERA, by assuring legal and political equality, would also bring about economic equality for women led them away from any systematic analysis of women's roles as wives and mothers. That some women might not wish to work outside the home because of their own socialization, because of their husbands' objections or society's disapproval, or because of the limited range of job opportunities available to unskilled or undereducated women did not seem to be ideas which occured to the NWP. Moreover, housework, after all, had not been socialized. As the supply of cheap, easily available household help declined drastically in the early twentieth century, most women performed their own housework and suffered a double burden if they worked outside the home. Rising standards of child care and "home management" during the twenties too often meant that the double burden became an intolerable burden.

The NWP's failure to analyze systematically the institutions of marriage and the family was significant because women's roles as wives and mothers had a direct bearing on the Party's major priorities: the Equal Rights Amendment and equal employment opportunity for all women. In the process of establishing legal equality for women, the ERA would remove certain protections, such as alimony, from married women. The Amendment might also endanger such legislation as maternity acts and mothers' pensions, and certainly would have barred all special provisions for women workers which limited hours and occupations or provided for special working conditions. The Party, of course, believed that women would gain equal pay, and even more importantly, equal opportunity to compete with men for satisfying jobs and careers. Yet the NWP's failure to explore the importance of women's roles as wives and mothers meant that the home was still considered a married woman's "place" and primary sphere of responsibility. A married woman who worked, especially if she had children, deviated from this norm and was conscious of society's disapproval. Even during the period of the depression when many women were forced to work outside the home by economic necessity, public opinion rejected such employment as neither right nor desirable.

Thus equal opportunities for long term success in a job field or career were not internalized as goals by most women, who saw themselves as temporary workers. The blatant wage discriminations of some of the NRA codes or the wholesale dismissals on the basis of sex which were threatened by the Government Economy Act could rouse women workers on a short term basis. But the failure of the NWP to develop a feminist ideology that went beyond the elimination of such legal and economic discriminations and offered a new, fuller identity for women meant that members often dropped out of the Party after their specific grievances lessened. If working women were concerned with legitimatizing this role and integrating it with women's other roles as wives and mothers, then the NWP had little to offer them.

NWP feminists, then, were correct about equality, especially economic equality, but the arguments with which they supported their demands were weak. In addition, the tactics they used to advance their aims were sometimes poorly chosen. The suffrage struggle had been long and hard, and to propose another federal amendment immediately was an error. A spate of amendments had resulted from the Progressive reform era, just as in the aftermath of the Civil War, and it was clear that neither the Fourteenth nor the Eighteenth Amendments were fulfilling their intended purposes. Many people were also disillusioned with the effects of the Nineteenth Amendment, since women were not voting as a bloc, and, in many cases, were not voting at all. Furthermore, since Constitutional amendments generally require massive support on the grass roots level, the NWP should have expected to have to do an enormous amount of educational work in the states. Yet the old guard members of the Party were impatient, and given the nature of their mistaken analysis of the NWP's role in suffrage, they were unwilling to engage in that sort of long term consciousness raising.

While it was a strategic error to propose another federal amendment during the twenties, the ERA was to prove particularly divisive. Both social and equalitarian feminists were convinced of the necessity of economic independence for women. But social feminists believed that special legislation for women protected them and made them better able to compete with men, while equalitarian feminists insisted that protective laws restricted women and lessened their chances for economic independence. The ERA would have destroyed protective legislation for women, and even in the New Deal years, the NWP was unable to convince social feminists to work for protective legislation based on the job rather than on the sex of the worker. During the economic fluctuations of the twenties and the depression of the thirties, economic opportunities for women were seriously jeopardized. The ERA, then, became an issue on which feminist compromise was impossible.

The equalitarian feminists used two other relatively ineffective tactics in the twenties but abandoned them by 1930. The English tactic of holding the party in power responsible for the success of the Amendment was politically naive at best—at worst, it was a kind of collective self-indulgence in dramatic posturing. But the NWP was hurt by the fiasco of its foray into the 1928 presidential election and the Party learned its lesson. Militancy, so much a part of the NWP's role in the suffrage campaign, was simply out of tune with the times. The issues were not clear enough, for even women's right to paid employment was controversial during the depression.

Other NWP tactics were far more effective. The Women For Congress campaign, along with the consistent support the NWP gave to the election and appointment of feminists to office, kept the issue of women's political involvement before the public. There were many women interested in politics, especially during the twenties, and the Party provided support for women seeking such careers. This strategy might even have provided a viable basis for cooperation with other women's groups, particularly with the League of Women Voters. Yet the NWP never put very much effort into this tactic after its 1924 campaign, and often insisted on allegiance to the ERA as the price of its support.

The NWP was very good at publicity, and this encouraged what its members would have called a sense of "sex-consciousness" among women. The celebration of feminist anniversaries and events, the support of women's history, the publicizing of the increasing job discrimination against married women—all these efforts helped to keep feminism alive in the interwar period. It was partly this sense of sisterhood which led the NWP into international equality work, although such international activities did spread the Party's resources too thin, diverting money and time to projects which had relatively little chance of achieving concrete results. The NWP cannot be blamed for splitting the European feminist movement, however, since the same division between equalitarian and social feminist viewpoints was already present in international feminism.

Although some personality clashes with social feminist leaders were probably unavoidable, especially during the 1920s, the NWP might have tried to reduce such disagreements. There were numerous women's issues on which cooperation would not have caused equalitarian feminists to compromise their principles. In fact, such cooperation might have shifted feminist attention away from the truly divisive issue of protective legislation. The most likely areas included jury service for women, the extension of the Shepard-Towner Maternity Act, the amendments to the Cable Act which gave women more nearly equal citizenship, suffrage for Latin American and European women, the support for women in political office, equal pay, the repeal of the married person's clause of the Government Economy Act, and relief eligibility and projects for unemployed women.

The changing membership in most social feminist groups (with the exception of the Women's Bureau and social feminist leaders closely associated with Mary Anderson) might have gradually helped to heal the suffrage wounds. But the NWP erred in its refusal to democratize in the thirties when it had gained new younger members, notably the professional and working women of the government workers' council and the industrial council, who were free from old suffrage antagonsims. These women tended to be associated with the reform faction of the Party and believed in the ERA as a long term goal, but wanted to do state work, often to protect women from job discrimination. The reformers were correct—national lobbying for the ERA had to be backed by constituent support, and state work did tend to "feminize" women, find and develop new leadership, and create solidarity among women's groups.

There is no doubt that the effectiveness of the equalitarian feminists was limited by some mistaken strategies and failures of judgement. Yet the NWP *was* the only "true" feminist organization in the United States during the interwar period. Recognizing the pervasive anti-feminist sentiment of the twenties and thirties, the Party feminists fought courageously for equal political, legal, and economic rights for all women. Caught in a world not of their making, they demanded freedom from artificial barriers as a basic human right. Yet they were also part of that world, unable to free themselves totally from the assumptions they shared as white, middle class, American women. Their feminism was reformist, not revolutionary—they merely wanted to close the gap between the ideals of marriage, motherhood, and work and the realities of most women's lives. In fighting for its vision of women's equality, the NWP kept feminism alive during the interwar years, alerted women to the legal and economic discriminations against them, and, I think, prevented many of these discriminations from becoming worse. Finally, in formulating the Equal Rights Amendment, NWP feminists pointed the way to a future equality before the law that, unfortunately, women do not yet enjoy.

SELECTED BIBLIOGRAPHY

PRIMARY SOURCES

MANUSCRIPT COLLECTIONS

The richest collection of papers for this study may be found at the Schlesinger Library, Radcliffe College, Cambridge, Massachusetts. Especially useful were the Alma Lutz papers which primarily cover the period between 1921 and 1945, and the Jane Norman Smith papers, the bulk of which consists of correspondence with other National Woman's Party leaders. Other NWP members' papers include those of Caroline Lexow Babcock, Inez Haynes Irwin, Florence Ledyard Kitchelt, Emma Guffy Miller, Lena Madesin Phillips, Doris Stevens, Helen Hunt West, Sue Sheldon White, Anna Kelton Wiley, and Mary Winsor. Also at Schlesinger Library are some of the papers of social feminists Mary Anderson, Mary Dewson, Maud Wood Park, Frances Perkins, Belle Sherwin, Mary Winslow, and Marguerite Wells, along with a small collection of the American Association of University Women papers. In addition, the library maintains a biographical file which is helpful in obtaining information on both equalitarian and social feminists of this period.

The Library of Congress also possesses a number of essential collections, including the papers of the National Consumers' League, the National League of

Women Voters, the National Women's Trade Union League, and the Women's Joint Congressional Committee. The Women's Bureau papers are at the National Archives, and the National Woman's Party Papers, 1913–1972, of which Series I (correspondence), Series II (minutes), and Series IV (financial records) are the most relevant, have recently been made available by Microfilming Corporation of America (Glen Rock, New Jersey, 1977).

BOOKS

Addams, Jane. *My Friend, Julia Lathrop*. New York: Macmillan, 1935.

Anderson, Mary. *Woman At Work: The Autobiography of Mary Anderson as Told to Mary N. Winslow*. Minneapolis: University of Minnesota Press, 1951.

Balsan, Consuelo Vanderbilt. *The Glitter and the Gold*. New York: Harper and Brothers, 1952.

Beard, Mary R. *A Changing Political Economy As It Affects Women*. Washington, D.C.: American Association of University Women, n.d.

―――, ed. *America Through Women's Eyes*. New York: Macmillan, 1934.

Breckinridge, Sophonisba P. *Marriage and the Civil Rights of Women*. Chicago: University of Chicago Press, 1931.

―――. *Women in the Twentieth Century*. New York: McGraw-Hill, 1933.

Buck, Pearl. *Of Men and Women*. London: Methuen, 1942.

Dangerfield, George. *The Strange Death of Liberal England*. New York: Harrison Smith and Robert Haas, 1935.

Dorr, Rheta Childe. *A Woman of Fifty*. New York: Funk and Wagnalls, 1925.

Goldmark, Josephine. *Impatient Crusader: Florence Kelley's Life Story*. Urbana: Ill.: University of Illinois Press, 1953.

Holtby, Winifred. *Women in a Changing Civilisation*. New York: Longmans, Green, 1935.

Hooker, Edith Houghton. *The Laws of Sex*. Boston: R. G. Badger, 1921.

Irwin, Inez Haynes. *Angels and Amazons: A Hundred Years of American Women*. New York: Doubleday, 1933.

―――. *The Story of the Woman's Party*. New York: Harcourt, Brace, 1921.

Kirchwey, Freda, ed. *Our Changing Morality: A Symposium*. New York: Albert and Charles Boni, 1924.

Knopf, Dr. Olga. *Women On Their Own*. Boston: Little, Brown, 1935.

Komarovsky, Mirra. *The Unemployed Man and His Family*. New York: Dryden Press, 1940.

LaFollette, Suzanne. *Concerning Women.* New York: Albert and Charles Boni, 1926.

Lippman, Walter. *Drift and Mastery.* Englewood Cliffs, N.J.: Prentice Hall, 1961.

Lutz, Alma. *Challenging Years: The Memoirs of Harriot Stanton Blatch.* New York: G. P. Putnam's Sons, 1940.

Lynd, Robert and Helen. *Middletown.* New York: Harcourt, Brace, 1929.

———. *Middletown in Transition.* New York: Harcourt, Brace, 1937.

Nestor, Agnes. *Woman's Labor Leader: The Autobiography of Agnes Nestor.* Rockford, Ill.: Bellvue Books, 1954.

Paul, Alice. *The Nationality of Women, Seventh Conference of American Republics, Montevideo, December 1933.* n.p., 1934.

Peck, Mary Grey. *Carrie Chapman Catt: A Biography.* New York: H. W. Wilson, 1944.

Schmalhausen, Samuel D., and Calverton, V. P., eds. *Woman's Coming of Age.* New York: H. Liveright, 1931.

Schneiderman, Rose, and Goldthwaite, Lucy. *All For One.* New York: Paul S. Erikson, 1967.

Stevens, Doris. *Jailed For Freedom.* New York: Boni and Liveright, 1920.

Strachey, Ray, ed. *Our Freedom and Its Results.* London: Hogarth, 1936.

PAMPHLETS

Gale, Zona. *What Women Won in Wisconsin.* Washington, D.C.: National Woman's Party, 1922.

Matthews, Burnita Shelton. *The Status of Women as Jurors.* Washington, D.C.: National Woman's Party, 1930.

National Woman's Party. *Alabama Laws Discriminating Against Women.* Washington, D.C.: National Woman's Party, 1922.

———. *Equal Rights Amendment: Questions and Answers.* Washington, D.C.: Government Printing Office, 1943.

———. *Florida Laws Discriminating Against Women.* Washington, D.C.: National Woman's Party, n.d.

———. *How Colorado Laws Discriminate Against Women.* Washington, D.C.: National Woman's Party, 1924.

———. *How Maryland Laws Discriminate Against Women.* Washington, D.C.: National Woman's Party, 1922.

———. *How Mississippi Laws Discriminate Against Women*. Washington, D.C.:
National Woman's Party, 1922.

———. *How New Jersey Laws Discriminate Against Women*. Washington, D.C.:
National Woman's Party, 1926.

———. *How New York Laws Discriminate Against Women*. Washington, D.C.:
National Woman's Party, 1922.

———. *How Virginia Laws Discriminate Against Women*. Washington, D.C.:
National Woman's Party, n.d.

———. *Louisiana Laws Discriminating Against Women*. Washington, D.C.:
National Woman's Party, n.d.

———. *Michigan Laws Discriminating Against Women*. Washington, D.C.:
National Woman's Party, 1922.

———. *The National Woman's Party, 1913, 1926*. Baltimore: Allied Printing
Trades Council, 1926.

U.S., Department of Labor, Women's Bureau. *The Effects of Labor Legislation on the Employment Opportunities of Women*. Bulletin no. 65. Washington, D.C.: Government Printing Office, 1928.

———. *Women At Work: A Century of Industrial Change*. Bulletin no. 115.
Washington, D.C.: Government Printing Office, 1933.

———. *Women in the Federal Service, 1923-1947*. Bulletin no. 230. Washington,
D.C.: Government Printing Office, 1949.

———. *Women's Occupations Through Seven Decades*. Bulletin no 232. Washington, D.C.: Government Printing Office, 1951.

PERIODICALS

Annals of the American Academy of Political and Social Science 143 (May 1929).
Equal Rights, 1923-1941.
Equal Rights Independent Feminist Weekly, 1935-1936.
Equal Rights: Weekly Bulletin of the National Woman's Party, 1922.
The Suffragist, 1920-1921.

ARTICLES

Adams, Mildred, "Did They Know What They Wanted?" *Outlook* 147
(December 28, 1927), 528-30.

Anderson, Mary and Dorr, Rheta Childe. "Should There Be Labor Laws for Women?" *Good Housekeeping* 81 (September 1925), 52–53.

Archdale, Helen A. "International Developments in the Woman's Movement." *Current History* 29 (October 1928), 48–52.

Austin, Mary. "Forward Turn." *Nation* 125 (July 20, 1927), 57–59.

Baker, Elizabeth; Van Kleeck, Mary; Lutz, Alma; and Gram Swing, Betty. "About the Women's Charter." *Independent Woman* 16 (March 1937), 72–74, 95.

Beard, Mary R. "Test For the Modern Woman." *Current History* 37 (November 1932), 179–83.

Belmont, Alva E. "Are Women Really Citizens?" *Good Housekeeping* 93 (September 1931), 99, 132, 135.

———. "What the Woman's Party Wants." *Colliers* 70 (December 23, 1922), 6.

———, and Matthews, Burnita S. "Next Step Toward Complete Independent Nationality For All American Women." *Congressional Digest* 9 (November 1930), 263–64.

Beyer, Clara Mortenson. "What Is Equality?" *Nation* 116 (January 31, 1923), 116.

Blackwell, Alice Stone. "Woman's Seventy-five Year Fight." *Nation* 107 (July 18, 1923), 53–54.

Blair, Emily Newell. "Are Women Failures in Politics?" *Harper's* 151 (October 1925), 513–22.

———. "Discouraged Feminists." *Outlook* 158 (July 9, 1931), 302–03, 318–19.

Blankenhorn, Mary Dewhurst. "Do Working Women Want It?" *Survey* 57 (February 15, 1927), 630–31.

Blatch, Harriot Stanton. "Can Sex Equality Be Legislated?" *The Independent* 111 (December 22, 1923), 301.

———. "Do Women Want Protection?" *Nation* 111 (January 31, 1923), 115–16.

Bromley, Dorothy Dunbar. "Feminist: New Style." *Harper's* 155 (October 1927), 552–59.

Brown, Gertrude Foster. "Editorially Speaking—Why the League Objected." *Woman Citizen* 11 (July 1926), 24.

Bruere, Martha Bensley. "Highway to Woman's Happiness." *Current History* 27 (October 1927), 26–29.

Bunand-Sevastos, Fanny. "What the InterAmerican Commission of Women Has Accomplished." *Congressional Digest* 9 (November 1930), 267–68.

Catt, Carrie Chapman, et al. "Should Congress Approve the Proposed Equal Rights Amendment to the Constitution? CON." *Congressional Digest* 22 (April 1943), 118–28.

———. "Too Many Rights." *Ladies Home Journal* 39 (November 1922), 31, 168.

Cramer, Jane S., and Parkhurst, Genevieve. "Should Women Support the Equal Rights Amendment?" *Independent Woman* 14 (May 1935), 171–74.

Dozier, Howard. "Women and Unemployment." *Review of Reviews* 85 (March 1932), 55–56.

Eastman, Crystal. "Alice Paul's Convention." *The Liberator* 4 (April 1921), 9–10.

Ellis, Havelock. "Equal Rights: A Paradox." *Pictorial Review* 26 (November 1924), 5, 120–22.

"Equal Rights." *Woman's Home Companion* 66 (April 1939), 2.

Evans, Elizabeht G., and Rehfisch, Carol A. "Woman's Party, Right or Wrong?" *New Republic* 36 (September 26, 1923), 123–24.

Evans, Nancy. "Good-by Bohemia." *Scribner's Magazine* 89 (June 1931), 643, 645–46.

Ferrero, Gina Lombroso. "Feminism Destructive of Woman's Happiness." *Current History* 25 (January 1927), 486–92.

Fletcher, Grace N. "He Wants My Job." *Independent Woman* 14 (May 1935), 154, 166–67.

Gilman, Charlotte Perkins. "The New Generation of Women." *Current History* 18 (August 1923), 731–37.

Hall, G. Stanley, "Flapper Americana Novissima." *Atlantic Monthly* 129 (June 1922), 771–80.

Havener, Helen, "International Board Meets in Brussels." *Independent Woman* 14 (November 1935), 376, 388–89.

"Heads I Win, Tails You Lose." *Independent Woman* 19 (August 1940), 228.

"Hearing on the Equal Rights Amendment." *Independent Woman* 17 (March 1938), 88–89.

Heneker, Dorothy A. "Our Part at Geneva." *Independent Woman* 17 (October 1938), 322, 335.

Herendeen, Anne. "What the Home Town Thinks of Alice Paul." *Everybody's Magazine* 41 (October 1919), 45.

Hibschman, Harry. "Equal Rights For Men." *Forum* 98 (December 1937), 305–09.

Hill, Elsie and Kelley, Florence. "Shall Women Be Equal Before the Law?" *Nation* 114 (April 12, 1922), 419–21.

Hinkle, Beatrice. "Woman's Subjective Dependence Upon Men." *Harper's* 164 (January 1932), 205.

"How Can We Raise Women's Status? A Symposium." *Independent Woman* 17 (September 1938), 280–81.

Irwin, Inez Haynes and Kelley, Florence. "Equal Rights Amendment." *Good Housekeeping* 78 (March 1924), 18–19, 158–65.

"Is the Younger Generation in Peril?" *Literary Digest* 69 (May 14, 1921), 9–12, 58, 61, 63–64, 66–67, 69–70, 72–73.

Johnson, Ethel M. "The New Woman's Party." *Survey* 45 (March 5, 1921), 827–28.

———. "Why Protection?" *Woman Citizen* 9 (August 9, 1924), 16–17.

Kenton, Edna. "The Ladies' Next Step, the Case for the Equal Rights Amendment." *Harper's* 152 (February 1926), 366–74.

Keyes, Frances Parkinson. "Equal Rights Bill." *Good Housekeeping* 76 (February 1923), 28–29.

Kirchwey, Freda. "Are You a Feminist?" *World Tomorrow* 6 (December 1923), 361–62.

Komarovsky, Mirra. "Cultural Contradictions and Sex Roles. *American Journal of Sociology* 52 (November 1946), 184–89.

———. "Functional Analysis of Sex Roles." *American Sociological Review* 15 (August 1950), 508–16.

Lee, Muna. "Pan American Women." *Nation* 126 (March 14, 1928), 294–95.

"The Legislative Journey of the Equal Rights Amendment." *Congressional Digest* 22 (April 1943), 105–06.

Lutz, Alma. "Shall Woman's Work Be Regulated by Law?" *Atlantic* 115 (September 1930), 321–27.

———. "Women and Wages." *Nation* 139 (October 17, 1934), 440–41.

Macy, John. "Equality of Woman with Man: A Myth." *Harper's* 153 (November 1926), 705–13.

Manning, Alice L. "Congress Upholds Women's Rights." *Independent Woman* 20 (September 1941), 276.

———. "Legislatively Speaking: Senator O'Mahoney's Substitute Amendment." *Independent Woman* 20 (December 1941), 372.

———. "May Day Surprise." *Independent Woman* 20 (June 1941), 184.

Martin, Anne. "Equality Laws Vs. Women in Government." *Nation* 115 (August 16, 1922), 165–66.

———. "Feminists and Future Political Action." *Nation* 120 (February 18, 1925), 185–86.

Mead, Margaret. "Sex and Achievement." *Forum* 94 (November 1935), 301–03.

"Miss Dunshee on Equal Rights." *Woman Citizen* 13 (March 8, 1924), 19–20.

Morann, Margaret. "Give Her the Fruit of Her Hands." *Independent Woman* 13 (July 1934), 200, 221–22.

Nation editorial. "Chivalry and Labor Laws." 127 (December 12, 1928), 648.

————. "New Program for Women." 117 (September 19, 1923), 285.

"National Woman's Party Explains Its Proposal for an Equal Rights Amendment." *Congressional Digest* 22 (April 1943), 102–04.

Nelson, Josephine. "She Supports a Family." *Independent Woman* 17 (March 1938), 81–82, 90.

New Republic editorial. "Equal Rights For Women?" 94 (February 16, 1938), 34.

Ninabuck, Avis Ring. "Panacea Is Questioned." *Woman Citizen* 14 (May 1929), 28–29.

Parker, Cornelia S. "feminists and Feminists." *Survey* 56 (August 1, 1926), 502–05.

Parkhurst, Genevieve. "Is Feminism Dead?" *Harper's* 170 (May 1935), 735–45.

Paul, Alice et al. "Should Congress Approve the Proposed Equal Rights Amendment to the Constitution? PRO." *Congressional Digest* 22 (April 1943), 107–17.

————. "Women Demand Equality in World Code of Law." *Congressional Digest* 9 (November 1930), 279.

Peet, Creighton. "What More Do Women Want?" *Outlook* 158 (August 5, 1931), 433–44.

Perkins, Frances, and Baker, Elizabeth F. "Do Women in Industry Need Special Protection?" *Survey* 55 (February 15, 1926), 529–32, 582–83, 585.

Pharo, Eugene. "Emancipating the American Male." *American Mercury* 44 (May 1938), 44–48.

"Proposal for A Woman's Charter." *Independent Woman* 16 (January 1937), 10.

Pruette, Lorinne. "Equal Rights or Easier Work?" *Woman Citizen* 14 (January 1929), 14–15.

————. "Why Women Fail." *Outlook* 158 (August 12, 1931), 460–62, 478–80.

Sands, Florence. "Why Many Woman Do Not Succeed in Business." *Independent Woman* 9 (October 1925), 12–13.

Seeley, Evelyn. "Equality, Norwegian Style: An Interview With Betsy Kjelsberg." *Independent Woman* 16 (December 1937), 373, 390–91.

Smith, Ethel M. "What Is Sex Equality?" *Century* 118 (May 1929), 96–106.

Smith, Jane Norman. "Where the Woman's Party Stands." *Nation* 106 (April 4, 1923), 393.

————, and Kenyon, Dorothy. "To End Discrimination Against Woman." *Independent Woman* 16 (May 1937), 132.

Snedden, David. "Probable Economic Future of the American Woman." *American Journal of Sociology* (March 1919), 528–65.

Stevens, Doris. "America Takes Her Stand Among Nations for Equality."
  Congressional Digest 9 (November 1930), 280, 288.
———. "Wages For Wives." *Nation* 122 (January 27, 1926), 81–83.
———, and Hale, Ruth. "The New Freedom in Divorce: A Debate." *Forum*
  76 (September 1926), 322–32.
———, and Hamilton, Alice. "Blanket Amendment Debate." *Forum* 72 (August
  1924), 145–60.
Strauss, Dorothy. "Independent Nationality Through National Laws."
  Congressional Digest 9 (November 1930), 281–82.
———. "I Swear Allegiance to. . . " *Woman Citizen* 15 (January 1930), 28–29.
"The Suffragist Fight Over Industrial Equality." *Literary Digest* 89 (June 12,
  1926), 10–11.
Swisher, Idella Gwatkin. "Program of the National League of Women Voters."
  Congressional Digest 9 (November 1930), 265–66, 288.
"They Stand Out From the Crowd." *Literary Digest* 107 (February 10, 1934), 9.
Thomas, Dorothy. "Equality or Alimony? Women Must Choose." *Independent
  Woman* 14 (October 1935), 338–39, 354–55.
"To Restrict Women is to Hamper the Race." *Independent Woman* 14 (August
  1935), 249, 276–77.
Tucker, Kate M. "Are Women Too Aggressive in Business?" *Independent
  Woman* 7 (January 1924), 5–6.
"Unemployment Among Women in the Early Years of the Depression."
  Monthly Labor Review 38 (April 1934), 790–99.
Vaerting, M. "Dominent Sexes" *Nation* 109 (September 17, 1924), 280–82.
Van Kleeck, Mary. "Woman and Machines." *Atlantic Monthly* 127 (February
  1921), 250–60.
Weed, Helena Hill. "The New Deal That Women Want." *Current History*
  41 (November 1934), 179–83.
Whittic, Anna Harbottle. "Defense of the Blanket Amendment." *Woman
  Citizen* 9 (June 28, 1924), 17, 29.
Wold, Emma. "Changing Legal Scene." *Independent Woman* 16 (April 1937),
  105, 123–24.
Wolfson, Theresa. "Equal Rights in the Union." *Survey* 57 (February 15,
  1927), 629–30.
"Woman's Party and Mr. Hoover." *Nation* 127 (October 3, 1928), 312.
"Women's Bloc?" *Nation* 109 (September 3, 1924), 230–31.
"Women's Charter." *Journal of Home Economics* 29 (March 1937), 180–82.
Woodhouse, Chase Going. "The Status of Women." *American Journal of
  Sociology* 35 (May 1930), 1091–1100.
Younger, Maud. "The NRA and Protective Laws for Women." *Literary Digest*
  117 (June 2, 1934), 27.

SECONDARY SOURCES

UNPUBLISHED DISSERTATIONS

Blahna, Loretta J. "The Rhetoric of the Equal Rights Amendment." Ph.D. dissertation, University of Kansas, 1973.

Johnson, Dorothy E. "Organized Women and National Legislation, 1920–1941." Ph.D. dissertation, Case Western Reserve University, 1960.

Ondercin, David C. "The Compleat Women: The Equal Rights Amendment and Perceptions of Womanhood, 1920–1972." Ph.D. dissertation, University of Minnesota, 1973.

Zimmerman, Loretta Ellen. "Alice Paul and the National Woman's Party, 1912–1920." Ph.D. dissertation, Tulane University, 1964.

BOOKS

Adams, Mildred. *The Right To Be People*. New York: Lippincott, 1967.

Baritz, Loren. ed. *The Culture of the Twenties*. New York: Bobbs-Merrill, 1969.

Bussey, Gertrude, and Tims, Margaret. *Women's International League for Peace and Freedom, 1915–1965*. London: George Allen and Unwin, 1965.

Carter, Paul. *Another Part of the Twenties*. New York: Columbia University Press, 1977.

Chafe, William H. *The American Woman: Her Changing Social, Economic and Political Roles, 1920–1970*. New York: Oxford University Press, 1972.

Chamberlin, Hope. *A Minority of Members: Women in the U.S. Congress*. New York: Praeger, 1973.

Ditzion, Sidney. *Marriage, Morals, and Sex in America*. Expanded ed. New York: Octagon Books, 1969.

DuBois, Ellen Carol. *Feminism and Suffrage: The Emergence of an Independent*

Women's Movement in America, 1848–1869. Ithaca, N.Y.: Cornell University Press, 1978.

Duverger, Maurice. *Political Role of Women*. Paris: UNESCO, 1955.

Equal Rights Amendment Project. *The Equal Rights Amendment: A Bibliographic Study*. Westport, Conn.: Greenwood Press, 1976.

Filene, Peter G. *Him/Her/Self: Sex Roles in Modern America*. New York: New American Library, 1974.

Flexner, Eleanor. *Century of Struggle*. Cambridge: Harvard University Press, 1959.

Freeman, Jo. *The Politics of Women's Liberation: A Case Study of an Emerging Social Movement and Its Relation to the Policy Process*. New York: David McKay, 1975.

Kraditor, Aileen. *The Ideas of the Woman Suffrage Movement, 1890–1920*. Anchor Books. Garden City, N.Y.: Doubleday, 1971.

Lasch, Christopher. *The New Radicalism in America, 1889–1963*. New York: Alfred A. Knopf, 1965.

Lemons, J. Stanley. *The Woman Citizen: Social Feminism in the 1920's*. Urbana, Ill.: University of Illinois Press, 1973.

Lifton, Robert Jay, ed. *The Woman in America*. Boston: Houghton Mifflin, 1965.

Lloyd, Trevor Owen. *Suffragettes International*. New York: American Heritage Press, 1971.

May, Henry F. *The End of American Innocence: A Study of the First Years of Our Own Time, 1912–1917*. New York: Alfred A. Knopf, 1959.

O'Neill, William L. *Divorce in the Progressive Era*. New Haven, Conn.: Yale University Press, 1967.

———. *Everyone Was Brave*. Chicago: Quadrangle Books, 1969.

Pivar, David. *Purity Crusade*. Westport, Conn.: Greenwood Press, 1973.

Riegel, Robert E. *American Feminists*. Lawrence, Kan.: University of Kansas Press, 1963.

Rothman, Sheila. *Woman's Proper Place: A History of Changing Ideals and Practices, 1870 to the Present*. New York: Basic Books, 1978.

Robotham, Sheila. *Hidden From History*. London: Pluto Press, 1973.

———. *Women, Resistance, and Revolution*. New York: Pantheon, 1972.

Scharf, Lois. *To Work and To Wed: Female Employment, Feminism, and the Great Depression*. Westport, Conn.: Greenwood Press, 1980.

Showalter, Elaine, ed. *These Modern Women: Autobiographical Essays from the Twenties*. Old Westbury, N.Y.: Feminist Press, 1978.

Smuts, Robert. *Women and Work in America*. New York: Schocken, 1971.

Sochen, June. *The New Woman: Feminism in Greenwich Village, 1910–1920*. New York: Quadrangle, 1972.

Walters, F. P. *A History of the League of Nations*. 2 vols. London: Oxford University Press, 1952.

Westin, Jeane. *Making Do: How Women Survived the Thirties*. Chicago: Follette, 1976.

ARTICLES

Bolin, Winifred Wandersee. "The Economics of Middle-Income Family Life: Working Women During the Great Depression." *Journal of American History* (September 1978), 60–74.

Burnham, John C. "Psychiatry, Psychology and the Progressive Movement." *American Quarterly* 12 (1960), 457–65.

Christy, Teresa. "Equal Rights for Women: Voices From the Past." *American Journal of Nursing* 71 (1971), 288–93.

Clements, Barbara Evans. "Emancipation Through Communism: The Ideology of A.M. Kollontai." *Slavic Review* 32 (June 1973), 323–38.

Davis, Allen F. "The Women's Trade Union League: Origins and Organization." *Labor History* 5 (Winter 1964), 3–17.

Degler, Carl. "Charlotte Perkins Gilman on the Theory and Practice of Feminism." *American Quarterly* 8 (Spring 1956), 21–39.

Freedman, Estelle. "The New Woman: Changing Views of Women in the Twenties." *Journal of American History* 61 (September 1974), 372–93.

Humphries, Jane. "Women: Scapegoats and Safety Valves in the Great Depression." *Review of Radical Political Economics* 8 (Spring 1976), 98–117.

Keniston, Ellen and Kenneth. "An American Anachronism: The Image of Women and Work." *American Scholar* 33 (Summer 1964), 355–75.

Lerner, Gerda. "Women's Rights and American Feminism." *American Scholar* 40 (Spring 1971), 235–48.

Nottingham, Elizabeth K. "Toward An Analysis of the Effects of Two World Wars on the Role and Status of Middle Class Women in the English Speaking World." *American Sociological Review* 12 (December 1947), 666–75.

Patterson, James T. "Mary Dewson and the American Minimum Wage Movement." *Labor History* 5 (Spring 1964), 134–52.

Rossi, Alice. "Sex Equality: The Beginning of Ideology." *The Humanist* 5 (September–October 1969), 3–6, 16.

Schwartz-Cowan, Ruth. "The Industrial Revolution in the Home: Household
     Technology and Social Change in the Twenties." *Technology and Culture*
     17 (January 1976), 1–23.
Trecker, Janice Law. "The Suffrage Prisoners." *American Scholar* 40 (Summer
     1971), 409–23.

INDEX

About the Author

Susan D. Becker is Assistant Professor of History and Chairperson of the Woman's Studies Program at the University of Tennessee in Knoxville.